Jane **Miller** was born in London in 1932 and educated at Girton
College, Cambridge, where she studied French and Russian. She has
wo............ in
the ....of
Lor ....

S ....*te*
Ma ....s.
Ess ....of
Ma ....d
Wo

Sed ....le
stuc il
Bak ....e,
and 1-
cies 1s
to a ....ir
live ....le
autl ....y
exp

D1465000

SEDUCTIONS
Studies in Reading and Culture

JANE MILLER

VIRAGO

Published by VIRAGO PRESS Limited 1990
20–23 Mandela Street, Camden Town, London NW1 0HQ

Copyright © Jane Miller 1990

Front cover photograph by Brassaï
© G. Brassaï

*A Catalogue record for this book
is available from the British Library*

Typeset by Goodfellow & Egan, Cambridge
Printed in Great Britain
Bookcraft (Bath) Ltd

For Georgia

Contents

Acknowledgements

A term's leave from the University of London Institute of Education made it possible for me to finish this book, and I want to thank my colleagues for letting me have that time. I have also been helped in different essential ways by Tony Burgess, by my father, Robert Collet, by John Hardcastle, Yvonne Kapp, Jane Lewis, Karl, Georgia, Sam and Daniel Miller, Ursula Owen and Ruthie Petrie, Carolyn Steedman, Richard Storey, Archivist at the Modern Records Centre of the University of Warwick Library, and Mary Taubman. Parts of Chapters 1 and 4 first appeared in the *London Review of Books*, whose editors I would like to thank for permission to use somewhat rewritten versions of them here. An earlier version of the final section of Chapter 1 was originally written for *The Don Giovanni Book. Myths of Seduction and Betrayal*, edited by Jonathan Miller and published by Faber & Faber.

Introduction

All I have to do is sit on the floor and cut frying pans out of the Eaton's Catalogue with embroidery scissors, and say I've done it badly. Partly this is a relief.

Margaret Atwood, *Cat's Eye*

Introductions are usually the last thing to get written and should probably be read last too. Yet it is hard not to write them as if you were really starting out and knew only very sketchily what was to follow. However, since this is a book about – amongst other things – reading books, the testimony of the writer as reader of her own work ought not to be thought absolutely negligible, or certainly no more so than an announcement of the 'intentions' from which the writing began. Even if the assertion that I have wanted this book to enact particular seductions and to display certain kinds of seductiveness amounts to scarcely more than a declaration that I have been seduced by my own argument, that is where I'll begin.

My interests as a feminist have always started from women's relations with a male and dominantly heterosexual culture. I have wanted to consider how women have thought and written about those relations and how feminism has conceptualised them and made proposals for changing them. There are feminisms more utopian than mine, more radical, more practical and more academic. As I explain in my first chapter, I came late to feminism, and the experiences underlying my resistance to its earlier voices characterise one version of the relations between women and male culture which are my theme here. For I was, and still am, seduced by men's systematic and exhaustive claims on our meanings and our realities through their occupation of everything which is thought of not as male, but simply as human. That sort of seduction even extends to aspects of feminism; for feminism has been shaped by the need to earn a place for itself within politics, within the academy and its disciplines, within 'common-sense' accounts of what is allowed as reasonable. So that feminism is required to justify what can look like its assault on the notion of 'humanity'. Then I am seduced by men themselves – or, at least, by one or two of them – men I know and men whose work I know. I dare say most of us are. Even women who have chosen to sever all connections with men have needed to fight their way out of the seductions which contributed to the desire to separate in the first place.

Seductions are dangerous as well as delightful, resistible as well as irresistible, and women may be ruined by them or made happy. Seduction is necessarily quite different from rape, though there are times when it may seem rather like a deflected or renamed rape. For in spite of all its slippery meanings and momentum, seduction must always return us to the fact of consent, to the eliciting of consent and the offering of consent. It is with the character of such consent, and with the traditions and pressures which bear on it, that I am concerned. Certainly seduction, as I mean to use it, is a shifty metaphor, sexual through and through – if always ambiguously and excessively so – as it spills into other aspects of women's lives: into their thought, their work and into the reports they have been able in one way or another to give of themselves. Seduction and the seductive entanglement may be thought of as analogies or metaphors, but they also provide the means by which sexual relations can be inserted into any understanding of how power is experienced in societies built on inequality. For by seductions I mean all those ways in which women learn who they are in cultures which simultaneously include and exclude them, take their presence for granted while denying it, and entice them finally into narratives which may reduce them by exalting them.

Women are seduced by more than the promise of sexual pleasure or escape from poverty, or even eternal devotion. They are seduced as well by the stories men have told about those seductions and by the vision of women which may be derived from such stories. And if women have given their consent to these stories and to the social arrangements they confirm as both natural and necessary, they have also withheld their consent and fought for alternatives. Critical women's voices have not always been heard for what they are, for the story of seduction repudiates women's denials as shrill and spoil-sport. It is clear too that such denials have not been much helped by those feminist writers who, in wanting to discover (or recover) for themselves voices and visions which were new and miraculously unadulterated by their subaltern history, have disconcerted the rest of us by their claims to be doing so. Women can no more escape being adulterated than they can escape being adulteresses; and it comes to seem urgent that feminism return to the divisions and tensions of women's actual lives amongst men and to the reasons why men and women who speak the same language have such difficulties with communication.

My first chapter contains three quite different approaches to this theme, to be read perhaps as a kind of triptych: associated panels rather than continuous narrative. There is, first, an autobiographical tracking of my recalcitrance as a feminist. This is followed by an attempt to define what I mean by seduction in relation to Gramsci's use of 'hegemony'. There is finally a reading of two novels, Samuel Richardson's *Clarissa* and Jane Austen's *Sense and Sensibility*, which focuses on their differences and continuities as novels about the seduction of women by upper-class men. So, autobiography, argument and rereading: the three parts of the chapter representing attempts to discover my starting point and the core of my preoccupations as a feminist. Singly they would fail, I think. Together they may go some way towards suggesting the scope and the intractable character of what I am after.

I have chosen to start from – and sometimes to 'lapse' into – autobiography on principle (not that there is anything particularly reassuring about that). In doing so I have wanted to insist on a particular history within which gender difference has been articulated and understood in particular ways. Naturally I hope that the experiences I volunteer and the connections I make between these and the books and ideas I am considering will prove recognisable. But it is not my purpose to extrapolate from my readings, my questions, my feminism, to other women's. Far from that. It is in some sense generalisation itself which is the problem. For generalisation belongs with other (usually academic) modes of thinking and writing which have ignored sexual difference so long as the level of truth aspired to could be regarded as impervious to all queries starting with the words, 'But who exactly . . .?'

Yet one charge against feminism which it has not always been easy to counter has concerned its tendencies to essentialism and its favouring of solutions which disregard differences between women and similarities between women and men. Some feminists have insisted on the supremacy of 'women' as a category in the teeth of passionate disagreement from other women – for whom being black, for instance, or working-class, or both, has mattered more, in their view, than being a woman has. I can take issue with neither group of women over this, especially since both strategies are found perfectly acceptable in other political contexts. But I am exercised as to whether writers and politicians on the Left can be trusted to include women as participants and women's lives as preoccupations within any politics developed out of analyses of power and the economic relations between classes. For classes have been envisaged principally as communities of men who work and have women at home.

As I have read my way into those men's texts, ideas and traditions which have seemed to me simultaneously seductive for feminism and excluding of women, I have been at least as unsettled by their inherent sexlessness as by their exploitation of sexual difference. Women find themselves absent rather than traduced for the most part within theoretical work. Indeed, feminism is especially threatened by the lofty representativeness of a tradition of philosopher kings (and by their contemporary incarnations as 'liberal ironists'[1]), for whom the sexlessness of important ideas and of thought itself is axiomatic, and whose style expresses only genial disapproval of an attention to differences between women and men which exceed the linguistic. What they write (and there is, of course, no reason why *they* should not sometimes be women) sings with the assurance that it could just as well be written by a woman or apply to women or be read by them. A specious scattering of female pronouns serves to remind readers – whatever the author's purposes may be – that women's notably slight presence amongst philosophers and linguists and critics and political theorists has got to be explained *somehow*. And if 'natural' explanations are to be dismissed with scorn, 'historical' ones can be dismissed less easily. For instance, the author of a recent article on Mary Wollstonecraft praises her for believing that 'mind has no sex'.[2] Only women have needed to make or heed such a claim. And the fact that it is a crippling one as well as an all too understandable one epitomises the tension of seduction, and, needless to say, the problem of men's refusal to see *themselves* as always and in whatever guise gendered people.

'The one great silent area'[3] of Chapter 2 is women and women's politics in the work of Raymond Williams. I have set out to trace, through a number of his theoretical and critical works and in his novels, his curious privatising of women and sexual relations and family life: their banishment from politics and even from history. This may be thought odd as well as disappointing in Williams, given his lifelong commitment to making connections between, for instance, intellectual work and other kinds of work, but also between levels of productive and cultural activity. As I try to show, the 'common culture' which was the organising aspiration of much of Williams's work never quite included women, either materially or imaginatively.

There are ways in which Williams has come to stand for me (as for some other feminists) as the quintessentially beguiling father, intellectual and teacher. This seduction is the first and the model for others. The invitation to join men in the interests of better understanding and even a better world is summarily and inexplicably withdrawn. A socialism which is potentially hospitable to women and to feminism abruptly shows them the door, while rebuking them for calling attention to themselves and for a hundred other adulteries (both petty and grave) of mind, body and soul. Women remain suppressed even within Williams's most moving revelations of history's suppression of whole classes; and in contrast to his celebration of working-class resistance, in the past and now, women's resistances are treated with suspicion and reproach.

In Chapter 3 I tell the story of my great-aunt, Clara Collet, a woman who may be thought to have succumbed but also to have stood up to fathers and intellectuals of her own. She began her career as a teacher, then worked for Charles Booth as a social investigator and statistician during the 1880s and went on to become one of the first professional women civil servants. The choice between marriage and a career was a hard and – to a considerable degree – an economic one for a woman like Clara, rather than a feature of (or even a metaphor for) kinds of contradiction that may be experienced by women nowadays. Equally hard were the learned disparagements of women's capacities built into what was a 'good' education for girls, an education which also offered the only weapons there were, in Clara's view, for contesting such disparagements.

I move in the fourth chapter to aspects of women's relations to imperialism, colonialism, slavery and racism. These relations, and what it has been possible to say about them, are set alongside two particular analyses of parts of that history. My interest in the effects of the colonising process as they are understood by Frantz Fanon and Edward Said is due in part to the neglected potential of both writers' arguments for a feminist account of class and race oppression. For both authors reduce women to metaphors for the colonised condition while extruding women themselves from the living as well as the discourses of colonialism and anti-colonialism. The chapter ends with a reading of Toni Morrison's *Beloved* and the possibility that a female perspective on the experience of slavery significantly expands on what we can otherwise know about it.

My final chapter collects together a number of reiterated themes from earlier chapters: education, reading, the learning of gender and the uneasy truce which may come to be assumed between feminism and femininity, or between a women's politics and women. These themes are exposed to the infinitely seductive theories of language and literature developed by Vološinov and Bakhtin in the Soviet Union during the thirties and afterwards.[4] Women are again absent from these theories, or most ambiguously present in them. Yet these are theories which insist on multiplicity and replace abstractions about language with a view of its transforming, interactive character, endlessly mediating between people who speak to one another out of relations of inequality. It is with the anomalous position of women with regard to criticism and subversiveness and jokes that I end, linking the treatment women receive in Bakhtin's wonderful study of

Rabelais with my own education and with the problems of educating girls to a critical awareness of their own possibilities: problems which are given imaginative life in Margaret Atwood's novel *Cat's Eye*.

Reading and rereading are method and substance here. My argument rests on readings and develops out of readings, even out of readings of readings and readings about reading. Feminist readings do not displace other readings, or settle once and for all the meaning and value of texts. As they challenge readings which suppress women they must also coexist and contend with such readings, even borrow from them. And since feminist readings necessarily pose the possibility of multiple readings, of alternatives, they promise no Eurekas, no final solutions, no right readings, not even themselves. And just as prevailing readings will persist to survive my criticisms of them, so there will always be something else, new exposures, new glimpses of who and what were inaccessible to the imaginative structures of particular writers and readers rooted in particular times and particular places. Awareness of specific historical impediments to kinds of empathy or identification, of the dynamics of conflict and of the levers of change: these have constituted strengths for feminism, just as the knowledge that feminism's entry into the field of criticism has transformed that field will defeat the elephantine orthodoxies which still deny it.

It would be disingenuous to leave it at that, however, with feminism as no more than a plucky contender in a proliferating, even infinite accumulation of additions and caveats. That might well reduce feminism's purposes and achievements to no more than a set of interpretative strategies, easily learned and easily applied, and completely untethered to women's histories and particularities, offering, therefore, no prospect of change. Feminisms, however multifarious, address the lives of half the world's population, and because that half has lived a vast range of dependencies the voices developed within these feminisms will be voices which have been heard only rarely and which, once heard, alter knowledge.

Antonio Gramsci, who was founder and leader for some years of the Italian Communist Party, was also the writer and thinker who, perhaps more than any other in this century, initiated a significant rereading of Marx in the light of a study of twentieth-century capitalism and the political and cultural relations which have maintained it. His distinctive contribution was in the area of this connecting of culture with political and economic activity. Although he focused on women only in their role as workers (and that, after all, put him well ahead of most other Marxist theorists of this century), his reconceptualising of 'hegemony' (which I shall go on to discuss more fully in Chapter 1) depends on an explicit linking of developing political consciousness with the emergence of new cultural forms and even a new group of artistic practitioners. He did not, of course, believe that new artists, a new culture, would simply burst into being, but he did believe that – as he wrote in the 1930s when he was in prison – 'one must speak of a struggle for a new culture', and that:

> A new social group that enters history with a hegemonic attitude, with a self-confidence which it initially did not have, cannot but stir up from deep within itself personalities who would not previously have found sufficient strength to express themselves fully in a particular direction.[5]

Gramsci envisaged that process as following from transformed relations between intellectuals and the people and between what he distinguished as hegemonic cultures and subaltern cultures. Those changes could not simply be asserted. They had to be wrenched out of an elaborated consciousness of what relations between classes really entailed. 'Subaltern', an important word in Gramsci's work, has made its way into feminist argument from time to time, and helpfully, I think.[6] For its double and connected meanings mirror the dual and pincer-like character of women's dependencies.

On the one hand, 'subaltern' carries the meaning of inferior (and is probably most familiar in its meaning of a subordinate rank in the army), but it also stands for the particular as opposed to (or as a part of) the general in logical categories; for the specific (indeed, the subordinate) rather than the universal. The *Oxford English Dictionary* illustrates the word's meaning, oddly and interestingly, with a pronouncement from the poet Southey – which could certainly be debated on quite other grounds – that 'Christianity, they say, has raised the sex from servitude but has condemned them to subalternity'. Southey's contrasting of the two states is illuminating. For the specialising of women and of discussion about women within arguments for which an altogether broader human relevance may always be claimed delivers a condition which, if it is not servitude, resembles something like perpetual marginality. This condition is marked by uncertainty, and is excluded from the kinds of generalisations about human life and what matters most to it which guide and shape societies.

I have dwelt on this notion of 'subalternity', and indeed on Gramsci's connecting of political formation with cultural production, because the seductions I am most interested in have more in common with Gramsci's account of the relation between social classes than with Freud's writings on the seductions of daughters by their fathers. Yet, as I've already indicated, my use of seduction actually spans – illegitimately, it may be thought – the spheres of political thought and of psychoanalysis, though I think of myself as more susceptible to the first than to the second: a proposition with which Freud would have felt no need to agree. It is also the case that seduction as a term and as an event in psychoanalysis has been very thoroughly explored by a number of feminist writers,[7] and though I make use of their work, I have not wanted either to emulate it or simply to rehearse their arguments.

I should, none the less, acknowledge a debt in this context to the work of Juliet Mitchell.[8] And having recently reread Jane Gallop's *Feminism and Psychoanalysis: The Daughter's Seduction*, which I must have read for the first time shortly after its publication in 1982, I need to confess that its connecting of the role of the seduction in analytic theory with the dangerous seductiveness of such theories and theorists for feminists bent on holding their own within academic institutions, or within especially abstruse and even criminally obscure intellectual traditions, must have influenced me more than I had realised. I cannot altogether have forgotten her puncturing of Jacques Lacan as a 'ladies' man . . . always embroiled in coquetry'[9], nor her irreverent name-calling of the sometimes impossibly difficult Julia Kristeva as 'the vulgar Bulgar',[10] nor, more seriously, her harking back to Luce Irigaray's speculation that

> it would be too risky, it seems, to admit that the father could be a seducer, and even eventually that he desires to have a daughter in order to seduce her. That he wishes to become an analyst in order to exercise – by means of hypnosis, suggestion, transference, interpretation bearing upon the sexual economy, upon proscribed sexual representations – a lasting seduction upon the hysteric.[11]

So perhaps one of the deadliest and least resistible of seductions for feminists is their seduction by theorists, by theories, by the theoretical. This book bears witness to my own vulnerable interest in the kinds of intellectual project whose vaporous abstractions and purest distillations encourage a soaring-off from the grit and distraction of women and their irritatingly unabsorbable condition. But the alternative inspires terror too: anti-intellectualism, the comforts of an unprincipled empiricism, of injunctions to turn for *real* wisdom to the anecdotal, the personal and private, to narrative, to fiction. Wary, buffeted, we look for compromise, settlement and, of course, for ways out, new forms, reconceptualised vantage points. It was heartening recently to read Kate Soper's firm statement of the problem in a review of a collection of essays by a number of

American sociologists and political theorists called *Feminism as Critique*:[12]

> For there is more than a suggestion here that the male theorist is being shown what his theory would have had to say about the subordination of women were he to have devoted more serious attention to it – a patience of theoretical disposition which has its echo in the suggestion here and there in the book that this or that bit of Marx or Habermas is 'not helpful' to feminism. (To avoid misunderstanding: I thoroughly applaud this kind of constructive engagement with non-gender-sensitive theories. I just wonder whether the theoretical ghettoization of feminism is not protracted by the modesty which allows such theories to be 'unhelpful' as opposed to seriously flawed.)[13]

Critical engagement of both kinds is now regularly undertaken by feminists within and across a whole range of academic areas: philosophy, political science, sociology, the physical sciences, psychology, and so on. Yet feminism's origins as a politics require such engagement to be doubly vigilant and self-conscious, not least because the presence of women within the academy has so short a history and is still by and large so circumscribed and unequal, and career routes and traditions of teaching and research are so little affected by women's arrival as workers (or indeed as students) in universities and polytechnics.[14] Besides, women doing intellectual work are by no means equivalent to feminists doing it. How could they be, given the conventions of sexless knowledge and thought I have alluded to and to which education at all levels is still in fact committed? More important still is feminism's central concern with material oppression and, therefore, with the predicament of the majority of women in the world, for whom an impoverished or nonexistent education may well be thought the least of their many deprivations.

The best feminist research addresses both kinds of problem simultaneously. For instance, in a study which begins from the determining effect of working-class women's voting on post-war politics in this country, Nicky Hart points out that

> had Labour succeeded in attracting women's votes as successfully as it attracted male votes then it would have been Gaitskell not Macmillan who would have presided over postwar 'affluence', and it would have been Callaghan and not Thatcher who would have profited from the legacy of North Sea oil.[15]

Serious questioning as to why such a substantial number of working-class women vote to the right of their husbands has not gone on. Instead, a number of surveys by social scientists have, since the end of the Second World War, relied on traditional explanations. They have been perfectly satisfied with the notion of women's 'deferential' voting, or with women's political and economic naiveté (the result of their limited access to the politicising workplaces and arrangements of their husbands), or with the narrowness of the purely 'material' aspirations so crassly preferred by women to 'their true political interests'. Hart's critique is directed at assumptions which conflate men's and women's class interests unproblematically, when, as she puts it,

> one concomitant of the diminution of class consciousness which accompanied the growing affluence of manual workers was a decline in gender inequality . . . One direct effect of privatization is greater equality within the conjugal household. When male workers spend their surplus income on their homes rather than themselves, the result is higher living standards for their families.[16]

Hart's study returns to historical work on the nineteenth-century spending patterns of working-class men and women and to beliefs in men's superior 'rationality' and economic sophistication. She points out that these qualities appear to have been learned from and to have accompanied many men's spending half or more of their earnings on their own pleasures, while their wives 'naively' managed to feed and clothe the entire family on the other half. The purpose of Hart's study is in part to refute the Left's obdurate clinging to myths promulgated by those political surveys which trivialise women's reasons for voting Tory. The pig-headedness of the Labour Party on this front has, after all, been immensely self-destructive. But behind these mistaken conclusions are the academic methodologies which promote and confirm them. 'The culture of masculinity which serves as an impediment to a decent standard of living,' Hart concludes, 'has also obstructed the search for intellectual understanding.'[17]

Work of this kind addresses crucial and current political questions. It also engages with the circularities of research methods and interpretation within an academic discipline fortified (as they all are) against even the enquiries of the uninitiated. Yet these are matters of great importance to men as well as women, and to the development of serious understandings about how class and other unequal oppositions are lived in the late twentieth century.

The purpose of feminism as I see it is to disturb, irrevocably, the steady male gaze and the unquestioning male possession of the structures of economic and cultural power. For, as the French writer Catherine Clément has put it, 'men's education suppresses its own violences'.[18] And those violences, and the powers they so silently and covertly buttress, are deeply seductive to women. This book is about the experience of that seduction, and about the possibilities for resisting it and answering back.

1

Seduction and Hegemony

> She could just imagine it printed in a seducer's manual: *in an intimate moment always tell the lady (whoever she is) that you love her. This alone and unaided can turn an act of banditry into the supreme compliment.*
>
> Lorna Tracy, *Amateur Passions. Love Stories?*

I

Some time ago I was given an old copy of *The Twentieth Century*. It was a special number on women: pink, with a palely gleaming Mona Lisa on its cover. It is odd really that I hadn't read it before, since it came out in August 1958 and contains what could be described as my first appearance in print. This particular copy belonged to a writer called Betty Miller, and it was in her article, which was called 'Amazons and Afterwards',[1] that I appeared, anonymously and representatively, as Afterwards. The journal's editorial includes me, too, as one of the pony-tailed generation, clones of Françoise Sagan and Brigitte Bardot, who seemed to show absolutely no interest in what the journal referred to as 'women's civic rights'.

When I first met Betty Miller in the early fifties she was becoming quite well known in a small way as the author of a good biography of Robert Browning. I had read two of the seven novels she wrote during the thirties and forties. I did not know her well, but I liked her, and that was unusual for me. I was a late developer in this respect as in the matter of women's civic rights, and I didn't much like people who were older than me. Since the relation between generations of women and questions of age and ageing have emerged for me as central dilemmas for women and are a theme of this book, this suspicion of older people needs signalling. I suppose that I didn't like their having done and known so many things before me. I didn't like what I took to be their too well-thought-out plans for my future, and I didn't like the messages I felt they communicated about the possibly spurious value I acquired simply by being young. Betty was different. She had no plans at all for my future, and when she talked to me it was about ageless things like the sort of day she'd had, the absurd cavortings of a writer friend who lived down the road and a few of the pompous and irritating things her husband had said or done during the last week or so. She wrote her first novel when she was twenty-one and I was not quite one, so there is no doubt of her belonging to an older generation. Besides, my younger sister was stepping out with her son, though they were both still at school at that point. I remember her, though, as someone only a little older – and taller – than I was, and similarly awkward, perverse – beady, perhaps. She was often very funny as well as rather despairing.

She rang me in about January 1958. She'd been asked to write a piece about the younger generation of what the journal's editor called 'thinking women', which meant no more than women with degrees. We had a laugh at what we took to be the implications of 'thinking women' and of their opposites (unthinking, thoughtless, mindless, just silly) and at her plan to refer to 'more than one young woman' when offering me up as her data. I responded to her questions with the verbose conviction of a recent convert and told her exactly how I had discovered the secret of life. I had been married for nearly two years and had a six-month-old baby. Since his birth I had given up paid employment and was living off my husband, who had been temporarily out of work but was now earning over £20 a week. In our tiny flat, with its views into the highest branches of huge plane trees on one side and across a row of white houses built for Queen Victoria's ladies-in-waiting on the other, I was, I think, happier than I had ever been. This was better than being a child, better than being a student and much better than going out to work. I played with my baby and read books while he slept. I learned to combine housework with his waking hours, so that he would kick and expostulate on one bit of the floor while I tackled the straw matting with a toothbrush and a safety pin on another. His sleeping time was too valuable to me to waste on such tasks, so he experienced me chiefly, I suppose, as an interlocutor of sorts, and as a cleaner and provider. I allowed myself £3 10s a week for food and cigarettes (stylishly, as I thought, Woodbines in those days) which was more than enough when mince was 2s 8d and small Cox's apples as little as 6d a pound. So there I was when Betty rang, jiggling my baby on a denimed knee and as smug as hell.

The view of older literary persons (who were at least as likely to be men as women) was, she explained to me, that my generation was a lethargic and ungrateful lot, insensible of our advantages and of the struggles of our grandmothers and mothers on our behalf. I had, it is true, grown up knowing that my grandmother and her sisters had been suffragettes. I had aunts and great-aunts who had taught all their lives. There were doctors and scientists and writers and civil servants and singers and painters and psychoanalysts and anthropologists and collectors of this and that amongst the women of my family on both sides. My mother had drawn or painted every day of her life, faithful to the exhortations of Henry Tonks at the Slade, but also to her sense of her own talent and needs.

Betty's tone in the article as she paraphrases and comments on my account of my position is initially quite approving, or at any rate neutral:

> Questioned as to her own private reaction at this giving up of her rights, one young woman most unexpectedly answered – 'I love it! I actually enjoy the feeling of giving up my rights. Do you know – in some strange way, it's a great relief?' And she went on to say that in thus relinquishing an arid competition with the outer world, such as the conditions of her job had forced upon her, she had found in the domestic sphere, above all, in the single-handed care of her first child, a wholly unlooked-for release and fulfilment. Instead of envying the career women, she now enjoys a novel life in which, for the first time, she is, within her own sphere, supreme arbiter, and in which the tempo of that life, its duties as its pleasures, are largely dependent on no other will than her own. Moreover – an added bonus, this – free of the office and its imposed routine, she is able to find more time now than ever before to read, and so to cultivate, unhindered, her own intellectual life.

Later in the piece Betty grows impatient with my complacency and with what seems to her a distinct retreat on my part:

> And the young woman of to-day is openly indifferent to her own 'Rights'? Is not this, perhaps, because no one, so far, has seriously attempted to wrest them from her? Let the attempt – the hint, the mere hint of an attempt be made – and just see what happens!

Read thirty years later, the writing expresses something of the exasperation I feel myself with this self-indulgent young woman, who knew so much better than her elders and seemed to care and know so little about other people's lives. But then I am now a good deal older than Betty Miller was when she wrote the piece. I have become one of those older women I'd have been wary of in those days. It also needs to be said that only a very few weeks after that telephone call I was offered a part-time job with a publisher, which I accepted: and that for two and sometimes three days a week for the next three years I paid another (much older) woman £3 of the £7 I earned to look after my son.

These were indeed sluggish beginnings for a feminist, and explaining my enthusiasm for motherhood and domesticity as some kind of resistance to an older and supposedly more serious generation of women would be inadequate, if not fraudulent. As one purpose of this book is to explore ambivalence and reluctance on the part of many women, in confronting the possibilities opened up by feminism, I want to do more anyway than apologise or blush for the heady unconcern of my younger self. It may be, of course, that I simply feel ignored by most histories of feminism, but I am conscious that any history which sticks too doggedly to the manifestations of its own definition of feminism is quite likely to miss other isolated, poorly articulated and disgruntled beginnings.

At any time during the last one hundred and fifty years women who became involved in a politics on behalf of women must have started from (even where they operated consciously against) political formations organised by men and likely – in a variety of ways – to be negligent of women's interests. Class, culture and economic dependence have worked to isolate women and to deter them from resisting the effects of what is expected of them by men (but also, and importantly, by an older generation of women). Issues of generation, conflicting time-scales, arise within any movement set to challenge political domination from the margins. This may be peculiarly the case for women, since their life-span can be made to seem fractured and discontinuous, measured as it is by their servicing role within a male economy. Women's perceptions may also, like their needs, change in adjustment to the stages of their lives.

I joined the Labour Party in my teens, and worked – not hard, and chiefly at election time – for the local party of my home town and later at Cambridge. By 1958, my involvement consisted of not much more than addressing envelopes and canvassing for a local party struggling with nearly the largest Tory majority in the country. If my embarrassing speech to Betty Miller issued from a wish to assert myself against my elders, I was also negotiating difficulties I had with what I knew to be the privileges of my upbringing, though I did not always experience them as that. My grandparents and most of the older members of my family also supported the Labour Party of those days. Some of them knew Stafford Cripps and Clement Attlee. So I was no sort of a rebel on this account. The university I went to was the one to which virtually all the male members of my family and a good many of the female ones had gone too. I had blown a brief and solitary raspberry by announcing in my teens that I would not go to university at all but would be a PE instructor, a gymnast – even a nurse. I fell into line shortly afterwards, however. I was prey, I know, to twinges of frustration and even, sometimes, to spasms of rage and destructiveness, but I certainly remained a complete stranger to anything sustained and thought-out in the way of resistance to the life which seemed, quite mildly, to await me.

In fact, my brief maternal idyll in the tree tops was produced in part by my determination *not* to be one of *The Twentieth Century*'s 'thinking women' (which included on this occasion Florence Night-ingale, Simone Weil, Marghanita Laski, Mary Warnock and Jac-quetta Hawkes), not to be special or creative or glorious or pampered, not to rely on servants or an unearned income, not even to depend on expensive domestic aids (because I knew most working-class women survived without them), and so on. If I now feel critical of those attitudes as romantic, irrelevant, foolish, it is because they remind me of a politics envisaged almost entirely in terms of my own conscience and peace of mind, which paid no attention to other people – let alone to other women – who were working for political change.

By the time I became a working mother (as we were called) at the end of the fifties I had at least tumbled to the fact that I would never earn as much as my husband, and that though some options were open to me which had not been available to an earlier generation, those 'civic rights' I was thought so carelessly to have relinquished were, in point of fact, pretty notional still. When (in the mid sixties) I read *The Captive Wife*[2] by Hannah Gavron, I think I was shocked to discover that my personal sense of being left out and behind by my male contemporaries had become a topic suitable both for academic study and for political action. Yet not long afterwards Hannah Gavron, whom I had met, killed herself. Her suicide mattered to me, though she had not been a friend. I think I felt that her attempt to translate her own predicament into a general and solvable one had – and somehow predictably – backfired on her.

By the seventies I had two more children and was beginning to read whatever I could about women's writing and women's lives. I taught English in a comprehensive school in London during those years and reviewed novels by the yard (most of them by women). I still worked – intermittently, but with a gathering enthusiasm – for the Labour Party. By now I was huffily backing away from a younger generation of women rather than an older one. I had sons and a daughter, whose schooling I often construed as a problem, while teaching black and working-class children, whose schooling was clearly much more of a problem. I found it as hard as most teachers did then to focus at all helpfully on girls as a category which overlapped with those other ones but was also distinct from them. I recognised and sympathised with girls' ambivalence about them-selves, but I don't think I believed there was much they or I could do about it.

When I finally, lingeringly and irritably, approached feminism, it was, perhaps oddly, for the absolutely invaluable intellectual vantage point it seemed to offer. I had been researching into – and writing about – bilingualism, immigration, cultural conflict and inequality,

as these things are experienced in schools and by children. There was
something I wanted to say, and found difficult to say, about power
and language and about the usefulness of understanding the ways in
which people are *not* straightforwardly part of a culture. Or rather –
and this was the important thing for me – there are great differences
in the ways people experience and are able to express their sense of
belonging and not belonging to groups and traditions. By now I was
working in a university education department. I had become in some
sense an 'academic'. The questions became focused for me round the
problems for women of 'mastering' a language and a set of theoretical perspectives which ignored sexual difference as a term in almost
all intellectual work; though its practitioners, like other people, lived
pretty uncritically according to social constructions of sexual difference in all other aspects of their lives.

Late as ever, hobbled by my own perversities, I really thought by
the eighties that I was catching up. Here was a political movement
which managed to attend to my dilemmas while addressing and
concerning itself – both actively and intellectually – with the most
important issues of a post-imperialist world. My life, my professional
concerns within education and literature, could perhaps contribute
to a politics which was no longer a mere idealistic grafting. Middle
age, the menopause, redeemed for me now from old views of them as
signalling the subsidence of a woman's life, promised settlement,
collaboration, the release of energies, a healing of generational
differences. Action might, after all, be possible. I did not expect to be
received with open arms. Pacemakers can't, after all, be expected to
wait around for stragglers making their last-ditch spurt. I think I had
hoped to find more enthusiasm for – and even a collective pride in –
the sheer breadth of the feminist achievement and the complexity and
richness of the terrain opened up and debated by feminists.

In fact, untroubled enthusiasm of that sort may be difficult to find
these days. There is exhaustion with men's deafness and with the
general disarray in which Left politics has found itself during the
eighties. Then there has been a systematic and malign hijacking of
feminism by the media to mean something like an extension of greed,
competitiveness and ruthless individualism to women. Meanwhile,
some apparently irreconcilable divisions have arisen amongst feminists, who are no more generous to their opponents than anyone else
is.

Yet for those of us for whom the interest and the commitment
remain, these divisions are in themselves generative ones which
detract not at all, in my view, from the sense that feminism is still
potentially the politics and the intellectual force of the last years of
the century. For even where the emphases diverge, the marking of

women's difference, of their absences and presences, the inconsistencies of their exclusions and inclusions in relation to class and race and imperialism, raises major questions, the answers to which have the potential radically to change the ways in which people live and work together. Those are grand claims, which probably far exceed the scope of this book, but they are the ones which have inspired its arguments. So that if I am to declare my purposes in relation to the long-term purposes and achievements of feminism I need to confront and characterise these different traditions in feminism, whose adherents are often so hostile or indifferent to each other, but from which I have, as have most feminists, inherited preoccupations and approaches.

Two books – incidentally published in the same week and by the same publisher, and each assembled as a necessary summary or landmark of current feminism – illustrate two divergent strains in feminist thought and their particular areas of overlap. Broadly, this divergence is between the practical, often sociological or policy-orientated research of a writer like Ann Oakley, on the one hand, and the ideas deriving largely from French feminism and psychoanalysis, which employ the tactics of deconstruction, on the other. *What is Feminism?*,[3] edited by Juliet Mitchell and Ann Oakley, could be said to belong in the first category (despite Juliet Mitchell's distinguished work in psychoanalysis) and Toril Moi's *The Kristeva Reader*[4] in the second. Both books depend on kinds of collaboration and on notions of the range of feminist concerns.

At its worst, *What is Feminism?* (which deliberately recalls the anthology of essays, *The Rights and Wrongs of Women*,[5] edited by the same writers ten years earlier) has too much honing of watertight definitions of feminism and too much reworking of old research topics, which have by now provided too many 'keynote' addresses around the world. Some of the book's contributors are old hands at the academic paper and may be thought from time to time to be too little abashed by their ease with the form. Toril Moi's merciless intellectualism and her utopian and deconstructive refusal to truck with the least hint of liberal humanism could be similarly parodied. These are parodies, however, and neither fair nor wise to utter at a time when the press, which has been making a good deal of the phrase 'post-feminism', encourages the idea that feminism has either died of inanition or spontaneous combustion or, having achieved its paltry aims, need bother us no longer.

What is Feminism? contains, besides useful pieces on social policy in areas like health, law, work and welfare, excellent theoretical discussion by Juliet Mitchell and Rosalind Delmar, both of them early and pioneering feminist writers. Mitchell's 'Reflections on

Twenty Years of Feminism' exemplifies feminism's maturity and feminist thinkers' inherent need to engage with diversity and contradiction, given their starting point. Rosalind Delmar[6] argues well for talking of feminism*s* and for 'an historical examination of the dynamics of persistence and change within feminism'. She also sees an active feminist politics as incompatible with those forms of psychoanalytic and critical theory associated with writers like Julia Kristeva:

> To deconstruct the subject 'woman', to question whether 'woman' is a coherent identity, is also to imply the question of whether 'woman' is a coherent political identity, and therefore whether women can unite politically, culturally and socially as 'women' for other than very specific reasons.

We do indeed need to listen to that cogently expressed doubt as to the usefulness of dissolving 'women' from a category of material experience to a construct of language. Yet the material experience of being a woman includes women's acquiescence in forms of oppression, and that acquiescence has to be understood as a cultural and psychological process mediated by language if women are to do more finally than insert themselves as individuals into the existing male order at a number of specified points.

With considerable exegetical lucidity of a different kind, Toril Moi makes sense for us of the extraordinary, often difficult and varied aspects of the French feminist Julia Kristeva's intellectual project, which Moi characterises as no less than an attempt 'to think the unthinkable'. And if Kristeva recognises the somewhat mystical character of this attempt, she is also a pragmatist and as revolutionary in her own way as Mitchell and Delmar. For instance, in her wonderful essay 'Women's Time', she reminds us that 'the assumption by women of executive, industrial and cultural power has not, up to the present time, radically changed the nature of this power'. And it is this power, and its endlessly dispersed dislocations, which she is out to undermine. A 'unity' of women *is* hard to achieve if the consequences of those dislocations are bypassed for the purposes of getting something done. 'Feminism' for Kristeva 'has had the enormous merit of rendering painful' the fundamental difference between the sexes, and there is a danger within feminism that this essential pain is too quickly relieved, soothed, even 'cured'. There can be no straightforward alignments of women so long as they remain the creatures of an infinite or universalised oppressiveness, of a kind and on a scale which prevents women from conceiving of their own existence outside the excluding inclusions of them within a diffuse and all too capacious patriarchy. Nor can women's lives change in isolation. For their lives are inextricably tangled with men's, with children's. It is with women's conscious and unconscious acquiescence in this oppressiveness and oppression that I am concerned, and with the ways by which they are seduced into that acquiescence.

I shall need to return to the divergence within feminism which is expressed by Delmar's scepticism and by Kristeva's. For though it may indeed constitute a testament to feminism's willingness to confront contradiction and to admit irreconcilables, it also represents a perhaps unscalable wall in terms of traditions of thought and proposals for action. And the divergence is multidimensional: political, first and foremost, a matter of alliances, tactics and priorities, but also intellectual and ultimately generational. Yet this tension is more productive than 'sisterhood' ever was, with its monolithic view of women and its denial of class, race and cultural difference.

These disagreements within feminism are themselves implicated in forms of seduction, for both sides shelter to some extent within powerful male and academic contemporary discourses, from which their modes of confrontation are also borrowed. Both nod, if implicitly for the most part, at their heroes and gurus. Yet they are both involved in resistance to those discourses, and this is what they share. For just as Mitchell and Delmar invoke a history of women's struggle against oppression, so Kristeva takes the ideas of writers like Bakhtin in order to reverse the apparent impotence of female discourse. Both kinds of feminist are engaged in restatement, reformulation, the possibilities of remaking language and human relationships.

So it is interesting to return to Betty Miller, who started all this for me and whose penultimate novel was reissued two or three years ago. *On the Side of the Angels*[7] is about the Second World War and women and hero worship. At its centre are two sisters. Honor is married and currently stupefied by young motherhood and by her dependence on a husband who is looking for glamour and success through association with the Commanding Officer of the military hospital where he works. Claudia is tougher, unmarried, a teacher of history. She often despairs of her sister: 'Honor sitting back with a sort of complacency, accepting everything, uncritical audience to all this male pirouetting. One couldn't seem to rouse her to any sort of consciousness of her real position . . .' Yet Claudia herself risks everything to run away with the 'hero' of the Corps, who is, it turns out, a pathetic impostor. Each of them is unsympathetic to the other's particular accommodations to men. The novel delicately illustrates the difficulties women experience even in recognising one another so long as they deny what has kept them apart: the character of their individual and collective susceptibility to both the meretricious and the heroic in male culture. The question continues to be asked by those who are seduced as much as by those who aren't: why are women seduced by men, and how do they live with and resist that seduction?

II

The word 'seduction' presides somewhat wilfully over chains and clusters of meanings which are contradictory, tautologically driven and embedded in and issuing out of a number of worlds and variegated accounts and visions of those worlds. Seduction alludes simultaneously to notions of conquest and of captivation, while relying absolutely on expressions of consent or acquiescence. If seduction is most obviously entangled with sex and sexual relations it frequently foots it out of there, as I hope to show, in order to impregnate quite other territories. Charm and fascination may be said to gleam at one end of seduction's possibilities. Suborning, bribery and coercion lurk at the other. There are delights and pleasures to be found within its purview. There are also errors, wrongs, betrayals. And if, most especially, a seduction is something other than a rape, it may also be thought of as a deflected or renamed rape, a rape annulled by an ambiguous assertion of consent.

Seducers are possessed of powers: sexual, magical, verbal, musical, political or intellectual powers; and those who are seduced consent to the exercise of such powers – if only temporarily – even when they know they may be harmed by them. Those who let themselves be led astray, into wrongdoing or wrong thinking, have only themselves to blame. They have been beguiled, enticed, lured, won over. The language of seduction spells out the ambiguities within an apparently shared responsibility. The seducer tempts. The one who is seduced yields to temptation.

Surrender, then, is intrinsic to the act of seduction. The intentions, the activity and the achievement of the seducer depend on passivity and responsiveness in the seduced. For a seduction which is resisted is bound to fail. Indeed, it at once ceases to be a seduction. The role of the seduced, of the deceived, of the misled, is to confirm the seduction, even to celebrate its success. Stealth and trickery and wiles – standard items in the seducer's arsenal – are bizarrely redeemed by the consent they have been shown to elicit. Blame shifts and slips easily from the deceiver to the deceived, for there can be no seduction which does not implicate the one who is seduced. Milan Kundera writes about his womanising hero's recent discovery that 'conquest time has been drastically cut'.[8] He reminds us of seduction's ritual character, its merely residual survival within sexual encounters enjoyed by consenting adults in what must now be regarded as a pre-Aids twentieth-century European capital. For the speed with which seductive manoeuvres may be performed and their end accomplished has less to do with improved skills than with those social changes which may encourage a swifter surrender. The perfunctory seduction in Kundera's novel comes to mimic other inhumanities of post-1968 Prague. Kundera returns us to the ambiguity of consent and to a history of its meanings.

There are obvious reasons – and less straightforward ones – for women's concern with seduction. We will be told, of course, about Delilah, about liberties taken by women, even about the essential androgyny of Don Juans. It has none the less been women who were most often seduced, and it has usually been men who asserted, in one way or another, that a woman had given her consent to what may thereafter be thought of as a seduction. And whereas analogies with events on sporting or battle fields may be thought appropriate to a male account of a seduction, surrender to desire and to pleasure is not only more complex and dangerous for women, it is riskier to represent, always anomalously admitted to. Seduction comes to stand for the tensions and their dynamic inherent in the unequal relations between women and men. Its reciprocities, like its inequities, are characteristic of women's dependencies on men and of women's apparent acquiescence in many of the conditions of those dependencies.

This is one reason why I have started from 'seduction' when I might well have borrowed Antonio Gramsci's 'hegemony'[9] and started from there. For I need to insert a different and distinguishing metaphor into ways of thinking about and understanding domination. Gramsci's 'hegemony' describes institutions and strategies of control in a class society, through which those in power elicit and receive the consent of those they govern. These strategies acquire in Gramsci's analysis some of the tension and the elasticity I have emphasised in my circling of seduction. For those who are seduced or governed or colonised or otherwise oppressed find themselves, through the processes of hegemony, validating their seducers or rulers or oppressors – indeed, cheering them on – through the self-fulfilling apparatus of a contract drawn up and underwritten by those in power. Hegemony, it should also be said, comes to mean more than this in Gramsci's account. For the loops and balances and reciprocities, the forms of organised acquiescence, the networks of negotiation, which Gramsci saw as characteristic of modern capitalist states, are also frail, vulnerable, in need of perpetual attention and maintenance and renewal. Change, in this view, is achievable precisely through an understanding and exploitation of the workings of hegemony, through a manipulation of its particular rigidities and flow.

So far I have concentrated on the overlapping meanings of seduction and hegemony. These words issue, however, from significantly different histories of use. Behind seduction lie the private, the hidden and personal, the secret, the sensual, the erotic, and pleasure. Gramsci's version of hegemony bestrides a map of metaphors involving force and military conquest, massed and public and – inevitably – male belligerence. Yet the subtlety of Gramsci's appropriation lies precisely in his use of the word within an analysis of civil and potentially non-violent control. The influence of the differences between seduction and hegemony bears just as heavily on my argument, I think, as all that the two terms share.

I have already suggested that seduction carries more than the meanings associated with an overture to an act of sex or, indeed, with the multiplicities of interpretation likely to follow such an act. In a number of rather different ways I mean to explore this idea of seduction and the seductive entanglement as a way of approaching the relation of women to predominantly male and heterosexual cultures. Within such cultures women's consent is continuously elicited to practices, values, theories and language, embedded in the material conditions of their lives, which are at best based on arbitrary habits of differentiation according to gender, and at worst ignore or diminish women. Seduction, then, is my theme: as an analogy or metaphor, if you like, but also as a means of inserting sexual relations as an absolutely central term for any understanding of how power is experienced in societies based on inequality.

It is in fact the character of ideological as well as sexual seduction that I am after, as well as the reasons for its being just as difficult to exonerate theories deriving from the Left as from the Right. Why, for instance, is Gramsci's use of the word 'hegemony' at once so tantalisingly attractive to feminist analysis and yet so wholly undeveloped in its potential relevance to women? What has encouraged the acceptance by so many women of notions of the family and its sphere of responsibilities coming from both Right and Left, when these so strenuously constrain women's energies and intelligence and perpetuate such an array of economic and social injustices affecting men, women and children? There are never simple answers to questions about the capacity of ideology to get around and establish itself for ideology, if its meaning can be pinned down or found to reside anywhere, must participate in and be learned in every aspect of our everyday lives. In trying to do justice to the complexities of women's seductions into ways of life, behaviour, beliefs and traditions which have the potential to undermine them, I have wanted to portray seduction as both multifaceted and diverse. And so – if only to match seduction's slippery pressures and ubiquity – I have needed

to resort to narrative just as much as to argument and to autobiography and biography as much as to criticism. This could be said to
reflect another well-worked dilemma within feminism, one to which
I have already alluded: the seductiveness of systems of thought
whose origins and style are implicated in institutional exclusions of
women.

Foucault and Lacan, for instance, are both theorists to whom
feminists have listened attentively. Indeed, it has become almost *de
rigueur* to rehearse their best-known theoretical positions in a good
deal of feminist work. Yet it is hard to think when, if ever, women
were explicitly addressed by either writer. Both men insisted above
all on the constitutive character of language and discourse, and such
views allow little scope for thought or subjectivity outside learned
forms of language. The sheer abstractness of their arguments denies
the substance rather than the formula of difference as it applies to
women. And the deconstructive strategy makes discovery and
criticism of dominant discourses within projects like theirs essential
tasks, but also − necessarily − impossible ones. For instance, how
would it be possible for a woman to argue her own absence or
suppression or extrusion from a discourse which she is herself
using? Toril Moi poses this question in relation particularly to the
work of Julia Kristeva:

> Many women have objected to Kristeva's highly intellectual
> style of discourse on the grounds that as a woman and a
> feminist committed to the critique of all systems of power, she
> ought not to present herself as yet another 'master thinker'.
> From one viewpoint, this accusation would seem to be some-
> what unfair: what seems marginal from one perspective may
> seem depressingly central from another (*absolute* marginality
> cannot be had), and one cannot logically set out to subvert
> dominant intellectual discourses (as Kristeva does) without
> simultaneously laying oneself open to the accusation of being
> intellectualist. However, from another perspective, Kristeva,
> with her university chair in linguistics and her psychoanalytic
> practice, would certainly seem to have positioned herself at the
> very centre of the traditional intellectual power structures of
> the Left Bank.[10]

Kristeva herself has answered this question differently at different
times. Broadly, however, she has enjoined on women the strategies
of negation and denial. She expresses the necessity for 'a feminist
practice [which] can only be negative, at odds with what already
exists, so that we may say "that's not it" and "that's still not it"'.[11]
Alternative tactics drive feminism into the impasse of accepting

essentialist accounts of sexual difference, she believes, and this is unacceptable, for

> the belief that 'one is a woman' is almost as absurd and obscurantist as the belief that 'one is a man'. I say 'almost' because there are still many goals which women can achieve: freedom of abortion and contraception, day-care centres for children, equality on the job, etc. Therefore we must use 'we are women' as an advertisement or slogan for our demands. On a deeper level, however, a woman cannot 'be'; it is something which does not even belong in the order of *being*.[12]

The tensions and ellipses here are potentially silencing. Many women have felt as rebuked by Kristeva's sibylline utterance as by Germaine Greer's contemptuous boldness or Dale Spender's maddening simplicities. Kristeva may even be thought to have seduced some of the most imaginative feminist writers into an obscure, virtually mystical terrain and into forms of linguistics and psychoanalysis which are perilously individualised, unsocial and inhospitable to productive scrutiny. Their endeavours have at times become divorced from those other (surely crucial) endeavours, for which Kristeva cavalierly recommends the retaining of slogans like 'we are women'. I have already outlined the kind of objection to this position offered by a writer like Rosalind Delmar.

In developing 'seduction' as a metaphor for women's relation to a male-dominated culture I shall need, none the less, to hear Kristeva's injunction to negate. But I also want to hear women's reluctance – even their refusal – to negate. I want to understand women's willingness to be led and spoken for by men, the attraction for women of theories from which women and feminist analysis are absent. The relief that many women express at conceding that they are inevitably *hors de combat* may in part be due to the difficulty of so many feminist ideas and the contradictions they set up in women's actual lives.

Many women will suspect a feminist approach to a problem on the grounds that it is likely to attend *only* to the interests of women, forsaking broader considerations in the name of such sectional interests. Women have traditionally regarded other people as their province, after all. Where women have been educated beyond a certain age they will have been educated into their culture's expectations and conventions of order, coherence, consistency, logic: into hierarchical levels of argument and into specialised disciplinary traditions of written and spoken discourse, of exposition and presentation of evidence and proof, and so on. Even where the forms of ordering knowledge and discourse are seen to differ markedly as between one kind of society and another – between, say, broadly Western societies and China, or between Hindu and Arab cultures – such forms will be valued above all for their universalising and generalising capacities. And areas of knowledge constructed by such theories – whether we are talking about the physical properties of the universe or the patterns of change in human societies – will reject gender, by and large, as a relevant or usefully differentiating category.

Women have rarely been allowed to participate in the developing of traditions of thought or in their renewal or rewriting. They share that with most of the rest of the human race, of course. Grand theory is so by virtue of the potential and scope of its explanatory power as underwritten by the academy. Social or psychological theories which began from female experience as characteristically human would court charges of overspecifying, of losing sight of more general human problems by focusing on detail, the exceptional, even the redundant. Race and class are treated as superordinate categories compared with gender in most critical work on the Left, and many women will find that quite unexceptionable.

Yet, as I shall hope to show, assuming women as simply undifferentiated members of the human race achieves the same, and as little, as marking them off for special – if secondary – attention. If their complicity is taken for granted, their needs are bound to be ignored. For many of the thinkers of this century who have potentially the most to offer a feminist politics, women figure as adjuncts of men's private lives and the objects of both their significant and their trivial dreams. This puts the most important events and decisions of women's lives bizarrely outside politics and into enclaves of individual responsibility and moral tussling. The problem may be articulated as a conflict between accepting the place offered them in men's lives and men's ordering of existence, or resisting that seduction in favour of the terrors of negation, of criticism and abnegation and silence. If we start to distrust our alliances with men, querying men's good faith and their concern for our welfare, we are stripped of everything, including a language in which to explain ourselves.

We need to start somewhere else: with seduction itself and its pleasures; with art and literature, perhaps. For these activities and their products are hardened seducers of women, enticing us with their accounts of who we are and indefatigably dodging our replies and provisos and denials.

III

Operas, for instance, have to seduce us. When they fail to we all too easily see through to the fumbling flasher, abjectly exposing his tricks and plans for our enchantment, embarrassingly resistible. Don Giovanni himself must be irresistible, certain to notch us all up. Murderer, bandit, burglar he may be, but to see through his seductions, to deny him ourselves, is to spoil the fun – his fun, our fun, and the complicity of the won-over audience. Seductions can seem to have equivalent meanings for women as for men in such a scenario. A woman, after all, may 'let herself be seduced' or even, Delilah-like, seduce. She may also, a Zerlina, resist (with a little help), her evasions read simply as confirming, titillating, encouraging, or as the attractive face of a hard-nosed peasant economic sense.

Most kinds of resistance will be accommodated already, and explained, within the desires and achievements of the seducer. What women may not do is cancel the seduction, deny its nature, rename it, separating and distancing themselves from its intentions and its fulfilment. To do that is not just to misname but (worse) shamefully to overreact. Yet it is possible to construe women's inclusion as willing participants in their own seduction as a sleight of hand disguising their exclusion from the language which performs it. Seduction contains and measures out women's incapacity to speak for themselves or to claim as unadulterated a sexuality independent of men's dreams of them. If women's testimony is assumed, written in, to the act of seduction itself, their interrogation of the act, like their interrogation of the narrative which announces that act, will be short-circuited and disallowed.

It is important to pornography, in its least exalted forms as in its most, for women to participate excitedly in their own and in other women's seduction. Moreover, accounts of seduction and of women's role as procurers of it, aiders and abetters of it, which purport to be written by women when they are not, are also common features of the genre. It is not merely that myths and legends of the *Don Giovanni* kind tell stories which place women anomalously in relation to men's designs on them, but that women who read such tales, or write them, are cast as androgynous, duplicitous and at fault. That casting is inevitable, perhaps, within stories which are intended to explain male sexuality, even to console men for its pains and confusions. The problems of all that for women are, as usual, multiple. For if seduction is stealthy and stolen it is also, necessarily, seductive and delightful, so that women are required to concede above all that seduction is different from rape, that they have wanted it and that their complicity has, more often than not, had dire consequences for men.

Foucault, who taught us to think about sexuality in terms of historical discourses and their articulating of power, none the less contributed to a tradition which has offered the libertine as a kind of libertarian, hero, free spirit and individualist.[13] That tradition focused on women only in so far as they were the generalised object of male desire, thus narrowly determining women's scope for choice and resistance within narratives of seduction and ignoring the account of events they might have given themselves, if asked. The same tradition bypasses women as readers of such narratives, though they are readers who might, after all, be in a position either to endorse or to deny them, or even to replace them with alternatives. If women readers are assumed or implied at all they must be presumed to switch allegiance effortlessly and often, from a man's view of it all to a receptive and womanly one. Such a woman would need to read a novel like *Les Liaisons Dangereuses*[14] through eyes which were not just male but mistily misogynous, so that women become for other women creatures who are variously complicit with men, either as predators or as willing, foolish or hypocritical prey.

It has, above all, been difficult for women to write of seduction and of seductive men and seducers within a tradition which has measured the seducer's claim to general sympathy or disapproval in terms of his making off with another man's property and thereby contravening civil law, divine law, or both. Women will have had other ways of considering that theft of themselves (and it will not always have seemed to be out of the frying pan and into the fire), but they will also have needed to contend with testimonies to their complicity in male versions, which have covered their tracks in mimicry and ventriloquism. It is necessary to unravel actual women's stories of seduction from the falsetto productions of men, as a first step towards challenging those accounts of sexual relations and sexual difference which have established them as natural, universal, even eternal relations and difference, when they are always in fact historically specific and are, moreover, controlled as practice and as discourse by men, in their own interests. A powerful convention within such discourse is the attributing to women of views which men need women to have. Byron, for example, consoles his Don Juan with a letter from Donna Julia containing this stanza:

> 'Man's love is of man's life a thing apart,
> 'Tis woman's whole existence; man may range
> The court, camp, church, the vessel, and the mart;
> Sword, gown, gain, glory, offer in exchange
> Pride, fame, ambition, to fill up his heart,
> And few there are whom these cannot estrange;
> Men have all these resources, we but one,
> To love again, and be again undone.'[15]

It is worth remembering that these famous lines were written and attributed by a famous seducer to a woman who has let herself be seduced away from her husband by the guileless and adolescent Don Juan. It is written from the convent where, as an adulteress and a sinner, Donna Julia is complacently ready to spend the rest of her days. Men have wanted and needed to hear women tell them, as Byron gets Donna Julia to, that it is all right for men to love them and leave them, for how else would the world's business – whatever that might be for a Don Juan – get done?

In considering two novels about seducers, Samuel Richardson's *Clarissa* and Jane Austen's *Sense and Sensibility*, I want to chart continuities and overlaps as well as gaps and discrepancies between them. For though the novels are separated by more than fifty years and by the sex and class of their authors, they also have a good deal in common. It is possible, anyway, to see Jane Austen's novel as one in a sequence, which might also include novels as different as Fanny Burney's *Evelina* and George Eliot's *Adam Bede*, novels by women which rewrite the seduction story, perhaps even *Clarissa* itself, from within its constraints. Those constraints involve women in collusion with their attackers and allow only so much resistance to assaults on their bodies and their integrity as consorts at all credibly with retaining their appeal for men.

Because Richardson made Clarissa a tireless writer, on whose version of events we are encouraged to rely, the novel has sometimes been read as championing women and deploring men. Readers of both sexes have certainly found it hard to resist the novel's seductions, for it is subtle and humorous and it tells us in marvellous detail and at extraordinary length about eighteenth-century life and gentlemen's treatment of women. Yet at the heart of this beguiling story is a rape. It is from Lovelace himself that we first learn of his raping Clarissa. It is an event he reports on with brief, evasive elegance in letters to his friend, John Belford:

> And thus, between terror, and the late hour, and what followed, she was diverted from the thoughts of getting out of the house to Mrs Leeson's, or anywhere else.

and then:

> And now, Belford, I can go no farther. The affair is over. Clarissa lives. And I am
>
> > Your humble servant,
> > R. LOVELACE[16]

Lest that laconic allusion to a savage act be thought to stand straightforwardly for the value a reader might be expected – either by Lovelace or by Richardson himself – to put on it, those lines need some context and explanation. Clarissa herself could be said to be spared her own rape in the sense that she is first drugged and then shocked into unconsciousness. She remains in a coma, it turns out, for a week. The rape is made Lovelace's alone, for it leaves intact – according to such an account – Clarissa's body and mind, even though it strengthens her will to die. It is necessary to the rest of the novel that she be beyond charges of either complaisance or resistance at the time of the rape, and that she be disqualified even as a witness to it. The novel's strategies are designed to make rape compatible with seduction. Lovelace must be forgivable, just as Clarissa must remain uncontaminated by the passions and the covetousness she inspires and provokes. Richardson has made of Clarissa a paragon and a saint, whose death in her nineteenth year and a white satin nightdress is hardly less than an apotheosis. She has been coveted by men since her childhood. She is favoured as heiress to her grandfather, pet of her unmarried uncles, valued by her brother and father for her services as precocious housekeeper. She is also a clever businesswoman, expert in matters of law and wills and property, indefatigably given to improving herself, flawlessly beautiful, a devout Christian, a gifted linguist (happier writing French than speaking it) and an accomplished needlewoman, who is not above coining somewhat elaborate maxims of this sort:

> a woman who neglects the *useful* and the *elegant*, which distinguish *her own sex*, for the sake of obtaining the learning which is supposed more peculiar to the *other*, incurs more *contempt* by what she *foregoes* than she gains *credit* by what she *acquires*.[17]

As John Stuart Mill put it, 'we are perpetually told that women are better than men, by those who are totally opposed to treating them as if they were as good'.[18] This woman is not only better than men: she is far, far better than all the other women in the novel too. Clarissa's mother and sister speedily and enthusiastically join in the general condemnation of Clarissa and leave her to Lovelace and his stratagems, while Clarissa's 'dear Miss Howe' answers her letters with dispatch but moves not a finger to visit her beleaguered friend. Clarissa is so idealised a man's woman that a woman reader may be forgiven for wondering whether she can be read as a woman at all.

Mrs Sinclair, the brothel keeper, who attends Lovelace and incarcerates Clarissa for him, is also meant to be a woman. She is a creature of brutish vivacity who is implicated in Clarissa's rape and in the novel's diffuse and violent antagonisms towards women. In one of his letters to his friend Belford, just preceding his admission of rape, Lovelace offers this description of Mrs Sinclair:

The old dragon straddled up to her, with her arms kemboed again – her eyebrows erect, like the bristles upon a hog's back and, scowling over her shortened nose, more than half-hid her ferret eyes. Her mouth was distorted. She pouted out her blubber-lips, as if to bellows up wind and sputter into her horse-nostrils; and her chin was curdled, and more than usually prominent with passion.[19]

That image is produced by Lovelace as he contemplates admitting to the rape he has committed. It may also be understood as in some sense filtered through the drugged and terrified perceptions of the hapless Clarissa. Its association with the rape, and with Lovelace's urbane and only direct allusion to the rape, chimes with some of the novel's central dilemmas.

The elements of that image of Mrs Sinclair are wilfully fragmented and overlaid. A composite monster – dragon, hog, ferret and horse – is distorted and curdled as it straddles and sputters. The strangeness of similar vocabulary is remarked on much later in the novel by Clarissa, who characterises as 'female words' 'battered' and 'flurried' and suggests that 'all female words, though we are not sure of their derivation, have very significant meanings'.[20] They are meanings, one might suppose, having something in common with the grunt and the snort, and they are assembled in passages of menacing violence. At all events, we have here a strangely imagined and fabricated beast, predatory, indefinite and protean, which is also its own victim.

This Beast could be said to consume its own Beauty. Ferocity is cornered, the hunter is caught, and the stench of fear, of cruelty and revenge are carried equivocally by the passage, which is so curiously overblown and overwrought that it seems dispersed by the hatred which informs it. It is an image which may be read as the expression of Lovelace's inadmissible terror of female sexuality, seen here as rampant, untamed, unmastered. In the words of Dryden, which Lovelace quotes as explanation of his behaviour, 'with revenge it glows'. The rape which is so bizarrely absent from the text itself has been displaced by the hatred it was intended both to express and to discipline. Mrs Sinclair, become monstrous, contains Lovelace's guilt and assuages it. She stands for his violent designs on women and for his rake's predilections and habits. His wry 'are not all rakes sad fellows?'[21] is scuppered by that snorting beast who is a woman and therefore a justification of sorts for those habits: their victim, but also the nightmarish embodiment of Lovelace's need to believe in the complicity of women. Richardson has him repeatedly resorting to that seducer's rhetoric, in which 'every woman is a rake in her heart', for '*no wickedness is comparable to the wickedness of a woman.*'[22]

Lovelace is, as he puts it to his friend Belford, 'a notorious woman-eater'.[23] The association of seduction with the hunting, preparing and eating of food is explicit and emphatic in the novel and is, of course, central to the value put on women and to the options open to Clarissa herself. She has learned from her brother that 'daughters are chickens brought up for the tables of other men'.[24] At the beginning of the novel Clarissa herself is not only possessed of 'delicacy', but is delectable and is also responsible for her father's larder and his table. By the time of her self-induced and anorexic death she is described as 'iced', of spun-sugar frailty, a proper dessert.

Yet for Lovelace women are also wild game, free for the taking and no man's property: there to be shot at, snared, trapped, surprised and netted. In this vein his language is closer to a hunter's than an eater's, for, as he points out, 'Does not the keen foxhunter endanger his neck and his bones in pursuit of a vermin which, when killed, is neither fit food for men nor dogs?'[25] The reformed rake Belford reminds Lovelace that women caught 'unprepared for being seen' are filthy, diseased creatures. Birds must be speedily drawn and plucked and cooked. Clarissa's death, for which she has so exquisitely and seductively prepared herself, is preceded by Mrs Sinclair's:

Her misfortune has not at all sunk but rather, as I thought, increased her flesh; rage and violence perhaps swelling her muscly features. Behold her then, spreading the whole tumbled bed with her huge quaggy carcase: her mill-post arms held up, her broad hands clenched with violence; her big eyes goggling and flaming-red as we may suppose those of a salamander; her matted grizzly hair made irreverend by her wickedness (her clouted head-dress being half off) spread about her fat ears and brawny neck; her livid lips parched, and working violently; her broad chin in convulsive motion; her wide mouth by reason of the contraction of her forehead (which seemed to be half-lost in its own frightful furrows) splitting her face, as it were, into two parts; and her huge tongue hideously rolling in it; heaving, puffing as if for breath, her bellows-shaped and various-coloured breasts ascending by turns to her chin and descending out of sight with the violence of her gaspings.[26]

How infinitely preferable will be Clarissa's 'lovely corpse',[27] dressed for the grave rather than the cauldron.

Richardson has done more than give Lovelace the best lines and all the jokes in *Clarissa*. His novel sympathetically enacts the compulsions and contradictions in this self-hating and misogynous seducer by incorporating the mutinous independence and those other forms of resistance in Clarissa which are so expertly designed to keep alive Lovelace's interest in her. Initially, the novel's plot could be said to hinge on the consequences of Clarissa's split-second decision to seek help from Lovelace in escaping her family and thwarting their plans to marry her to the unprepossessing Solmes. Thereafter, the novel's remarkable suspense and excitement are maintained – as Lovelace's interest is maintained – through Clarissa's increasing provocations.[28] The novel itself, seducer-like, lovingly, gloatingly, lubriciously, watches a young woman recoil from the unbearable encroachments of a threatening man into the progressive divesting of that very physicality in herself which has inspired both lust and vengeance in her tormentor.

Anorexia, illness, death become in the novel simultaneously a means of escape and the aphrodisiac ruses of a predatory woman. As Clarissa works to concentrate her entire bodily existence into vapour, spirit, an early death, she is also being congratulated for affording Lovelace the most intense sexual and emotional experience of his life. Clarissa's apotheosis is also Richardson's way of controlling his heroine, mastering her and bringing her to heel. Dying and dead she is 'prepared for being seen', totally possessed, seemly, contained within the pages of the novel, a man's woman. Had she followed the advice of her family and friends she might have redeemed the situation for herself by marrying her abductor, her seducer. Lovelace himself has prefigured the kind of triumph that would have been for Clarissa, and the kind of humiliation it would have spelled out for him: 'To be *despised by a* WIFE! – What a thought is that!'[29]

Guardedness, a withholding of favours and a judicious coolness are the least of what is enjoined on young women in novels where seducers prowl. Clarissa's preparation for her death, her purchase of her own coffin and her use of it as a bedside writing – or so-called 'occasional' – table, may be said to constitute the last word in guardedness: and as double-edged a weapon against Lovelace as it is meant to be, since it simultaneously excites his lust and protects her from it. In *Sense and Sensibility* it is precisely Marianne's 'Romantic' conviction that guardedness is squalid and that only the strongest emotions are worth either having or expressing which so alarms her sister Elinor on her behalf. Marianne's openness and generosity with the enchantingly handsome Willoughby go with preferring Scott to Pope and crooked trees to straight ones. In a novel which begins and ends with money and with the particular economics of women's dependence on fathers and husbands and brothers within the poorer sections of the early-nineteenth-century gentry, such behaviour in a beautiful sixteen-year-old is seen as inviting abuse. At this rate she will end up poor as well as miserable. Would Elinor regard her sister as less culpable, more virtuous, if she kept dalliance and money apart, as Willoughby does? In this, as in much else, Jane Austen expects higher standards of women than of men. Seducers are hazards which sensible young women must learn to detect and avoid.

Willoughby's first appearance, with his dogs and his gun, establishes him as a gentleman. Elinor, just as enthusiastically as Marianne and Mrs Dashwood, responds at once to his beauty, his voice, his frank and graceful manners. The Dashwoods are relieved to learn that he is due to inherit from a rich old lady and that he already has a small estate of his own. Even at the point when he rushes back to London, leaving Marianne in tears and everyone in confusion as to his intentions towards her, Elinor is able to say to her mother, 'I love Willoughby, sincerely love him; and suspicion of his integrity cannot be more painful to yourself than to me.'[30]

Yet Willoughby is not just seductive, he is a seducer. It is not only, of course – as he later reveals – that his intentions towards Marianne have not been honourable, but that he has seduced Colonel Brandon's fifteen-year-old ward and abandoned her with a child. It is this act which makes Willoughby a serious seducer, and it is at the centre of the novel's ambiguous treatment of the subject. It is an act which is condemned particularly as one 'which no man who can feel for another would do'.[31] Marianne's mother will later be certain that her daughter could not have been happy 'with a man of libertine practices! With one who had so injured the peace of the dearest of our friends, and the best of men!'[32] It is easy to feel that both these remarks register the injury to Colonel Brandon as more important than the injuries done either to his ward or to Marianne. It is significant too that it takes a man to detect the bounder in another man.

Jane Austen's novels are principally concerned with the lives and the possibilities of women, usually with very young women and the brief adventures they may embark on during what we would describe as their teenage or adolescent years, which will perhaps lead to marriage, and will end there. *Sense and Sensibility* does not, as *Clarissa* does, concern itself with the hunt, with the ways in which a libertine's appetite may wax and wane or be systematically maintained or increased. Indeed, the seducer's motives are of interest only in so far as they might be able to provide some comfort to the young women who have been deceived and abandoned or who may feel that he has made fools of them. Yet Jane Austen was also writing within a tradition which saw the seducer, provided that he was also a gentleman, as a kind of sportsman. Young women had only themselves to blame if they let themselves get caught. We are, of course, meant to find absurd as well as cruel the words of John Dashwood to his sister Elinor when he first sees Marianne again after her disappointment with Willoughby, yet their absurdity lies chiefly in their being uttered so blatantly and insensitively. They express quite recognisable and acceptable anxieties:

> At her time of life, anything of an illness destroys the bloom for ever! Hers has been a very short one! She was as handsome a girl last September as any I ever saw, and as likely to attract the men. There was something in her style of beauty to please them particularly. I remember Fanny used to say that she would marry sooner and better than you did: not but what she is exceedingly fond of *you* – but so it happened to strike her. She will be mistaken, however. I question whether Marianne *now* will marry a man worth more than five or six hundred a year at the utmost, and I am very much deceived if *you* do not do better.[33]

The male tradition of seduction narratives focuses on female sexuality as a valuable commodity, worth a certain amount of money on the open market. It is a commodity owned by men and prized. The seducer of women disrupts the ordinary process of bargaining and exchange, intruding on the transaction by appealing to the woman herself and to her sexual nature.

If a seducer steals a woman from another man he will necessarily be seen to be doing so with the woman's consent (for otherwise it would be rape). And the woman's consent will justify the controlling of women by men, since it will demonstrate once again that women are sexually unbridled as well as undiscriminating. It is significant, I think, that Lovelace ensures by his abduction of Clarissa that no other man is likely to lay claim to her. Jane Austen has made Marianne fatherless and beyond her brother's direct economic control. To this extent she breaks with the tradition which makes the seducer's crime primarily an offence against a man. Yet Willoughby's seduction of Colonel Brandon's ward and his success with the woman the Colonel loves and wants to marry mark out the extent to which Jane Austen accepts a male account of it all. Her dilemma lies in reconciling this male view of Willoughby's transgression with her almost maternal need to believe some good of him, to make him credibly seductive, likeable, lovable, and a young man of quite a different sort from Lovelace, one whom an intelligent young woman – if a rash one – might plausibly trust as well as love.

At the end of the novel, when Marianne seems after all likely to recover from what was nearly a fatal illness, exacerbated at the very least by Willoughby's betrayal of her, Willoughby himself appears.

His attempts to gain Elinor's sympathy through elaborately alternating passages of self-exculpation, self-pity and abject apology work on the clear-headed and upright Elinor as a kind of seduction. He knows – and plays on – Elinor's (and perhaps the reader's) passionate wish to have been mistaken about him. She is gratified to learn from him that he was and still is attached to Marianne, and that he regrets his marriage to another woman. She takes in her stride his tales of debts, the reasons for them and even the view that they made marriage to any woman without a fortune of her own out of the question. Though she is occasionally stern she is also won over, even by his callous account of his treatment of Colonel Brandon's ward:

> I acknowledge that her situation and her character ought to have been respected by me. I do not mean to justify myself, but at the same time cannot leave you to suppose that I have nothing to urge, – that because she was injured, she was irreproachable, – and because I was a libertine, she must be a saint. If the violence of her passion, the weakness of her understanding – I do not mean, however, to defend myself. Her affection for me deserved better treatment, and I often, with great self-reproach, recall the tenderness which, for a very short time, had the power of creating any return.[34]

Elinor will remember him after their conversation as 'poor Willoughby', will allow herself a rudimentary wish that he might one day become a widower and available for remarriage, and will often feel a 'pang' for him, a pang which is not on her sister's behalf alone:

> Willoughby – he whom only half an hour ago she had abhorred as the most worthless of men – Willoughby, in spite of all his faults, excited a degree of commiseration for the sufferings produced by them, which made her think of him as now separated for ever from her family with a tenderness, a regret, rather in proportion, as she soon acknowledged within herself, to his wishes than to his merits.[35]

The novel may laugh in the end at passionate love and at romance, and may come down in favour of moderation and of young men and women marrying sensibly and with an eye to comfort and economic security. The excesses – and certainly the morbidity – of *Clarissa* have been frowned upon. But the pain of these struggles for young women, their unmet longing for male love, is not evaded.

Stories and novels could be said to be bent, like operas, on seduction. They are out to cajole complicity from readers imagined in postures of mutinous independence; though these may only, of course, be provisional. So long as the narrative of male seduction ignores the woman as its reader — or at best assumes her to be androgynous and on men's side — the text will have closed in on itself, protecting its embalmed view of men's and women's libido, as *Clarissa* does, by identifying an independent sexuality in women — their refusal of the seducer — with the rampant, the chaste or the corpse-like. Jane Austen was writing from within that tradition. She was constrained, as women writers have been — and still are in most cases — by the defeats that that tradition predicts for women. *Sense and Sensibility* can be read, however, as challenging *Clarissa* and any account of seduction which settles for women being beasts, nuns, fools or dead. Jane Austen allows women to find men seductive and necessary to them. She also emphatically requires of women that they take responsibility for their sexual behaviour. She certainly expects them to survive their errors and humiliations. Most importantly, she asserts the possibility of a woman's morality and a woman's resistance, even as she perpetuates the tradition which has made both so necessary and so difficult to represent.

2

The One Great Silent Area

Even if they have read, listened to lectures, toyed with accomplishments, their miscellaneous information does not constitute culture.
Simone de Beauvoir, *The Second Sex*

I

The English publishers Verso have brought out a posthumous
collection of essays by Raymond Williams and have called it
Resources of Hope,[1] which is a neater version of a title of his own.
The portrait of Williams they've used on the cover is magnificently
hieratic in its strength and seriousness and in the sense it gives of
mental and physical activity – and, indeed, speech, for he is speaking
in it – stopped abruptly in their tracks and set in bronze. It seems
right to start from this, from the span of the essays themselves
between 1958 and 1987 and from the book's message of a life
impressively, even heroically, achieved, though so arbitrarily stopped. I am intimidated (though also exhilarated) by the thought of
actually formulating the questions I have cumulatively wanted to put
to Williams; nonplussed by his death and by the simultaneous
vulnerability and impregnability death has conferred on him. I write
in the wake of more than a year's obituary offerings, which have
been admiring, bereft, taken aback. I too am admiring. I am also sad,
though I did not know Williams and have occasionally wished that I
did. But this is no funerary wreath, simply some thoughts about
reading Williams and some enquiries, which have been put together
too late for him to take note of.

In one of the book's essays, 'You're a Marxist, Aren't You?',[2]
which Williams wrote in 1975, he wrestles with the ways in which he
felt ready as well as quite unready to describe himself as a Marxist.
Fabianism he rejects out of hand, for its 'most crucial underestimate
of the enemy' and its consequent faith in administrative and institutional change. Yet he feels able to accept what he regards as the
constraining Marxist 'label' only if this is understood to include the
particular emphasis which Gramsci developed round the idea of
hegemony within Marxism. This emphasis is essential, Williams
suggests; for without it culture and ideology are separated off from
the practical and daily experiencing of class in people's lives:

> We could then say that the essential dominance of a particular
> class in society is maintained not only, although if necessary, by

power, and not only, although always, by property. It is maintained also and inevitably by a lived culture: that saturation of habit, of experience, of outlook, from a very early age and continually renewed at so many stages of life, under definite pressures and within definite limits, so that what people come to think and feel is in large measure a reproduction of the deeply based social order which they may even in some respects think they oppose and indeed actually oppose.[3]

This is quintessential Williams. The language of the analysis can seem oddly abstract as it connects with its theme of all that is concretely understood within individual consciousness and individual histories. The passage also contains Williams's particular insistence on the sheer power and pressure of dominant cultures to influence and appropriate, whilst expressing with equal firmness his absolute refusal to ignore the living-out of contradictions. It is also characteristic of Williams to confront unsentimentally, as he goes on to do, the prospect that any significant change in the fundamental structures and relations of society would – precisely because of these lived contradictions within a hegemony – entail the most strenuous and painful effort. Far from rebuking those who are uncertain about aspects of their commitment to achieving such change, or are racked by their sense of conflicting allegiances, the essay takes to task those tendencies on the Left which encourage easy optimisms or treat with disdain the thoroughgoing effectiveness of the enemy:

I learned the experience of incorporation, I learned the reality of hegemony, I learned the saturating power of the structures of feeling of a given society, as much from my own mind and my own experience as from observing the lives of others. All through our lives, if we make the effort, we uncover layers of this kind of alien formation in ourselves, and deep in ourselves. So then the recognition of it is a recognition of large elements in *our own* experience, which have to be – shall we say it? – defeated. But to defeat something like that in yourself, in your families, in your neighbours, in your friends, to defeat it involves something very different, it seems to me, from most traditional political strategies.[4]

It may even be that this capacity in Williams to unearth and explain the ways in which we are all seduced by dominant accounts of the world, by ruling-class values and their translation into 'nature' and 'the universal' and 'common sense', marks out most exactly where Williams could be both subtler and more generative than any other writer about literature and politics during the last thirty years. It undoubtedly accounts for his importance for feminist analysis and, I suspect, for some of the dismay and shying away amongst feminist writers, both at finding themselves largely absent from his work, but also – and I think more significantly – at the ambiguous place accorded women generally within a social and cultural theory which appears at first blush to be so obviously hospitable to them.

To return to that essay and to the moment in it when Williams writes of learning 'the reality of hegemony': that kind of writing needs to be set alongside the quite different undertaking, *Marxism and Literature*,[5] which he was working on at the same time. The book deals with similar questions, but theoretically here, in a series of short, densely argued chapters, which offer collectively the lineaments of a sociology of literature. From the book's opening chapters on culture and on language (an exciting short history of how language has been conceptualised over time) and on literature and ideology, the argument moves into ten central concepts within Marxist theory and ten related (or implied) themes in literary theory. The book's impetus is towards the necessary connectedness of these levels of analysis. His extraordinary life's project – for that is what it was – was moving into its final phase. A reworked historical and cultural materialism (which refers to Gramsci and introduces the work of the Russian theorists Bahktin and Vološinov, but is finally and notably Williams's own) is assembled and used to illuminate key problems. For Williams these were above all connections between class and culture, and between the selective traditions operating on language and literature and what he defined for us as 'structures of feeling' (with uneasy reverberations round 'structures'), the practical social consciousness and knowledge people develop from inside their own shared histories.

The project was remarkable for its scale and scope and internal diversity, for its resilient imagination and for its consistent holding together of his own life and a range of historical, cultural, theoretical and political perspectives, which he investigated and used and taught and demonstrated in more than twenty books of quite different kinds. The project is unusual too for combining a passionate belief in the possibilities and the virtues of 'community' and a 'common culture' with what Terry Eagleton has described as

a rock-like sense of self-sufficiency which sometimes merged into solitariness, though he was paradoxically the most social and public figure one could imagine. It was not the quirky introspection of one shut out so much as the arresting originality of one out in front; you had a sense of having struggled through to some theoretical position only to find that Williams had quietly pre-empted you, arriving there by his own personal, meditative route.[6]

Williams's work was continuously fed by the use he made of a dramatic transition in his own life: from growing up in a farming and railway valley in South Wales during the twenties and early thirties to Cambridge, and then his adult life as a teacher and scholar and writer. This move – which he never represented as a split or break – came to map, in a literally geographical way as well as historically and theoretically, the cultural contradictions and continuities which the transition itself emblematically contained and produced. In an early essay, 'Culture is Ordinary', he angrily and movingly links the two worlds he inhabited through his own imaginative knowledge of them and through the fundamental unity underlying their opposite – indeed, opposed – histories:

> I was not, by the way, oppressed by Cambridge. I was not cast down by old buildings, for I had come from a country with twenty centuries of history written visibly into the earth: I liked walking through a Tudor court, but it did not make me feel raw. I was not amazed by the existence of a place of learning; I had always known the cathedral, and the bookcases I now sit to work at in Oxford are of the same design as those in the chained library. Nor was learning, in my family, some strange eccentricity; I was not, on a scholarship in Cambridge, a new kind of animal up a brand-new ladder. Learning was ordinary; we learned where we could. Always, from those scattered white houses, it had made sense to go out and become a scholar or a poet or a teacher. Yet few of us could be spared from the immediate work; a price had been set on this kind of learning, and it was more, much more, than we could individually pay.[7]

If Williams's work on culture begins from the displacements of his own life, it is organised round literature and, more specifically, in relation to a series of arguments about how literature has been thought of historically. These arguments have taken Williams deeply into a variety of areas of study and have re-emerged into the five novels he published. The arguments have been about the practice, the activity of writing itself, the relation of texts to their readers and the processes by which both texts and readers may be all too easily abstracted and isolated from their social and economic production – so that, for example, he has needed to engage with the history of education and of Standard English. For his study of English pastoral poetry and then of the novels of the eighteenth and nineteenth century in *The Country and the City*[8] he needed to gather a history of the changing relations between the growth of cities, the agricultural use of land and the spreading of Empire, with its exploitation of new world markets and productive potential. Within these and other

undertakings Williams has wanted to rescue the writing of literature
from disabling idealisations and return it as practice and history to
'the process and the result of formal composition within the social
and formal properties of a language'[9] – to divest literature, that is, of
its pre-emptive privileges. It is very clearly part of Williams's purpose
that that process and that result be distinguished from those traditions within which literary texts possess 'an undifferentiated
equivalence with "immediate living experience"'.[10]

If literature is neither life itself, nor yet a simple telling about life,
what kind of thing might it be? In a variety of theoretical and
historical studies of texts and authors and traditions Williams first
extended the notion of literature beyond its specialised meanings of
aesthetic value, great texts, particular genres, to include the actual
practices of reading and writing and communication. He next offered
literature as implicated in the whole of the economic and social
formation. He expresses it like this in *Politics and Letters*:

> But what one then has to go on to say is that it is ultimately
> impossible to treat the industrial revolution as a process which
> had external effects in a literature subsequent to it. For the
> industrial revolution was among other things a revolution in the
> production of literacy and it is at this point that the argument
> turns full circle. The steam press was as much a part of the
> industrial revolution as the steam jenny or the steam locomo-
> tive. What it was producing was literacy; and with it a new kind
> of newspaper and novel.[11]

This example comes within a conversation with Marxists about the
relation of 'base' to 'superstructure', of modes of production to
cultural institutions and practices. There are many other places
where Williams has argued against the traditional Marxist version of
this relation and proposed instead an account of culture as itself
produced by and also constitutive of the determining productive
functions of societies. The argument is also, and significantly, made
within moments of personal testimony. At the end of what I think of
as his most comprehensively imaginative work, *The Country and the
City*, he connects the historical and analytical work he has been
doing with movements in his own life:

> We can overcome division only by refusing to be divided. That
> is a personal decision but then a social action. I can only record
> what I have myself learned. Others will learn it quite differently.
> But I grew up, as I said, where the division was visible, in a land
> and then in a family. I moved from country to city, and now live
> and work in both. I learned, in many forms, the shapes of this
> history, its ideas and its images, in the society and the literature

which had earliest and most thoroughly experienced a change that was to become universal or at least an offered model for universal development.[12]

This passage carries and validates diverse kinds of learning and knowing from childhood to maturity, from immediacy to study. What was learned was a set of vital realisations about the world he inhabited. Wealth, property, land, capitalism had skewed and suppressed understanding of the past and then the present. Without that understanding people could not contemplate change, for the destructive effects of inequality and division come to seem inevitable. Yet it is emphatically not Williams's purpose to promote some levels (that is, abstract or schooled levels) of knowledge over others, though he is ready to differentiate between them. Solidarity may be built only on knowledge that is shared, common. 'The personal is political' is by no means Williams's slogan, and even within feminism it has sometimes risked reductiveness through its implied *faute de mieux*. Yet Williams has always indicated the dynamism of the idea itself, its utterly necessary connecting of the private and the public, the individual and the social.

While Williams was engaging in difficult debates on the Left, so that he would sometimes adjure us to beware abstraction and specialisation in language marked by both qualities, he also wrote, in his novels and elsewhere, with the utmost simplicity and directness. Always he argued for synthesis and against those analyses which seek to isolate levels of experience in the interests of controlling the frameworks available to people for understanding and accounting for their own lives. The project was also an intensely political one, a life's critical and evolving commitment to socialism (almost always outside any political party); even if, as Francis Mulhern put it in a review of *Towards 2000*, he 'offers an estimate of "resources", not a strategy'.[13]

Here, then, is a twentieth-century thinker who is braced for struggle, and whose life is spent reworking, revising, redescribing the detailed as well as the general connections between history, culture and experience. Here is a theorist who is always historical and a reader who is able to be theoretical. Culture, literature, language: these become ways of describing and understanding human societies and of inhabiting them. As Williams himself puts it, 'A definition of language is always, implicitly or explicitly, a definition of human beings in the world.'[14]

II

Unsurprisingly, my concern is with 'the one great silent area'[15] (as his interviewers called it in *Politics and Letters*) of Williams's social theory of culture. Women have seemed to many readers of Williams to be only intermittently and then peripherally present in his work, and feminism to have made virtually no impact on him at all, despite some rather clipped allusions to it at the end of his life.

I need to start by attempting to explain this charge, for it is not always easy to distinguish between very general kinds of language in his writing about human societies, which avoid specification and categories of other kinds than gender, and something much more troubling at the heart of his position. The charge I am making is directed at all aspects of Williams's work, though the ways in which women may be read as present or absent in particular parts of it differ significantly. There are, for instance, several female characters in his novels, and I shall come to these and to the novels themselves. He wrote at length and well about women writers like Jane Austen and George Eliot. *The Country and the City*'s dedication is 'For the country workers who were my grandparents James Bird, Mary Ann Lewis, Joseph Williams, Margaret Williams'. In *The Long Revolution* he starts by making families, generations, nurturing, essential ingredients of any social theory, though this is not finally developed in the book:

> People did not need telling, by the new psychology, that their ordinary experience as parents and children, brothers and sisters, husbands and wives, was of central importance in their own development. If social thinking excluded this experience, by its insistence on man in social relationships based on economic activities, then it was so much the worse for social thinking: we simply separated our family and personal life from the life of society. But of course it is clear that the family, in its changing forms, cannot be separated from society. Either it gets the reduced status of an instrument of supply and training, or it gets the idealized status, that only family relationships are real.[16]

So Williams did acknowledge that families, anyway, are vital to his account. There is no doubt either of his sporadic willingness to remember that besides having some role in families, women may also be workers and even writers. Yet there are obviously some difficulties with a notion of families which simply contain or absorb women without explaining how, and how variously, this actually comes about. To do so would entail an account of the relation of families to communal and economic life and, indeed, to culture and socialism.

But it is not only women who are made to disappear into a family so divorced from the social. The meanings made of sexual difference, sexual activity, human development itself all disappear into this private and hidden enclave of the family. Indeed, the family, in such a view, becomes a surprisingly handy container for both the natural and the socially anomalous. Nor would it be unfair to suggest that the only obstacle to a removal of the family from theory altogether is that it is, after all, where male lives begin, before men move out into the world and acquire families of their own (for which they are entirely responsible) and move on again to varieties of work, to other men, to the world's business. What is so extraordinarily suppressed here is women in the culture, women as participants and transmitters and as makers and readers of culture. For that 'saturation' to which Williams alludes in his account of hegemony refers precisely to a world in which women make and control many of the most significant cultural meanings.

I feel bound to speculate as to whether Williams – and indeed the question might be asked of many other writers – ever actually envisaged women reading his work. And if he did, were there then adjustments to be made, sniping to be countered or avoided? Could a woman ever be the 'implied' reader of such texts? In *Culture and Society*,[17] an early work, written during the early fifties and published in 1958, Williams ends with a series of Beethovian finales and, more specifically, with two short sections called 'The Idea of Community'[18] and 'The Development of a Common Culture'.[19] These were important statements for many readers at the time, for their clear commitment to 'criticism of what has been called the bourgeois idea of society'[20] and to new kinds of solidarity developed in the interests of such a criticism and of change. Throughout – and in ways which readers must have found unexceptionable in 1958 – Williams writes of men rather than of people (though there is one mention of 'the men and women' amongst whom Williams grew up). It is still, of course, possible to interpret his use of 'men' as no more than a pre-feminist lapse and to assume that his utopian blueprint for a genuinely egalitarian community will not only contain women but fully include them. Such a view is difficult to sustain, though, when one reads into the detail. Consider a passage like this:

A skill is only an aspect of a man, and yet, at times, it can seem to comprehend his whole being. This is one kind of crisis, and it can only be overcome as a man becomes conscious that the value he places on his skill, the differentiation he finds in it, can only ultimately be confirmed by his constant effort not only to confirm and respect the skills of others, but also to confirm and deepen the community which is even larger than the skills. The mediation of this lies deep in personal feeling, but enough is

known to indicate that it is possible. Further, there can be no
effective participation in the whole culture merely on the basis of
the skill which any particular man may acquire. The participation depends on common resources, and leads a man towards
others.[21]

Here is a vision of a society in which working relations and the value
attaching to kinds of skill and kinds of labour will be radically altered
from the hierarchies and oppositions produced and held in place by
profit and by competition. We could assume that Williams is covertly
including the whole population in his new world only by assuming in
our turn that by men he means, in fact, men and women, and that by
work he means unpaid as well as paid work. We will have difficulty
sticking to such an assumption, not least because women have rarely,
if ever, been characterised in terms of their skills but – quite the reverse
– according to the value placed on the skills (or the property) of their
fathers and husbands and sons. Indeed, the problem for working-class
women (and it is more often than not a problem for middle-class
women too) has been that their labour, their skills, their talents have
not been differentiated and specialised at all, but dumbly anticipated
and relied on and rarely, if ever, appropriately paid for.

In *Politics and Letters*, his interviewers taxed Williams with this and
later failures to include families and women within an analysis which
so intrepidly set out to connect every level of experience within a social
and cultural theory.[22] Williams accepted the criticism, but instantly
levelled one of his own at the women's movement: for failing to
confront the contradictions inherent in specific forms of liberation for
women within a capitalist order poised to exploit women's willingness
to enter it on any terms. Feminism becomes no more than a rationale
for the success of individual women in a 'man's world'. He gives no
sense of the traditions of solidarity within feminism, nor of that other
solidarity, which goes back at least as far as 1966 and Juliet Mitchell's
significantly entitled 'Women: The Longest Revolution'[23] and her
ringing assertion that 'We should ask the feminist questions, but try to
come up with some Marxist answers'.[24] Years of important and
passionate debate between feminists and between feminists and socialists are ignored in favour of a kind of dispersed 'mood' amongst
women encouraging them individually to emulate and to join men. As
Williams himself concedes, it is not a satisfactory answer, and he
follows it with a notable apology:

> These are the kinds of contradiction within the very real process
> of liberation that I would have tried to analyse. I wish I had done
> so in *The Long Revolution*, and I also wish I understood what
> prevented me from doing so, because it wasn't that I was not

thinking about the question. I think that the likelihood is that I had such a comparatively unproblematic experience both in my own home and in my own family, which were very good ones, that I was not as intensely aware of disorder and crisis in the family as I was in other areas. But it was nevertheless an intellectual failing not to confront the problem, especially since I had identified it.[25]

There is anyway, as I have already pointed out, a difficulty about invoking women solely in relation to family life, and unhappy family life at that, as if half the population were in some sense *equivalent to* the family and to the bringing up of children, while the other half adopted in sequence a series of positions in relation to the family: dependent, supportive, responsible, parasitic, and so on. Men are identified with their families too, after all. Nor can there ever have been a time in Britain's history when a large percentage of women was not also part of the workforce. Indeed, it could be said that neglect of these kinds of facts has been produced by exactly the sort of 'selective tradition' which Williams blames for other manifestations of historical suppression.

Williams himself points to the peculiar ironies of domestic labour, of servant work, and its prevalence within the nineteenth-century economy, though he doesn't dwell on women's position within this, nor on the surely uncomfortable thought that if women are to be dissolved into families, then it has to be noted that a very large number of women have always been engaged in the maintaining of families which were not their own. Williams actually mentions the fact that members of his own family left Wales for Birmingham and domestic labour there, and that women were often the first to leave the villages in search of work.[26] Even where women could somehow be disposed of within an economic account of social relations as no more than members of a family, there is still a problem about their class, and it is a problem to which non-feminist Marxist theory has given only the most rudimentary attention.

The French economist Christine Delphy goes so far as to lambast Marxist feminists above all for their refusal to regard women as a class of their own:

> To think of yourself as a class is primarily to think of yourself as a *man*, and, furthermore, to think of yourself as a man of the most *glorious* category. It is to raise yourself to the rank of the cultural heroes.[27]

This could be said to hit one target whilst missing another. As she reminds us that gender lags behind class and race as an analytic category and tells us why, Delphy may be seen to sidestep the dilemma for women of dealing with what is experienced as a double bind. But the difficulty of theorising women, either as a single class or solely in relation to accepted accounts of class (even within competing analyses), does not — as one might easily be led to believe — mean that women do not live their lives within deeply known allegiances to class and race and within quite specific relations with other women and with men. The blind spot of thinkers on the Left who, like Williams, undertake so scrupulously to reveal the operations of suppression and selection within historical accounts of communities, constitutes an aspect of these very operations. Williams was far from alone as a Marxist in exhibiting ignorance of and impatience with feminist debate. Yet the question still has to be asked: why should a thinker who was throughout his life prepared to revisit and rethink absolutely central tenets of Marxism be so unwilling to countenance even the questions which feminists have addressed to Marxism?

III

So how might Williams — or for that matter, how might I — connect and understand the women who fleetingly make an appearance in the first hundred or so pages of *The Country and the City*? I have already mentioned his two working grandmothers. They are echoed in Williams's early memory of 'the women in headscarves, outside their cottages, waiting for the blue bus that will take them, inside school hours, to work in the harvest'.[28] Juvenal's women, who were 'shaggier than their acorn-belching husbands',[29] are recalled to give context to a whole rhetoric of rural innocence. And the field workers, 'all the men and women whose land and work paid their fares and provided their spending money',[30] are preyed upon by 'the land-owner's wife and her prospecting daughter',[31] the 'endowed' heiresses, the virgins fattened and adorned for dynastic marriages and the nuns who chose an alternative to such marriages. Even the prostitutes of the city are blameworthily — and surely inaccurately — linked in Williams's account to the court, and are seen to come 'from, some on their way to, what was called an aristocracy'.[32] And presiding over a pastoral paradise corruptly maintained on the proceeds of City and Empire trade and exploitation are 'a proprietary lord and lady'.[33]

It is all too easy to read these women, whether headscarved or heiresses, field workers or dynastic virgins, as sharing only their position as human beings envisaged and ultimately measured and understood outside a politics, independently of the economic and socially shaping relations within which they lived and are actually now perceived. Even the London whores are made personally responsible for their fate, which has been chosen either as a consequence of a decadent and probably upper-class upbringing or in preparation for some parasitic attachment to a wealthy man.

A later chapter considers the eighteenth-century novel's preoccupation with 'the problems of love and marriage',[34] and specifically with the relation of marriage to property. Williams sees Fielding's Squire Western, who 'uses his daughter to unite the estates, as if it were the most natural thing in the world',[35] as part of an 'openly cynical scramble for land and for heiresses'.[36] Land within this conflation at least retains its value and integrity. Heiresses, who have only themselves to blame, do not. Virginity, which Williams never actually specifies as female — as it must surely be in this context — becomes in his argument 'an asset which must not be surrendered without the necessary security of marriage'.[37] The implication is that a woman's desire to retain her virginity is of the same order as her father's, and as squalidly venal.

I have plucked these references to women and to marriage out of an argument which, in a general way, seeks to develop connections between certain literary traditions (pastoral and country-house poetry and the eighteenth-century novel) and developing bourgeois ideologies in the period. Williams shows how a deliberate polarising of, for instance, rural innocence and urban iniquity, or pastoral peace and beauty and cities sullied and blackened by industry and commerce, contributes to the invisibility, the ignoring of the lives of both the urban and the rural poor. The romance with landscape and with the grandeur and the replenishing of great country houses and estates had the effect of miraculously emptying the countryside of those workers whose appalling pay and living conditions and backbreaking work sustained this pastoral dream. The bogus purifying of the countryside entailed in fact successive displacements: so that the human exploitation involved in certain families' amassing of wealth was hidden from the vulgar, concupiscent gaze, either on distant colonial plantations or within a new view of the countryside as consisting of naturally and endlessly rolling acres rather than of the old busyness and exhaustions of smallholdings and farmyards. Similarly, the poverty of the mass of city-dwellers (especially in London) was progressively thought of as impersonally produced by some evil emanation of the city or as the ingrained and virtually ineradicable character of the poor themselves.[38]

These processes and their relation to a literature produced by — and even, necessarily, productive of — the capitalist ethic itself, are argued for by Williams through his reading of particular texts. Most startlingly clear-cut and striking within this argument is his image of erasure, of the scratching-out of whole generations of people from a land which had been stolen from them and which they laboured to maintain as some idyll of nature requiring no human hand to work it.

Yet – and this is the difficulty – it is possible to feel that women too have somehow been erased and scratched out; that they are only vestigially present within the landscape Williams has redrawn for us as a replacement for the prettified one he has exposed and anatomised. Women lurk, we are presumably to suppose, behind – or perhaps alongside – their menfolk. There will be children clinging to their skirts. There will also be those other women, richly dressed and proudly complicitous in the marriages arranged for them, which will accumulate the wealth of two families through the conduit of their overdressed white bodies. What is left out, reduced to an insensible stump in this reseen landscape, is the mental life of the women who were destined to see themselves only within this shadowy, dependent relation to men and to marriage within different classes.

In another characteristic moment of the book Williams queries those histories which have drawn on evidence of the sterling independence exhibited by a few individual men, during and after the enclosing of land which ruined their own and so many other people's lives:

> The question we have to put to this version of social history is not whether some men emerged and survived – they will always do so, under any pressures – but whether, taken as a whole, the way of life could sustain a general independence.[39]

The answer Williams gives is, inevitably, no to a question which so exactly defines what he asks us to think of as a minimum requirement for any community. But within the kind of historical distortion and suppression he is seeking to dispel there are other suppressions which Williams ignores. Individuality, independence: these could not even be aspirations for all but a handful of women. Even those women writers whose gender he politely ignores in his reading of their work could barely consider such freedoms except as men possessed them.

Still further into the book, in a fine chapter about Hardy's novels, Williams returns to the issue of marriage, its meanings and, in Hardy, its particular susceptibility to class and to what Williams calls 'an insecure economy'.[40] What he characterises as Hardy's 'false' marriages are in some sense produced by the communal disruptions inherent in capitalism, and Williams contrasts them with an oddly idealised and individualising view of what marriage either is, in some essential way, or should be: 'the personal choice which is after all a choice primarily of a way to live, of an identity in the identification with this or that other person'.[41]

How is it that marriage, of all social relations, escapes Williams's vigilant understanding of the connection between feeling and economic structure? Or rather, why are bad marriages produced by capitalism and good ones made in heaven, or untethered to any political social theory? Marriage, like women, like the family, comes to occupy for Williams (in his novels and in his other writing) the private, personal part of a man's life and his choices, an area to be spoken of in tones of prudish as well as squeamish protectiveness. In this view a man's choice of a wife is a significant fact about him, standing for his commitment to a person (or to a kind of person), to a way of life and to a politics. It will be marked and prefigured in some respects by his own childhood, by his own experiencing of family life; and it will be, as Williams put it himself and provided it is not incurably 'false', 'an unproblematic experience'.[42]

It is not only, of course, that there is an absolute neglect within this account of women's experiences and needs and, indeed, mental life of any kind. More intractably, in the end, we are left with the sense of women skulking, hovering, on the edge of, slightly behind or somehow contingent to, the argument and the theory. They *are* there, but they are spoken for by those men who have responsibility for them, whose moral sensibility they may reflect. They are included, whether in the exploiting or the exploited classes. They are never, however, represented as pivotal to relations between individuals or groups; and their consciousness is not at issue as itself produced by and productive of culture, ideas, values, language.

Certainly it has been an immensely difficult task – and will continue to be for feminists as well as non-feminists – to theorise women in ways which start from and hold to a classical class analysis founded on economic determinations. There have, of course, been notable attempts, and by no means all have, as Christine Delphy has, exasperatedly thrown such accounts of class to the winds and redefined women as a class in themselves:

> But if only the capitalist mode of production is considered – as is usually the case – and if the same criteria are applied to women as men, then it can be seen that all women who do not work outside the home are outside the (proletariat/capitalist) class system. What is more, such women can only be reintegrated into the class system by determining their class membership according to non-Marxist criteria (that is, by attributing to them the class of their husbands). By pretending that women belong to their husbands' class, the fact that wives belong, by definition, to a class *other* than that of their husbands is hidden. By pretending that marriage can take the place of relations of production in the capitalist system as the criterion for class

membership in this system, the existence of another system of production is masked, and the fact that the relations of production within that system place husbands and wives into two antagonistic classes (the former benefiting materially from the exploitation of the latter) is hidden. The 'reintegration' of women into classes by defining them as the property of their husbands has as its objective precisely hiding the fact that they really *are* the property of their husbands.[43]

Many socialist feminists will have found such an analytical solution unsatisfactory, though they may welcome the boldness of the critique in the light of the kind of privatisation of women which I have tried to characterise in Williams. They may also have been sympathetic to Delphy's claim that such a redefinition makes a positive contribution to Marxist thought. The removal of women, of families and children – and, above all, of sexuality and sexual relations – from politics, even from history and culture and theorising itself, works above all to avert our gaze from male sexuality, particularly in its more violent manifestations, as also beyond politics. It also reduces women to what Cynthia Cockburn has called 'metaphorical material':

> . . . woman is, for Left as for Right, *metaphorical material*. The outcome is that Left men do not really see women as part of the socialist project. Rather they are a territory of the imagination, destined to absorb the desires and fears of men.[44]

Williams's relegation of women to men's care, whether benign or not, to men's private lives, to their inner worlds and their own narratives, deprives women of nearly everything: their bodies, their will, a voice, even – and crucially – their difference. They become unavailable for either heroism or innocence, and they are debarred from the myths which at any time may provide the terrain for the exploring and the contesting of heroism and innocence.[45] Yet, devastatingly, as if by some inadvertence or sleight of hand, they are also profoundly implicated in every form of human viciousness, weakness, cowardice. Williams's reading of Marvell's 'Upon Appleby House' sets the poem's 'composition of different ways of seeing' alongside his own outrage – at once predictable and dispiriting – at the 'unbearable irony' of confronting the poem's

> elaborate formal praise of the beauty and innocence of the daughter of the house, and to be directed forward to her marriage . . . The irony is not only the personal destiny that this marriage was to be to the appalling George Villiers, 2nd Duke of Buckingham, within a few years of the idealization in the

poem. It is that the fruit of this new house was to be that kind of political deal in which property and title were reconstituted.[46]

That 'personal destiny' is not merely put in its place by the more significant economic meaning, the political deal, assigned it in Williams's reading. It is inwardly vitiated by the young woman's assumed class complicity in transactions which exploit a body and a life denied all access to beauty and innocence, let alone independence.

Some of Williams's unwillingness to see women within class becomes clearer in his chapter on D.H. Lawrence, and specifically in the part of it where he comments on Lawrence's contrasting in *The Rainbow* of male and female vitalities, wherein physical activity, particularly on the land, is contrasted as male with mental activity, which is female. As so often with Lawrence, this nonsensical separation becomes a pretext for casting suspicion on female energy, for finding it dishonourable. Williams has no difficulty with this, nor with Lawrence's next elision. As Williams explains it, 'this feeling is already entangled with class: the lives of the vicar and the curate, the squire's lady, which the woman sees as superior'.[47]

A separated and unrooted mentalism, out of touch with the authentic sources of life, becomes a feminine principle and glides into the experiencing of class only as the most superficial snobbery. This is what so much envisaging of women's class experience comes down to: this sort of withering and dismissive assertion. For women, class is not allowed as the living of hegemony, the living of the most intense contradictions, but instead is whittled down to no more than an aspect of themselves, of their narcissism, their confined choices and allegiances, just one of their acquired characteristics. Within such an account there can be no resistance and no defeat. Neither feminism's birth and growth within a socialist politics, nor the kinds of solidarity it has worked for, are acknowledged. Women, dispersed, fragmented, vulnerable, protected – if they are protected – by a single burly male form, are to be plucked like wild oats out of the corn.

IV

Williams's Welsh trilogy of novels, *Border Country*,[48] *Second Generation*[49] and *The Fight for Manod*,[50] were written and rewritten and eventually published between 1958 and 1979. Their writing, as he recounts in *Politics and Letters*,[51] presented him with immense difficulties, so that the planning and writing of his theoretical and critical books seemed, by comparison, straightforward. It is possible to feel that Williams cared more about his fiction than his other work, and that his struggle for a productive form for it, for a voice which connected the worlds he wanted so passionately to connect, and his sense that neither publisher nor readers would permit him to write novels of the length he wanted to write, met finally with several sorts of disappointment. Even Williams's greatest admirers find it hard to like the novels wholeheartedly, though they are bound to read them with curiosity and care.

Each of the novels of the trilogy is about an aspect of the Welsh diaspora in this century. Yet Williams most especially set out to write against those versions of a working-class dispersal which were either elegiac or novels of escape. These, he thought, 'lacked any sense of the continuity of working-class life, which does not cease just because one individual moves out of it, but which also itself changes internally'.[52] Instead, he wanted to write within what he called 'a continuing tension, with very complicated emotions and relationships running through it, between two different worlds that needed to be rejoined'.[53] These worlds were equivalent in many respects to the worlds Williams himself inhabited during his adult life. Elsewhere, he characterises the relation between them as 'the relation of learning to labour',[54] the expression of a possibly idiosyncratic preoccupation for Williams, as it has been for so many male writers who feel themselves to be in some sense renegade sons of the soil. I think of Seamus Heaney's 'Digging' and its final lines:

> The cold smell of potato mould, the squelch and slap
> Of soggy peat, the curt cuts of an edge
> Through living roots awaken in my head.
> But I've no spade to follow men like them.
>
> Between my finger and my thumb
> The squat pen rests.
> I'll dig with it.[55]

This desire for the father's approval is expressed by Williams, as by Heaney, in the form of an assertion that the two kinds of work *are* alike, even equal. It is none the less possible to see this assertion as the other side of a fear that learning, writing, literature may be associated for many working-class men with their unmanning, with weakness, triviality and most of all with women. Williams's romance is always with his father and with a male world like his father's, and forging links between that world and the world of the university becomes an urgent imperative for him. The trilogy develops — scrupulously, if not always convincingly — material for the history of such a connection, with roots spreading more widely and more deeply than the example of his own life.

Matthew Price – whose father, Harry, is the undoubted hero of
Border Country – teaches in a university and specialises currently in
'population movements into the Welsh mining valleys in the middle
decades of the nineteenth century'.[56] The novels begin with a sum-
mons back to the village where he was born and where his father has
just suffered a stroke. Matthew's visits during the last months of his
father's life generate the novel's organisation of his own memories of
childhood and his learning and telling of his parents' life before his
own birth and up to the beginning of his own memories. The narrative
places individual knowledge within a continuity which enlarges it. The
story is told through Matthew rather than by him, and central to this
adult experiencing of the shape of his own life and of his parents' lives
is his registering of 'a change of substance'[57] between places and
between ways of life, which, he is now able to imagine, 'must also have
been for them, when they left their villages'.[58]

Ellen, Harry's wife and Matthew's mother, is pregnant and yellow-
haired when she arrives in the village, intent on finding a home and
permanence in the wake of the First World War, having trailed behind
her husband as he was shifted from one railway station to another. At
last Harry gets a relatively secure job on the railways as a signalman.
The couple put down roots. The ageing woman who is now caring for
her dying husband is still girlish, oddly unformed and indefinite, her
hair coloured so that for her son 'it was almost the yellow he remembered'.[59] Her husband, in contrast, has always had a hard physical and
moral presence and the kind of incorruptibility which provokes his
oldest – and more flexible, but also corruptible – friend to remark, in
words which Matthew understands and endorses, that 'He's been too
good a man'.[60] The child Matthew takes more after his mother, but his
love – marvelling, caressing, total – is always for his father, for his
father's 'pale, delicate, beautifully formed' hands, and later for

> his smile . . . so easy, so open, and still very young. It was the
> surprise, perhaps, of the sudden break from the ordinary serious-
> ness. The lines of the face were set very deeply now, and the black
> hair had thinned and receded, leaving a high, prominent fore-
> head. He had thickened considerably in the body, especially in
> the chest and shoulders. The grey shirt, with no collar, was open
> all down the chest. The braces were drawn tight on the heavy
> black serge trousers, of which the top button, at the waistband,
> was always undone. The belt was wide and stained black. The
> black boots were clean but not polished, light working boots.[61]

Yellow (which is not gold) becomes the base pinchbeck of mild frau-
dulence when seen against the authentic density and blackness of the
father.

The novel circles Harry's life and his son's growing up in relation to that life: the railway work and the union and the Labour Party, the disruptions of the General Strike, the father's small-scale yet heroic makings and maintenance of home and family and garden amidst the rocky, mountainous Welsh landscape. The mountains are the Black Mountains, and the men are hardened and blackened too: by work, by the mines, by the railways, by the war, by their political struggles during the twenties and thirties.

Ellen often weeps for her way, but she yields too. Only once, and almost wordlessly, does Harry accept *her* determination, which is that there will be no more children. It is a moment of potential explosiveness, an unexplained and passionate denial, which is dissolved, as so many other moments like it in the novel are dissolved, by something between squeamishness and realistic reserve. Through her making of curtains and cushions and her buying of pretty, unnecessary things for the house, Ellen shows that she has an eye, good taste. The pair cannot agree on a name for their son. For his mother and for the rest of the village he is always Will; but Matthew (his father's name for him) is the name he takes with him when he leaves home. It is the name of the grown man, connecting him with his father and with a man's world. Williams also had two names, and dropped Jim for Raymond when he left home for Cambridge.

This oedipal trio is skewed, for the son loves his father, and cannot love the woman who loves his father too. Returned home to his own wife, Matthew says nothing to her about the mother who has limited his access to her dying husband, delaying her son's visits to him with offers of food and other distracting motherly blandishments. Mother and son, each of them needy, dependent, are in competition for the dying Harry.

The birth of children sets off this competition and its separations. From an upstairs room in Harry's own home come barely human screams and the bustlings and ministrations of women. Harry 'went indoors and along the passage to the foot of the stairs. Then he knew he must turn back, and walked slowly out through the porch to the back-kitchen'.[62] There is a similar scene in *The Fight for Manod*, in which Peter, a husband of a younger generation, also watches his wife go upstairs and away from him to her secret biological destiny, which is not for men's eyes. Once again the father is told of his own child's birth by an older woman he barely knows (this time by telephone).

It is not, of course, that women's lives are directly denigrated by such separations, for there is a kind of reverence in these scenes. Rather, this insistence on the mysterious and on the shared animal knowledge (and courage) he attributes to women puts them outside the community's everyday values and, more importantly still, beyond the deep moral and political convictions, and the stamina and endurance, available to their husbands as part of those everyday values. Sexual love and intimacy between men and women become potential impediments to honourable commitment and then to action.

This theme is more explicitly tackled in *Second Generation*, a novel in which Williams 'hoped that by taking something as basic as the division between intellectual life and manual life, coexisting within one city, I could at least show the real theatre in which these confusions were occurring'.[63] The novel is about the working and family lives of two brothers, Harold and Gwyn Owen, who left Wales for Cowley and the car works there in the thirties to escape unemployment. Now, in the sixties, they are next-door neighbours, living in almost soap-box contiguity, with a passageway linking their houses and an 'understanding' between Harold's son Peter and Beth, who was born to Myra before her marriage to Gwyn. Place and boundaries are vital to the novel: the relation of Cowley to Oxford, of the car works to the university and, in the background, the emptied Welsh village transformed now into a caravan site, a holiday place. The separation of the university and the car works is irreducible, though it is perilously crossed in the novel; and it is, above all, with the lure of an illicit and deadly sexuality and with a sour, second-hand and cowardly involvement in left-wing politics that a transgression of the boundary between town and university is associated.

Williams was clearly not, as Terry Eagleton pointed out, someone 'one would think of as a particularly feminist writer': yet, Eagleton maintains, '*Second Generation* is as searching a study of the relations between work, politics, sexuality and the family as one could envisage'.[64] There is something to this claim, despite the novel's curious evasions and the sense in the end that clever and political women may present even more dangerous distractions to their single-minded husbands than their more vacuous and compliant sisters. Kate, Harold's intelligent and dissatisfied wife, a woman who has brought all her energies to supporting her husband in his gruelling union work, moves with cold deliberation into an adulterous affair with a cynical don she knows through the Labour Party (itself charged with treachery towards the striking car workers); and their son Peter — a graduate student at the university — rounds off a phase of alienation and destructiveness by having an affair with a manipulative married woman, who almost cooks his goose. Both mother and son have settled, by the end of the novel, for forms of sexual accommodation. Kate is received back by her bitterly hurt husband. Peter will eventually marry Beth, who loves him and will keep her job at the bank in order to support him through a series of posturing flights and reversals, which fail to satisfy either his gifts or his beliefs.

The sexual theme is in fact a good deal more intricately explored than I have suggested. Beth is implicated in Peter's unfaithfulness to her because she won't sleep with him until she is sure they'll marry. The guilty Kate criticises her simpler, more conventional sister-in-law, Myra, for hypocrisy in lying about her premarital 'lapse'. Sex within marriage is vulnerable to the exhaustion and despair that Harold habitually brings home from his work, and there is no solution to this. Yet anything smacking of 'sexual radicalism' or liberation is repudiated for its separation of sexual energy from the heart of family and feeling and community.

There are echoes in this of D.H. Lawrence's unique brand of sexual puritanism. Perhaps Williams's interviewers in *Politics and Letters* thought this too when they argued that 'to identify the presence of social reaction with the absence of sexual integrity appears to be a dangerous aesthetic simplification', having asked him whether there were not 'upholders of the bourgeois order, whether in the economic, political or cultural domain, whose private lives are of reasonable rectitude – say, the Keith Josephs of this world?'[65] There was, of course, no possibility that Williams would have accepted the idea that the 'reasonable rectitude' of right-wing gentlemen in public life had much to do with what he was writing about – and quite right too – so that he avoided answering their question and turned instead to a contemplation of what he knew about treacheries amongst certain intellectuals in the Labour Party. There is something quite diverting but also inattentive in the descent of an initially high-minded discussion of Williams's attitude to feminism into jocular speculation about possible sexual shenanigans in the Tory Cabinet.

Back in *Second Generation* Kate's lover, Arthur Dean, marvels at her intelligence:

> He was again surprised by the range of her intelligence. He had known that she was much more intelligent than her background would have led him to believe, and she was still limited by lack of training. But what he found increasingly – it was an odd admission to have to make – was an intelligence quite equal to his own, capable of the last surprising reaches and insights that couldn't be taken for granted anywhere. Yet when he tried to talk to her about their own relationship, it was different. There he felt no control, and could find no bearings. Usually, indeed, she would put him off with some joke. The only direct thing she

said was that she wasn't a young girl, to be dreamy and overwhelmed; she was a woman perfectly capable of managing her own life. And in the link which most mattered between them this seemed, against all his doubts, unquestionably true.[66]

Though we are not encouraged to approve of Dean, this is offered as an honest enough expression of arrogant male bewilderment and thwarted expectations. Williams does not endorse it. Yet Kate's sturdy and unusual presence in the novel is doomed to waste and idleness and frustration, and the pain suggested by her clenched body and her bitter speech is neither mourned nor deplored. There is a moment's sympathy, perhaps, when her father's death is remembered as preventing her from going to university (hence her untrained mind), but none at all for her now that her son is distancing himself, his mother's encouragement of his intellectual powers having borne fruit and delivered the 'training' she never had. The desperation out of which Harold assaults his wife so furiously is felt in a way that Kate's painful dilemmas never are, though the registering of intelligence and creativity blocked is part of the novel's subject matter. The curious unpleasantness of the scene in which Kate first makes love with Dean may be due to its vision of her sexual neediness as arid, even shocking, and finally injurious to her lover.

Kate does represent, none the less, a determined attempt by Williams to enter the life of a working-class woman who is a wife and a mother, and the practical and moral possibilities and constraints she encounters. She is by no means stereotypical, though it is possible to feel that there is something primitive and unresolved in her uneasy living of the discrepancy between female sexuality and intelligence. The novel is bent, however, on checking this life. Kate is firmly reprimanded and punished. The accommodations required of her are quite different from the accommodations required of her husband or of her son. Yet she *is* offered a kind of destiny, even if it is a resolutely subaltern destiny. She has a role: to devote her intelligence and love to her husband's life and political work, and warmly and uncritically to nurture him sexually. One is bound to recall Williams' sense of family life as 'unproblematic' in the light of this exorbitant expectation.

The novel deals, in fact, with a range of relations. The brothers' marriages are quite different (and still alive, as the glimpsed middle-class marriages are not) but also intimately interdependent and defined by their difference, as happens in families. Harold's struggles in the union are seen from his family's point of view, but also from the viewpoint of other workers, his brother, academics, members of the Labour Party: that is, within a connected and public politics.

Williams's purpose was to write novels about working-class life, but to do so in a way which did not rely for its focus on the distanced, omniscient observer, but instead worked within a range of contemporary views of events and from a set of closer vantage points. Ultimately, he came to see that what he most wanted 'was to find a fictional form that would allow the description both of the internally seen working-class community and of a movement of people, still feeling their family and political connections, out of it'.[67]

This was ambitious, calling for the kind of scope and the containment of a novel like *Felix Holt*, yet needing a more ambiguously authoritarian narrative voice. The difficulty, as some have seen it, is that this closer view of a working-class community through the eyes of one of its members who is on his way out of it (and it will, inevitably, be his, not hers) effectively isolates the village, the railway station, the small farm, the car works, especially the family. In neither *Border Country* nor *Second Generation* are there embodiments of the ruling class, of landowners, industrialists, the Tory Party. In the place of the institutions and personnel of capitalism Williams has civil servants, university teachers, middle-class Labour Party supporters: capitalism's middlemen, all vulnerable to the blandishments of an established world of power and wealth which remains outside the terrain on which class is enacted here.

Williams conceded this absence in his novels and explained it partly as a genuine reflection of working-class people's limited experience of the centres of power and partly in terms of the perhaps uncharacteristic nature of the community in which he grew up.[68] The effect of this absence in the novels is, however, to individualise moral and political dilemmas so that they are wrestled with in a kind of privacy, amongst family, friends, colleagues. This may even account, in the first two novels of the trilogy at least, for the pressure on women to uphold the family's feeding and watering of the male struggle in an exploitative world. The sense is not, finally, of a joint enemy, a class enemy, but of specific oppressions experienced by working men in relation to their work, which are damaging to their standing and their integrity as much as to their capacity to earn a living for their families. Ellen in *Border Country* never quite understands this. She is weak because she offers her man food but not sustenance. Kate offers neither food nor domestic warmth, and she is also damned for taking sides in a political struggle independently of her life's central commitment, which must be to the maintenance of her husband's integrity.

The Fight for Manod brings together Matthew Price from *Border Country* and Peter Owen from *Second Generation* (two characters Williams once described as versions of himself). Both are employed as academic consultants to advise on the building of a new city in the heart of the emptied Welsh mountains. In this novel, as in the later futurist thriller *The Volunteers*,[69] there has been a shift of focus to work and family life which are now middle-class, though attachments to place and to working-class childhood are important. In both novels the institutions of power and their administrators are included, though both novels are also organised round the impossibility of ever locating the sources of power, which diffuse and dissolve in a kind of inverse ratio to the intensification of the process of trying to track them down. Matthew and Peter in *The Fight for Manod* – ostensibly on the same side – come to represent the alternative possibilities of engagement and settlement with power available to those who leave working-class communities for a world which is corrupt, but also too powerful for intelligent men to ignore if they wish to have influence and effect change.

The mysteries at the heart of both *The Fight for Manod* and *The Volunteers*, and their heroes' frustrated efforts to unravel them, could be said to reiterate both novels' confusing of power with knowledge and of control with analysis. By the end of *The Fight for Manod* both Matthew and Peter have been routed. Matthew's exertions have led to a heart attack, from which he recovers to admit that the problem has been beyond him: 'I couldn't resolve it. All I've got to know are the pressures. The conflicting pressures.'[70] Such satisfaction as he can feel is an intellectual's satisfaction in at least understanding something of the arcane machinations and alliances of the powerful. Peter, meanwhile, has resigned, fled in protest; though it is a protest which, as his wife Beth knows, has become a habit, a kneejerk reaction to the forces of evil:

> . . . she had come to understand why there was no easy way out. Seeing his time as he saw it, as a civilisation and a society systematically repressive and false, there was a hard, bitter choice very early: to acquiesce or to oppose. No ordinary settlement had ever been possible. He would either fight that world in the open or, afraid to fight it or having taken its knocks, learn the means of pretence and disguise: despising all he joined, all he did, all he tacitly affirmed.[71]

These appear to be the choices for men: understanding the workings and the devastations of power from within and from a distance, with a mind 'trained' to make connections and proposals for the future; or furious flight, refusal, separation. Williams later characterised his own *Culture and Society* as 'negatively marked by elements of a disgusted withdrawal'.[72] This is also a description of Peter Owen, the young, but probably ruined, intellectual. And women? Their best, most wholesome choice is still marriage and loyalty to a man and to their children, even where as a wife a woman may know, as Beth knows, that her husband is wrong. By *The Volunteers* Williams could be said to have given up on the younger generation of women, who are either by now indistinguishable from men as they engage in new kinds of terrorist politics of both the Right and the Left, or melted down into 'bimbos', mistresses, second wives.

Meanwhile, Kate returns in *The Fight for Manod*, now become, as she puts it, 'the statutory co-optable woman ... It's an adaptive strategy. And by the way they don't even listen. It's just a limited natural break. Like the tea being brought in.'[73] This is well caught as self-disparagement, though it might also be read as trivialising this woman's sense of her life's futility, as always less than knowledge, less than accommodation, less even than honourable failure.

V

Politics and Letters, to which I have referred pretty extensively, takes its name from the journal Williams edited during 1947 and 1948. It's a remarkable book, compiled from conversations between Williams and three *New Left Review* editors, Perry Anderson, Anthony Barnett and Francis Mulhern. It was first published in 1979 and stands as a sort of spoken autobiography and as a series of arguments around some of the principal political and literary issues raised by Williams's work. His interviewers are not afraid to be critical, and they do indeed tax him – from the most detailed knowledge of his work and out of great admiration and affection for Williams himself – with neglects and confusions. Williams responds naturally and helpfully to what they say, and he could even be said at times to repudiate his early work and his early positions too yieldingly for comfort. Nor can the three male interviewers be faulted for avoiding feminism, though there can be no doubt that their questions would not by and large be the ones a feminist woman might have asked.

Such a reader may wonder, for instance – and by no means as a sniper – about the women Williams remembers in his own life. How did he think his mother (who 'had her own opinions' even if she was also in 'the classic situation of a Labour Party woman. She makes the tea, she addresses the envelopes, she takes them round – she does not have very many political activities in her own right'[74]) felt about the way she had spent her life? And what happened to the six girls who won scholarships to the local grammar school when Williams, the only boy, won his? He tells us only that girls 'would usually go only as far as the fifth form and would then leave'.[75] It is hard not to feel disappointed oneself as Williams registers the disappointment *he* felt when his Workers' Educational Association classes attracted not the working men he had hoped for, but 'commuter [*sic*] housewives at Haywards Heath who wanted to read some literature'.[76]

Later in the conversations Williams parries criticism of *The Long Revolution*, in which he at first proposes four essential social systems: economic, political, cultural and familial, but then drops the familial. The difficulty, as he expresses it, is in integrating truths about families and reproduction and the bringing up of children 'with an analysis of advanced capitalist society, where commodity production has become so much more extensive, while central areas of human life have been excluded from the category of production altogether'.[77] There is, indeed, an immense difficulty in integrating truths of these very different kinds, but it is precisely the sort of difficulty with which Williams grappled all his life in relation to men and to the individual women he chose haphazardly to include with or as men.

'The reality of hegemony', from which I began my discussion of Williams, is exactly the starting point needed for a social theory grounded as securely on gender differentiation as on class and race. So why did Williams – who was prepared to think of himself as a Marxist only so long as hegemony, in Gramsci's formulation, became its pivotal term, transforming the determinist rigidities of the base/superstructure relation between an economic level and a cultural – repeatedly and obdurately fend off feminism as simplistic, hopelessly overgeneralised, incompatible with a class politics and a class analysis, and dangerously prone to burrowing itself irretrievably into the charlatanry and false explanations of psychoanalysis?

The answer to this question lies, I think, close to the idea of 'the reality of hegemony', to the living of conflict, the experiencing of seduction. For instance, I have often felt as freakish, illegitimate, this desire I have to condense into a daughter's feeling for a father the simultaneous admiration, rebelliousness, affection, rage, regret and resentment Williams and his work provoke in me. It is easy to sympathise with Williams's known reluctance to be everybody's intellectual father. Yet in this process of trying to come to grips with Williams's formidable strengths, as well as his omissions or failures of nerve, I have found myself face to face with *his* living of hegemony as well as my own.

I think I know now that the male romance which was available to men of Williams's generation and background (indeed, both of his backgrounds really) did not include women. The romance was always with the harshness of landscape and the harshness of labour in relation to that landscape. It was a romance with and about men, which was at the same time profoundly homosexual and profoundly homophobic, always bound up with physical labour, with men's bodies and the solidarity amongst those of them who worked together. David Storey, less anxiously than Williams, recently remembered the pain of that romance for the man who undertakes to celebrate it at the moment when he leaves it:

> I remember, vividly, just after I had taken this Pauline decision to devote my life to art, my father coming home from the pit knackered, and there I was, painting a picture. Now, I'm physically bigger than my father. Built to be a miner, and there I am painting clouds, or writing poems about them. When I came to London, I had that feeling that I had to go down for eight hours, do my equivalent shift. It's a sort of moral justification for doing something useless.[78]

Women have always been a term in all this, a necessary and distinguishing feather in the cap, proof of virility but also of a capacity for gentleness. But their presence has been a peripheral presence, a useful embellishment and not much more, so that the romance and the intimacy and the politics (which could at times seem interchangeable) always excluded them and contrived to matter most when women's backs were turned. It may be inferred from this that women's presence has also been feared for its disruptive potential.

Even mothers – who are likely at least to be young children's first and most significant interlocutors, and therefore irrevocably implicated in their earliest dialogic or conversational forays into the world – are outside the romance, perhaps they most of all. Yet it is surely within those first conversations, those shared sightings and namings, that the specificity, the material detail and concrete knowing of the world are learned as values within an actual, evolving culture. The development from this first learning to children's (and especially boys') movement away from mothers, away from home, will vary vitally according to class, place, time. Gender is always learned, however, and by children of both sexes, through these earliest articulations and manifestations of difference and similarity. It seems probable, indeed, that such differences are perceived and interpreted even before differences of class and race in most children's lives.

In the succession of working-class women's lives so movingly recalled by Carolyn Steedman in her *Landscape for a Good Woman*[79] it is clear, in Steedman's words, that 'it was the women who told you about the public world, of work and politics, the details of social distinction'.[80] Ruqaiya Hasan,[81] as a linguist, and Cathy Urwin,[82] as a social psychologist, have demonstrated, through a number of highly persuasive examples, exactly how women come to assume responsibility for transmitting the culture's most controlling articulations of gender division and difference. That responsibility and that process – which has meant women learning to disparage their own femininity within particular class constructions of it – is continuous with the ways in which, as mothers, they will also have learned to protect their sons (and often their daughters too) from everything that a particular class culture may construe as undermining or dangerous in femininity.

That is the sort of learned doubleness, the uncertainty and ambivalence in relation to dominant values and dominant people, which Williams so clearly accounts for in working-class experience – so that it is difficult to imagine how a man able to write like this:

> ... it seems probable that the English working class was struggling to express an experience in the 1790s and 1830s which in a sense, because of the subordination of the class, its lack of access to means of cultural production, but also the dominance of certain modes, conventions of expression, was never fully articulated[83]

was unable to hear the very similar message which feminists have been offering about women's experience in the past and now. Why, for instance, when Kate, in *Second Generation*, says to her son, 'They say power corrupts and perhaps it does. What I know, in myself, is a quite different thing. That power corrupts the people it is exercised over',[84] can Williams not allow her to think of herself as a woman as well as the adjunct of a class? Why had he no interest in (or sympathy for) all that has been potentially corrupting of women and is also inherent in the forms their oppression has taken? Squalor begets squalor, and women have often been driven to exploiting the limitations which men's views and uses of them can seem to have enjoined.

VI

Carolyn Steedman's *Landscape for a Good Woman* is a book about, as she puts it, 'lives lived out on the borderlands, lives for which the central interpretative devices of the culture don't quite work'.[85] The book links her own 1950s childhood and growing up in South London with her mother's life, and before that with a grandmother and a great-grandmother who had been employed as servants and later became workers in the weaving sheds of Burnley. One part of the book's purpose is to disturb those male accounts of working-class childhoods which are suffused with nostalgia, but are also preferred unproblematically as guarantees of their own political authenticity and as simple demonstrations of the unity of class consciousness and class analysis. The disturbance to which Steedman alerts us is a radical disturbance:

> When the mental life of working-class women is entered into the realm of production, and their narrative is allowed to disrupt the monolithic story of wage labour and capital and when childhood and childhood learning are reckoned with, then what makes the old story unsatisfactory is not so much its granite-like *plot*, built around exploiter and exploited, capital and proletariat, but rather its *timing*: the precise how and why of the development of class-consciousness.[86]

Steedman's argument, then, is not just that women have been left out of working-class histories and political analysis. The reorientation required once their lives are told and heard alters the history, unsettles the politics and delivers almost entirely new versions of how and when class and gender are learned. And the emergent narratives will be very hard to read and to accept, for both their themes and their form will seem impermissibly raw and untreated, and offensively pallid from non-exposure to daylight:

> My mother's longing shaped my own childhood. From a Lancashire mill town and a working-class twenties childhood she came away wanting: fine clothes, glamour, money; to be what she wasn't. However that longing was produced in her distant childhood, what she actually wanted were real things, real entities, things she materially lacked, things that a culture and a social system withheld from her. The story she told was about this wanting, and it remained a resolutely social story. When the world didn't deliver the goods, she held the world to blame. In this way, the story she told was a form of political analysis, that allows a political interpretation to be made of her life.[87]

Raymond Williams reviewed *Landscape for a Good Woman*,[88] a book which both explicitly and implicitly acknowledges a debt to him. He wrote about it at some length and in detail, conceding that it was 'important' and deserved, therefore, some 'hard questioning'. He also submitted it to some wilful and punishing misreading, and its author (and even women writers generally) to some unwarranted end-of-term report put-downs of the kind: 'This is little developed, theoretically, and is based on what seems very limited reading'. And elsewhere:

> In fact, she might have added, following a wider perspective on this heavily contested area [Williams is referring to the origin and nature of class consciousness], that it reduces the consciousness and lives of many men, who were all also (it has sometimes to be

noted in following some styles of contemporary women's writing) children.[89]

These kinds of comment are not to be picked on as trivial stylistic points. On the contrary, they are characteristic, I think, of Williams and of many other writers on the Left, and of their readiness to listen to feminist argument only on their own terms – for what it adds to Marxism, not for what it finds unsatisfactory in Marxism – and to counterattack with flailing, hit-or-miss randomness, though always finally on grounds of narrowness.

Just as seriously, Williams charges Steedman with collapsing her mother's 'desire' for 'a New Look skirt, a timbered cottage, to marry a prince' with what he stigmatises as 'the rejection of socialism, in the enchanting name of a generalised "desire" by a whole group of French intellectuals'.[90] But the desire Steedman is writing about is as far as it is possible to be from such an abstraction. Quite the opposite: Steedman represents her mother's 'wanting' as a precisely and historically defined concentration of one woman's desires and needs, which a particular period of capitalism in a particular society is shown to have produced and, indeed, to have flagrantly endorsed and publicised. Far from constituting 'a rejection of socialism' in the name of a generalised desire, Steedman is asking serious questions from within socialism about its failure to theorise lives like her mother's, for which it must surely admit some responsibility, as it must also for the politics and even the autobiographical narrative the culture makes available to her.

Landscape for a Good Woman contributes necessary insights to a developing tradition of socialist feminist historical work. It also engages – on theoretical terrain many would see as having been opened up and explored with special efficacy by Raymond Williams – with how culture and identity connect in language and through literary form. The task of describing the changing dynamics of sexual relations within a predominantly Marxist account of class is, as I've said, an immensely hard one. It has not been helped by the separate and opposed hostilities directed at it by socialists and by feminists, of which Michèle Barrett writes at the end of her *Women's Oppression Today. Problems in Marxist Feminist Analysis*:

> By generations of socialists we stand accused of bourgeois diversionary, individualist reformism. By our sisters we are charged with betraying feminism in favour of a sexist, male class struggle.[91]

By no means all feminist politics in this country is or has been socialist, but a significant part of it has. Compared with the best-known work of French and American feminists, for instance, it would be true to say that from the mid sixties until now the most productive aspects of the debate in this country have centred on the relation of feminism to forms of socialist and Marxist analysis. Yet as the women editors of the History Workshop Series volume entitled *Language, Gender and Childhood* amusingly put it, the relationship was not always reciprocal:

> 'People's history and socialist theory', the last History Workshop to be held in Oxford, was a dividing place for more than the Workshop itself. It brought a tradition of people's history and workers' writing into direct confrontation with new sources of socialism from Europe, and there was a dramatic enactment of this confrontation in the darkness of a deconsecrated church in Walton Street, where titanic figures of the left boomed the struggle in imperious male voices; and the only woman on the platform stood up to say that, excluded from the form and rhetoric of the debate, she could only stay silent.[92]

Marxism – and perhaps most particularly the Marxism that Williams elaborated in all his work and throughout his life – cannot fail to be seductive, indeed irresistible, to feminism, for its determined connecting of those levels and areas of social life which both a conservative and a liberal humanist politics have expediently kept apart for us: the economy and psychological development, for instance, class and culture, ideology and institutions. Theoretically, Marxists have worked towards coherence; and this has, in principle at least, allowed for the inclusion of issues like child-rearing, education, cultural form as well as cultural production and distribution, and the character of practical consciousness, within understandings about history and social structure.

Within this potentially embracing project, families, women, children, have sometimes been remembered, for they were, after all, to be found within classes and could therefore be accounted for within the framework of class struggle. But an unwavering attention to that struggle has occluded other struggles and has falsified their character by a process of elision. Struggles between men and women, and even between Marxism and feminism, are characterised by the fact that the contestants are locked – and not just metaphorically – in matrimony. None is quite able to contemplate divorce, but neither are they able to withstand the propensity of marriage to inhibit constructive disagreement or re-emphasis.

Where feminism is extruded from the central ground of Marxist analysis, sexual relations are naturalised and privatised, and more than half the population (for small boys tend to slip unnoticed into the argument on this side, in much the same way that they slip into girls' schools and ladies' lavatories) is disenfranchised from a politics whose analysis and strategy have been addressed to the diversity of material experience in history and to inherent injustices. Concomitantly, feminism without Marxism is bereft without a history of inequality and plans for revolutionary change.

In the last chapter of *Towards 2000*, which was published in 1983, Raymond Williams salutes the first stage of feminism, as he also salutes the peace and ecology movements.[93] He distinguishes feminism from the other two movements for its relative stability, which he attributes to its 'more immediate identities and bondings'.[94] He speculates that movements like these may prefigure the forms, the themes, the interest bases of the future, and he goes on to warn against their tendency (particularly feminism's) towards narrowness, sectional concerns, a dangerous ignoring of the need to transform the economic base.

But feminism has grown out of exclusion, oppression, marginality, some forms of which are not susceptible to a class analysis. Feminism labours still with definitions which are meant to keep it in its place, away from the centre. For all that, its concerns have been broader, more inclusive, than all those politics which ask women to wait their turn and listen to their betters. Feminists cannot, by and large, be taken to task for their 'limited reading', since they find it impossible to deny their reliance on men's ideas and texts and power. Meanwhile we wait, with gathering impatience, for men of the Left, men — supposedly — of good will, to pay attention to what we say, with just a fraction of our kind of respect.[95]

3

An Odd Woman

> They fear we should excel their sluggish parts,
> Should we attempt the sciences and arts;
> Pretend they were designed for them alone,
> So keep us fools to raise their own renown.
> from Sarah Fyge Egerton's *The Emulation*

I

C.E. Collet is scarcely a name to conjure with. It makes an occasional unfussy appearance as a footnote or as an androgynous Index entry in a few studies of nineteenth-century social history. In one or two places it follows, decently enough, the name C.D. Collet, who may be mentioned in relation to a long correspondence with Karl Marx, in which Russia – even then an 'Evil Empire' – and the British press are somewhat obsessively discussed and, indeed, linked by Marx, as dangerously colluding.[1] C.E. Collet was, in fact, the second daughter and the fourth of the five children of Collet Dobson Collet, campaigner for a free press and author of a history of newspaper tax,[2] and his wife Jane, who owned and ran a laundry in North London. The C stood for Clara, though she was Miss Collet to all who knew her outside the family. The novelist George Gissing wrote to her at least once a week for ten years, and he never called her anything but Miss Collet. This was a title to which, as her father's second daughter, she had – as she would have been the first to point out – no right by convention, whereas I, as her great-niece and her nephew's eldest daughter, was, if nothing else, at least a genuine Miss Collet.

Clara Collet lived from 1860 to 1948. I remember her as a small, neat and formidable person, with an immense double chin and chilly ways. She once asked me about my plans for the future and was disappointed to be told that I meant first to be an Olympic diver and thereafter a PE teacher. I was no more satisfied with her answer to *my* question. What, I wanted to know, would happen after their death to all that she and her sisters absorbed from the two books a day delivered to their door by a van from the local library? 'Nothing will happen,' was her reply, 'absolutely nothing whatever.' I am sure that she assumed, and rightly, that I was as critical of all that useless reading as she was of my (shorter-lived) dedication to standing on my head, diving, and climbing anything which might be expected to cause my parents almost as much terror as it actually caused me. It was not the 'boyishness' of these pursuits which dismayed her, but their frivolity.

My few memories of my Aunt Clara have her in a large wooden bungalow, rimmed by a deep verandah and perched on the enticingly sheer cliffs at the edge of Sidmouth in Devon. As the member of the family with the best pension and the soundest experience of the world, she had moved them all from Hampstead in 1936. There was a big, square room, with a grand piano and four card tables set as far apart as possible. Here, during the last years of their long lives, Carrie, the eldest, Harold, the second son, and Edith, the baby, sat at their books and their Solitaire — inwardly railing, perhaps, at the high-handed way in which Clara had transported them there. It is remembered in the family that Clara had had a breast removed at about that time, that Geoffrey Keynes had performed the operation and that during a brief convalescence in Sidmouth, Clara had decided to sell the family house in South Hill Park Gardens and move them all to the coast. It is also remembered that she did not consult the others at all adequately about the move.

How hard it is for children to believe in the past! I assumed that these four people had always been old. Aunt Carrie had always worn her hair in a thin white plait at night, just as she had always dressed in black silk with a silver châtelaine for her pince-nez clipped to her belt during the day. Aunt Edith's mind had always sweetly wandered and she had always found dressing a confusing affair. Uncle Harold had always sat smilingly amongst his cricket and golf mementoes. It was not possible for me to imagine him as a good-looking young man who actually made use of these things. And Aunt Clara had always been bossy and worn grey stockings and what was known then as a navy costume. I never bothered to wonder how Wilfred had fitted in. He was my grandfather and would have been nearly as old as Aunt Carrie, had he not died before I was born. My sisters and I liked dressing up in his old clothes: white ducks, but also a suit covered in gold braid and a cocked hat, for he had been a governor of some sort, we knew, and a pretty stout one, if his uniform was anything to go by. Old people had always been old, and were different from us in that respect especially. I supposed that these ones had simply had a particularly long time to consider and prepare for death.

My father's mother had died in 1910 when he was five years old. Aunt Clara recorded her sister-in-law's death in her diary, adding to the medical report of it the words 'She had a beautiful character'. Thereafter, my father lived with varying combinations of aunts — Edith being the constant one — as his father was usually overseas governing in his braid and cocked hat. I know now that in my father's stories his aunts are sometimes young. He told me once that Clara felt that her mother preferred Wilfred to her. This image of two ancient people squabbling for position on the maternal lap was to be treated with contempt. My father was telling me about their childhood, of course, but they could never be young to me. Perhaps their having had no children of their own made it harder to imagine their having had childhoods of their own. Old age was their province as far as I was concerned. Uncle Harold was known to have 'failed' – in business, I thought, because I was once shown a school report of his which commended him on several counts. And Clara? Well, Clara was always less lovingly portrayed in my father's stories than her siblings, anyway. She did not suffer fools gladly, and she returned my mother's letters to her with spelling mistakes marked in red. She even returned Christmas presents as both inappropriate and unnecessary. She had opinions and was not, it seemed, always sensitive to the more trivial of human preoccupations. There were aspects of her character which it was thought I might have inherited. I was known to adhere a bit tenaciously to my 'little opinions' in ways which bore traces of the Clara will. Such comparisons did not endear her to me. I was fifteen when she died, and I don't think I mourned her at all. I had feared her a little and certainly felt rebuked by her at times, though never reproached. I know that I dreaded becoming at all like her, for wasn't she old and plain, serious and heavy with knowledge, unmarried and not very popular?

Yet in retrieving this woman for myself, as she was between the ages of sixteen and about fifty-five, I have not just been indulging in family reminiscences, family history; though paradoxically she would have applauded such an exercise, I suspect, while warning me to steer clear of sentimentality.[3] Nor is it simply that I want to record something of the life of a woman who was an intellectual and an impressively effective professional person in an era when this was still rare – though I do want to do that. What I am after is a way of making connections between the determining constructions put on women like Clara Collet as they prejudiced my sense of this woman's achievement and destiny when I was growing up in the forties, and her own complex learning of 'femininity' seventy or so years earlier.

Central to my childhood belief that my aunts had always been as they were when I knew them was the idea that there had been no struggle for Aunt Clara. She had always known what she wanted – had, indeed, 'chosen' to have a career and 'chosen' not to marry. This complacent ascription of effortless 'choosing' was produced in part by the callousness of youth. There is more to it, though. For these 'choices' were understood in some way to chime with her 'nature', and that 'nature' was to be understood by reference to all that it was not. The language used to describe a woman who, like my Aunt Clara, 'never married' and pursued a 'male' career in the peculiarly hobbled fashion a handful of trained and educated women were permitted to do in the last quarter of the nineteenth century is disparaging.[4] 'Mannish', 'assertive', 'domineering', 'opinionated', 'old maid': such language combines reference to a denatured femininity (undermined as much by its proximity to masculinity as by its absolute non-equivalence to masculinity) and to a femininity rejected as such by men. Freud could be said to have developed his theory of sexuality out of the contradictory accounts of women's 'natures' which caught and exercised control over so many women's lives during the second half of the nineteenth century.

I am interested in how women have internalised such contradictions and limiting disparagements – as well as the life possibilities they allude to – differently and according to class and other historical and cultural specificities. I need to insist on these differences, for it would be unhelpful to reduce an account of this woman's life to a set of analogies or correspondences – with mine, for instance, or even with contemporaries like Beatrice Webb, with whom she had a good deal in common, despite some crucial differences.[5] The connections I shall want to make between the difficulties I had as a girl with much of what this woman represented, and the ambiguities which marked her developing independence as a woman, reveal a history of significant changes in women's lives as well as a bizarrely unchanging quality in the character of discussions about these things.

One way of characterising Clara Collet's development is as a lifetime's struggle with and a lifetime's accommodations to the seductiveness of male lives and voices and invitations. There are many ways of submitting to such seductions and many of resisting. Emulation, imitation, joining are ways of consummating the seduction, and so is marriage. And both ways of yielding to the seduction may entail their own kinds of resistance. Yet a constant feature of all such accommodations must surely be the internalising of those disparagements which lurk in the language, with its pairs and its opposites, poised to home in on 'the weaker sex'. Tensions and conflicts of this sort characterise many women's relations with a male and heterosexual culture. I am concerned here with a particular experience of the seduction, with its pleasures and its pitfalls. Clara may be said, for instance, to have been enticed by the prospect of intellectual and financial independence to join men in their professional endeavours, and to have resisted – and at times regretted – what she came to see as her consequent solitude. She could be exasperated, however, by any idealising of independence for women which ignored its economic reality.[6]

Clara's brother Wilfred – my grandfather – was knighted in 1914 for his services to the Colonies and the Crown. The presence of his medals and his cocked hat in our dressing-up box may indicate a lack of respect. I don't believe that my father was especially proud of the father he cannot have known well and who chiefly communicated with his small son by letters addressed to Phoebus Apollo and signed Zeus. His achievement, however, was of a recognisable and describable kind. He had done well in his field, and doing so had certainly not interfered with his marrying a woman with 'a beautiful character' and even a beautiful face, who had borne him three sons. His was a destiny and a career which straightforwardly involved effort, choice, change and rewards. So did his sister's, of course. Yet her life and its anomalies were already perceptibly ambiguous to me even as a small girl. If she was as she was because that was her nature, what about my nature? I wanted to be 'boyish', if not 'mannish'. Could you be those things and at the same time be loved and admired by men for being almost entirely different from them? For how could men possibly approve of qualities in women which they worked so hard (as it seemed to me) to expunge in themselves? That was the question which dogged my childhood and which was, I suspect, not unknown to the young Clara.

My Aunt Clara undoubtedly shared some of those views which required her to sacrifice aspects of her woman's 'nature' in order to earn her living by the use of talents and interests which became, by this process, 'unnatural'. What seems surprising, given the kind of coercion she must have felt subject to at times, was her continuing interest and faith in men. She acquired and kept close women friends, but there is no evidence that she was ever sexually involved with a woman, and much more evidence that she continued to be as drawn to men as to the lives they led.

I have been piecing together Clara Collet's life – from her diaries, from her unpublished as well as her published writing, from friends' letters which she kept and from some memories of her, my own and my father's. I want to track her doubleness about her own life and her experiencing of sexual difference, and I want to do this in relation to echoes and elaborations of the versions of her life with which I grew up. For if these confusions were implicated in my plans for myself, they also marked out territory which was to be avoided at all costs.

II

In 1910 Clara wrote in her diary:

On the 2nd June I sent in my resignation for two reasons (1) in order to speak freely about the way in which the women's side of the Labour Exchanges is being organised, capable women being subordinated to men who know nothing & care nothing about women's interests and (2) because there was nothing to stay for.

She was nearly fifty when she wrote that and seriously contemplated truncating a successful career as Senior Investigator at the Board of Trade. In the end she was persuaded to stay on for another seven years; I shall return to this. Her two reasons for wanting to resign carry some of the doubleness of her career. First, her professional and public position was felt at some level to inhibit her speaking 'freely' as a woman, especially about issues of paramount importance to women, like wages. In 1891 Clara had been one of four women asked by the Royal Commission on Labour to report on women's 'sweating'. H.J. Mundella, the Head of that Commission, became President of the Board of Trade the following year and at once appointed Clara to a post as Labour Correspondent with special responsibility for women's industrial conditions.

Hilda Martindale[7] describes how Clara's department grew steadily, in line with a general increase in attention to women's work, so that before long she was permitted to appoint her own assistant investigator. For four consecutive years the four clever young women she appointed were obliged to leave as each of them married and was forced by the marriage bar to relinquish the post. By 1903 Clara had been appointed Senior Investigator for Women's Industries in the Commercial, Labour and Statistical Departments of the Board of Trade and had at last acquired a woman assistant who did not fall foul of the marriage bar. Clara herself had become by this time a recognised expert on statistics. She was that extremely rare phenomenon, a woman civil servant, who worked with men, in institutions organised by men and for men and according to male traditions of professional behaviour and procedures. Yet her specialism was women's work, women's education and training, and women's pay. Her professional life was constructed out of and also split on gender lines.

During the thirty or so most active years of her professional life, between 1890 and the early 1920s, Clara lived as a man of her position might have done – an unmarried man, that is. She lived alone in rooms, 'chambers' or flats, at first rented, but by the end of her working life owned. She took her friends and colleagues to restaurants. She belonged to clubs and spent a good deal of her time on the committees of professional and academic associations. In 1884 she was elected to the Council of the Charity Organisation

Society – a significant step, to which I shall return. She was also a
founder member of the Councils of both the Royal Statistical Society
and the Royal Economics Society.

There are ways in which Clara may be understood as belonging to
a generation of active and intelligent middle-class women, many of
them born into Unitarian families, who, during the last thirty years of
the nineteenth century and the first decades of the twentieth, were
involved in public life and particularly with the problems of urban
poverty. Yet if I am to make sense of Clara's particular choices and
developing opinions it will be essential to distinguish her from some
of her contemporaries. Where Beatrice Potter was able to assure
Sidney Webb in 1891 that she had an income of £1,500 a year on
which they might live, Clara always expected to earn her own living.
She never earned a large amount, certainly less than her male
colleagues, but she was always financially independent and she
enjoyed giving friends and relatives small gifts and occasional loans.
She had, as she might well have put it, 'done well for a woman'. Yet
she would inevitably remain subordinate to men less expert than she
in her field, just as her specialism would always be subordinate to
questions about men's work and men's wages. And though she was
one of a handful of women whose career offered some security and a
pension, her entry into the Civil Service and her position within it
remained quite outside the established career routes, and there was
never any possibility of serious promotion or of mobility for her
within the Service.[8]

It is clear from her diaries that she thought often, if guardedly,
about the difference between her life as a working woman and the
life of wives. Her professional preoccupations centred on the class,
economic and educational aspects of women's lives. She came to
believe, I think, that middle-class married women had, by marrying,
committed themselves to wasting any training and professional
qualifications they might have in order to perform the duties of wife
and mother. She may also have felt, somewhat exasperatedly, that it
was the duty of married women who were not poor to withdraw
from competition for the kinds of jobs which were gradually
becoming available to women at the end of the nineteenth century.

She often registered a sense of the oddity of being a woman
amongst men. For these were, of course, men married to women, and
wives were transported by marriage into a sphere from which she, as
an unmarried woman, was significantly excluded. This was not
always a painful matter, by any means. Indeed, she was often amused
as she contemplated her colleagues' wives. On one of her extra-
curricular committees, for instance, she encountered as its treasurer a
Lady Dudley, who had come

straight from Paris to the Ctte. She was in a light gray dress that looked very summery near our dark dresses although I suppose it was merely her travelling dress. She spoke very prettily to me afterwards saying that her husband was a colleague of mine; that he said he had never seen me but he was always interested in my work. She reads the Labour Gazette right through. She evidently means to make her husband a success.[9]

Wives may well have been capable of showing an interest in public issues – may, indeed, have been genuinely well versed in them – but as wives they became, for women like Clara Collet, pampered and patronising, but also, of course, fair game for her own condescension – justified, since these were women who had opted for becoming useful primarily to her male colleagues.

Throughout her life Clara sought – and enjoyed – friendships with men. In her twenties and early thirties it seems likely that she thought of these (proudly and privately) in relation to a possible marriage. She also envied 'George Eliot for her friendship with George Lewes'. 'The worst of friendships with men', she writes in her diary, 'is that one can't cultivate them for any length of time; they must simply come up & die without any attempt being made to water them.'

George Gissing, as we shall see later, confided to Clara details of his three impossible marriages, which he did not discuss with anyone else. Other male friends talked to her about their relations with women. One, a Mr Higgs, wrote to her about his marriage. She found his letter odd or interesting enough to make it worth quoting:

My wife is a very old friend of 14 years, but our engagement was one of 14 days. She is quite the 'competent housewife', likes a country life, her happiness is in her home and she is a good Churchwoman with a tender heart for the sick and poor. I am afraid that the COS would not approve of her![10] But so far as I can judge after 5 weeks we are not likely to have any 'incompatibility of temper'.

Another friend, a Russian called Mr Ibry, with whom she spent time in 1909, is reported as 'evidently now hoping to meet his ideal & marry. I hope he will.' Such equanimity (if that is what it was) about men loving and marrying other women, and about the kinds of relationship which it was then possible for her to have with men and with their wives, was won painfully, I believe. If she was once able to assert that a woman might possibly escape 'being old maidish by coming into daily contact with men professors and students', her capacity to identify with men in their sexual relations with women relegated her at times to a position of uncomfortably asexual support, which was cheerfully exploited by women as well as by men.

In returning to her adolescence, young womanhood and middle age I mean to attend to this developing double view of herself. Her concern with women's issues became a professional concern, from which she distanced herself, even while maintaining an insider's knowledge and sympathy for the women she interviewed and referred to in her writing. She began her investigative career with Charles Booth and his *Survey of London Life and Labour.*[11] Her published work originated as chapters for this survey, as reviews and articles, or later as Reports or Memos for her political masters at the Board of Trade. She did not call herself a feminist (indeed, this word appears not to have been used at all widely until this century) and she came to regard herself as a suffragist but not as a suffragette. Though at various periods of her life she was a President of the Association of Assistant Mistresses and a Governor of Bedford College for women, she was probably prouder of being the first woman to be made a fellow of University College London.

Compared with an even slightly older generation of women (her sister Carrie, for instance, who was five years older) she was fortunate. She was only in her eighteenth year in 1878 when London University approved the admission of women to degrees on the same terms as men. This opened up a wider set of professional possibilities for women who wanted to have careers outside teaching. For Clara, questions about personal happiness were always linked with her need to earn a living and with her lifelong faith in rationality and in the value of independent intellectual effort. Whereas contemporaries like Beatrice Webb and Eleanor Marx were to a considerable extent self-educated, Clara had learned a great deal at school, and besides being a qualified teacher had a BA and an MA from University College London. As a child she was competitive with her older brothers and aware of having interests and personal qualities which, if they were not thought 'masculine', were also not associated with girls or women. And if manly qualities and achievements were targets for unequivocally honourable aspirations, 'mannish' ones were ambiguously tainted by implications of the concomitant and likely denaturing of womanly ones. Yet she seems not to have been unduly concerned about such things, and she was also unselfconsciously interested in ideas.

Clara Collet lived to be eighty-eight. Rather than following her life through from its beginning to its end, I shall concentrate on four phases of it and use her voice and experience to illustrate some of the themes I have outlined. These phases are, first, the last two years of her schooldays in London, between 1876 and 1878; then the seven years spent as a teacher in Leicester until 1885. Third, there are the years of her new work as a social researcher, and then as a civil servant, and of her friendship with George Gissing between their meeting in 1893 and his death in 1903; and, finally, the years between 1902 and the First World War, during which she did some of her most interesting work.

III

Clara began her diary on 10 September 1876, her sixteenth birthday. Sometimes she wrote in it every day. Later, she tended to write reviews of weeks or months, drawing on notes she had made of events in an 'accounts book'. There are long gaps, sometimes of years, and there are gaps which are probably the consequence of her destroying portions of what she wrote. For her sixteenth birthday she received small items of jewellery and five books, most of them by women. She also went to Unitarian chapel that day and did 'nothing in the afternoon and the same in the evening'. The nearly two years of her diary until she left school in the summer of 1878 to become a teacher herself at seventeen are filled with family and friends, with her reading, with school and exams and with an anxiously glimpsed future beyond all this. She is humorous, confident and cheerfully iconoclastic, precocious perhaps in her determination to develop a style and wit for herself which will eschew cant and, above all, sentimentality.

Her family are the source of good times and presents. They are also ridiculous, and the male members have inherited a disagreeable saintliness. She is not fond of good boys. But there are visits to the theatre (her father sang for a time in the chorus at Covent Garden, and the family are musical). Even her brother Wilfred, who once invited easily the ugliest person in the world to tea and sometimes talks 'a lot of bosh', particularly about young women, has his points, particularly when he arranges Shakespeare evenings. Sometimes these are at the Collet home in Coleridge Road in Crouch End; sometimes at the Marxes' in Maitland Park Road. Eleanor Marx (Tussy or Tussie to her family and friends) is marvellous as Rosalind and 'perfect' as Lady Anne in *Richard III*. Eleanor is five years older than Clara and secretly engaged to Lissagaray, of whom Marx disapproved. The sixteen-year-old Clara can't wait for Tussy to return from Carlsbad, where she has been with her father. And when Tussy does return, the younger girl is grandly impatient with Lissa, as she conspiratorially calls him, for monopolising her friend. She wishes he could be induced to fight 'a fifth or sixth duel (I don't know which) and get done for; he is not half good enough for her'. Perhaps, she muses soon after this, he might 'commit forgery & suicide'. The Shakespeare readings are formalised. Clara records the establishing of the Dogberry Club in August 1877 and a reading of *The Merchant of Venice* in November of that year. The Maitland girls, Dolly and Clara, as well as several less acceptable male members of the Maitland family, become members of the club too.

She is intrigued by the young men she meets, though she is also defensively critical of their looks, their brains, their tendency to extreme conceit and to discussing topics on which they are ill-informed. She is highly entertained by a young man seen waving to his wife from the train as it passes her window. Such attentiveness to a wife who is still in bed when her husband leaves for work is absurd, unwarranted and unlikely to last.

Occasionally she goes to bed early because there is nothing left to read. She records vast and eclectic reading, from children's books to philosophy. After reading a life of Byron she announces: 'He was bad but he is the only person that I ever loved (whom I am not personally acquainted with). I hate his prim prig of a wife with all my heart & all my soul.' To the story of a daughter who voluntarily joined her father in Botany Bay she responds, 'Catch me going to Botany Bay for anybody unless myself.' She will never of her own free will 'read a single page of that detestable hound Leigh Hunt'. Even Florence Nightingale, whom Clara had admired, wrote 'sickening' letters. John Stuart Mill is 'dull & no mistake'. She is impressed by a sermon on an Anne Askew, which suggests that she was 'not bad for a woman'. She reads and loves Elizabeth Gaskell and Charlotte Brontë, and is delighted by Gaskell's biography of Brontë. One criterion for judging a book is for what it offers 'the female portion of the world', and it may be failure on that front which provokes her condemnation of Goethe's autobiography, 'the most conceited book I ever read . . . the man himself is disgusting'. George Lewes's life of Goethe is far better, and by the end of it both Lewes and Goethe have somewhat redeemed themselves in her eyes.

A favourite relative is Aunt Sophia, a writer herself and an authority on the Brahmo Somaj, a development within Hinduism which was welcomed by Unitarians.[12] Aunt Sophia also has good stories to tell about Louisa M. Alcott, with whom she once stayed, and about Emerson. The Alcotts were, Aunt Sophia told her, satisfyingly like the March family in *Little Women* and *Good Wives*: 'Mr Alcott was always talking about celibacy as though everyone ought to practise it. His wife got so sick of hearing him talk about it that she left him. Mr Alcott bore it for one day and then fetched her back.' And 'Emerson used to put a bank note into Alcott's desk or some place where he would be sure to find it, when

Alcott was hard up. Neither of them said anything about it to each other.'

School is central and interesting, though it is not allowed to take up too much of her time. Girls who take more than three hours to do their homework must surely be 'duffers'. She is doing Chemistry and Physics and Maths. Chemistry experiments are disgusting and she once actually failed an applied Maths exam. She is best at English, French, German, Latin and Philosophy. Her school was the North London Collegiate School, founded in 1850 and still at this point on Camden Road, though it moved to the site now occupied by the Camden School for Girls shortly afterwards. The school was still in the ardent and capable hands of Frances Mary Buss, who seems to have taken as kindly an interest in Clara as in all her girls. There are visits to museums and plays. One to the South Kensington Museum is 'dreadfully instructive': the only really interesting exhibit a 'machine for measuring the intensity of thought'.

After a visit to *Romeo and Juliet* she buys herself a print of which she cannot totally approve: 'Romeo should caress Juliet rather than Juliet Romeo.' Her favourite teacher, Miss Oswald, is shocked that Clara does not admire Goethe's *Hermann und Dorothea* and regards as 'something fearful' Clara's 'want of poetic appreciation'. Sometimes Clara and two other girls are sent to Dr Edward Aveling for a statistics lesson: the same Edward Aveling with whom Clara's friend Eleanor Marx will spend many years of her life. There are exams. She does well in most of them. There are occasional prizes. She expresses no great pleasure about these in her diary, but they are duly recorded. She thinks about writing, even about becoming a writer. Her diary is a problem. There is always the risk of being ridiculous, a risk she reckons is seldom quite avoided by the human beings of her acquaintance. There is the associated hazard of self-consciousness. Then:

> the worst of a diary is that when anything happens you have no time to write about it, when you have time nothing happens . . . I have come to the conclusion that if I ever wish to write anything worth writing I ought to make note of my own thoughts & opinions more than I have done; it will give me ease in writing and provided I do it truthfully it will be amusing to compare changing opinions. The most difficult thing in a diary is to write totally for yourself; try as hard as one will there is always the arrière-pensée about what people would think if they read it.

There is little doubt that Clara wrote her diary with some such thought in mind from the beginning. She alludes·more than once to having omitted painful events on the grounds that she is unlikely to forget them and they would be of no interest to anyone else. Later, she destroyed the section of her diary which coincided with a crisis in her friendship with George Gissing. She even edited a version of the diary she wrote during her seven years in Leicester and had it typed (with significant omissions) and entitled *Diary of a Young Assistant Mistress 1878–1885*. Even at seventeen she saw herself as writing for 'imaginary admirers', and there were aspects of her interests and ambitions which were already ebulliently public. She expected to be heard and listened to.

It is possible to see Clara's considerable intellectual energy and confidence as learned within her family and strengthened by her teachers. Her father (possibly more than her mother) encouraged the girls just as much as the boys to read and think and have opinions. The school offered a broader and probably better-taught curriculum than the majority of boys' public schools and encouraged the maximum academic ambition in its pupils, despite the relatively exiguous prospects available to them.

To some extent Clara's family had come down in the world since the middle of the eighteenth century. A good deal of money had been made and lost, in India and elsewhere. And then her grandfather had died young, in 1829, leaving a somewhat impoverished family of six children, most of whom went to make lives for themselves (as Dobsons) in New Zealand. Only Collet and his sister Sophia remained in England. Both tacked Collet (which was the name shared by their two grandmothers) to their names, and both revived the family's traditional Unitarianism, which had been deserted for Anglicanism by some members of the family in more recent times. Clara's own family seem always to have employed at least one servant and to have lived fairly comfortably; but it was expected of the children that they would support themselves, and Clara's two brothers left school at sixteen to work in offices, though Wilfred proceeded eventually to the Colonial Office and an external Law degree from London University.

IV

Suddenly, Clara's diary records the end of childhood and schooldays. She announces this unceremoniously: 'Next Saturday I am going to Leicester; I am not sure whether I shall like it; but I do know I shall like it better than being at home. The Marxes and Miss Oswald are the only people I care for here.' With this ungracious adieu to family and friends, she embarks on her adult life. Her sister Carrie has already begun to teach, and the experience is not encouraging: 'Her children are demons. They kick & swear & do nothing else but play cards.' The post of assistant mistress at Wyggeston Girls' School[13] will not present problems of quite that sort, but there will be others.

Clara noted later:

Very shortly after the announcement of the admission of women to degrees Miss Buss sent for me to her room. With a splendid disregard of her previous insistence on the necessity of my entering a training college before entering the teaching profession she told me that she had recommended me for a post in the new Wyggeston Girls' Grammar School to be opened in Whitsun week. I should only have £80 a year to begin with but Miss Ellen Leicester, the headmistress, would give me every facility for preparing myself for the Intermediate Arts examination in July 1879 and the Final B.A. in October 1880 (1st BA and 2nd BA in those days). Masters from the Boys' Grammar School would give me lessons in Greek and applied mathematics and I could manage Latin and English subjects by myself. A little lady who had been spending some time in our classrooms turned out to be Miss Leicester. Interviews followed with my father first and myself afterwards. I went down to Burlington House on Saturday, 15th June, saw my name on the alphabetical honours list of matriculation and was just in time to catch the train to Leicester with no refreshment other than a petrified bun at Kentish Town station. My brother Wilfred met me there and gave me the extra five shillings necessary for a first class ticket.

If she arrived 'hardly expecting to enjoy myself', she in fact found it 'delightful'. Clearly, her pleasure in her work at this stage, in the new friends she was making, in her grown-up life, were such that she began 'to get quite nervous as to what particular pain I am to suffer. I have almost presentiments that it will come soon and unexpectedly, otherwise I was never so happy in my life before.' Already, a year after starting as a teacher, she has completed her '1st B.A.' in the 'First Division'. She is studying Greek. She enjoys being a pupil as well as a teacher. Besides teaching and studying and discussing critically, but with interest, the sermons she hears, she skates and walks and swims and takes part in amateur dramatics. By 1880 she has a wide circle of friends and acquaintances, most of them connected with school or with the Unitarian community she discovers in Leicester. She spends a few days in Cambridge with her current headmistress and Miss Buss. A debating society is started at school, and the first topic is 'The occupation of girls on leaving school'.

In the holidays she goes home to Coleridge Road, sometimes taking a friend with her. There are visits to the theatre and to concerts. She goes to France with her sisters during the summer holidays. A plan to study for an MA waxes and wanes with the tides of enjoyment she feels in her life and her studies. Logic and Psychology are added to Greek, and she works hard at Calculus for a time. There is a sad, cryptic reference to TM (Tussy Marx), with whom there appears to have been some rift. There are no other mentions of the Marx family during all these years.

She is working very hard:

> ... with the work for school, the mathematics I do, and the mental science I ought to do, my time is filled up. This term however we seem to have been out a great deal & my mind shows a power of feeling excitement about nothing which makes me feel most unwilling to work at anything regularly difficult.

At an occasion organised by the Unitarian chapel she meets the three Gimson brothers, Ernest, Alfred and Sidney. Later, she admits to dancing with Sidney and even approving of him. Alfred comes in for a good deal of scorn. Sidney is different:

> I liked him better that night than I had ever done before. He seemed very sensible, a fact that surprised me. Since I have come to the conclusion that he is even more than that. He knows & has read ever so much more than A.H. [Alfred] and although I think he is shy he has a good deal of self-respect – I think –.

She is walked home, sometimes by Sidney, more often by Sidney and Alfred. Ernest is younger and less in evidence (though she kept up with him in later life and on one occasion 'he summoned up courage to put his arm round my waist & I nerved myself to corresponding deeds of heroism.') Occasionally, Sidney dances with Clara's friend Polly Blackwell too. These occasions are noted. So is the possibility that Sidney 'is not a downright Unitarian but rather a Secularist'. This is probably in his favour and inspires another admission that she likes him very much, though with a 'sisterly regard'. She is happy, 'drifting along with the current'. She gets a Valentine with a Cupid on it breaking his bow at the sight of a lady graduate.

Small shadows fall. Sidney is beginning to show a more obvious interest in Polly, and Clara dreams that Polly is engaged to her brother Harold. Sidney gives her his confessions to read 'on the way home by the light of the lamps', but 'our evening walks are over now', she comments, and 'Ainsi soit il'.

She thinks a lot about religion and God, and discusses these matters with Sidney, who calls himself an agnostic, as she does not yet, though he believes in God more than she does. 'I believe in God,' she writes,

> because the people I admire most do and because some of their best qualities seem founded upon or at any rate coincident with that belief; sometimes when I feel blissfully happy or dreadfully miserable I believe in him myself but I don't feel any real faith or trust.

A lecture by Arnold Toynbee entitled 'Are Radicals Socialists?' draws more enthusiasm for his looks than for his argument, which anyway seemed even less good later than it did at the time. Sidney, who had given her a ticket for the lecture, defends Toynbee's genuineness against her strictures, and Clara admits that people think her hard-hearted. Perhaps she is.

Her impatience with all the sensible sermons she hears increases, though one, in which it is mentioned that 'Longfellow was one of us and must be regarded as the poet of rational religion . . . made me feel a thrill of triumph.' There are picnics and rehearsals with the girls at school, impromptu as well as organised parties, when the young people make speeches on subjects like Women's Rights and Love and Matrimony and they dance, and Sidney sometimes sings, surprisingly well.

There are more frequent allusions to depression, restlessness, when reading is hard and study impossible. Sidney clearly has something to do with this, though it is not discussed. She still sees him, but he has 'quite dropped off into a properly polite bowing acquaintance'. There are rumours that he is to be engaged to Polly Blackwell. Then, in March 1883:

> I have been indulging in a fit of hysterical crying tonight. I feel so perfectly wretched & miserable & hopeless & worthless & tired. Instead of working for my exam I have been studying Physical Geography. I can't work for the Exam. The worry of school & the feeling of incompetence make me feel miserable. I do wish I could go to Girton or Univ. College or give up teaching or emigrate.

Years later Clara put a characteristic gloss on this passage: 'Partly to escape from teachers' meetings at school I was presenting myself at the first examination for the diploma [a teaching qualification] in 1883. The literature of educational theorists was responsible for this inspissated gloom.' There was clearly more to it than that. Clearly, too, however, Clara was finding teaching both dull and demanding by 1883 and was beginning to wonder whether it would be possible to earn her living in some other way. She is becoming bitter but resigned about the men she meets. One man she likes 'immensely' has been married for a week and a half: 'such is life'.

By now she has accepted the fact that Sidney will marry someone else. She is generously prepared to concede that at least he 'is entirely independent and even if he marries a perfect horror would not necessarily be ruined by it only warped'. There is a hurt, angry moment when it seems that the Gimson brothers have left the Collet girls out of plans to put on another play (for Carrie has by now joined Clara at Wyggeston). She confronts the pain and, as she always did on such occasions, accepts that it may be due to something difficult in her character.

> I shall never have any intimate friends and I know that I undoubtedly possess to a remarkable degree the faculty of offending nearly everyone. This is partly why I have decided to take to study as hard as I can first in order to ensure my always being able to hold a good position as a teacher and secondly to have something to fall back upon when life seems rather dismal. My school work is interesting and to a certain degree satisfactory, but my views on every subject are growing more and more unpopularly unorthodox and I doubt very much whether I shall be able to teach children much longer; what I care about no one wants taught and I do not know other subjects well enough to hold my own as a first class teacher. I think I am leaving off being a girl.

She admits that this may be only a temporary discontent, but in contemplating the future she is now firmly 'facing facts' and 'emotionless'.

As part of her teaching diploma she is required to give a demonstration lesson. This – on Robert Walpole and at her old school, North London Collegiate – is watched by Miss Buss and other formidable judges. She passes, but it is a wretched experience, confirming her determination to leave teaching and go for an MA. She expects bad news – presumably the news that Sidney Gimson has become engaged – and though she has no clear aim she tells herself that the moment has arrived when she must plan her life, despite having 'no particular ambition . . . no special power'.

A visit to the House of Commons during the school holidays is 'very amusing', especially 'seeing them all at prayers', during which 'there certainly was not much hypocrisy of attitude. Gladstone struck me most as looking so clean. Randolph Churchill did not speak but I conceived rather a sneaking affection for that worthless young man' – a worthless young man whose son Winston would one day be her political master at the Board of Trade. Her scorn for Parliament and for national politics is extreme, and was to persist in milder form in later life:

> It does not seem possible to feel any enthusiasm for any party whatsoever, they all seem untrue and interested. Parliament is the biggest sham imaginable, local government is grand in comparison; perhaps the reason why women have only individual enthusiasms is owing to their extra penetration; perhaps also it is not.

In May 1884, back in Leicester, she records Sidney Gimson's engagement to a Miss Lovibond, but says nothing about it. Then, with no warning, she writes that 'E.W. asked me to marry him'. It is not possible to identify this suitor, although it seems likely that he was one of her tutors from the Boys School. She refuses him twice, and is almost obliged to do so a third time. After describing a happy three-week visit to Newnham College, Cambridge, where she took classes in Logic and Psychology (presumably in preparation for her MA) she returns to this proposal. 'The E.W. affair' has made her 'miserable and low'. She distracts herself with study, describes classes at her old school with Mrs Bryant, whom she rather hero-worships, while recognising that her feelings are unrequited. Work, reading, philosophy become interesting again, though her admiration for George Eliot is accompanied by 'depression at the thought of how wanting my life will be in the fullness of living owing to my inability to care much for anyone but myself'. George Eliot stood for Clara – as she also stood for Beatrice Webb – as a reminder that women had to be better than men at whatever they did if they were to succeed. However, it is not always easy to decide whether these bouts of candour are inspired by defensive vanity rather than realistic self-appraisal.

By the middle of 1885, when she was drawing to the end of her time as a teacher in Leicester, she had done a good deal of work on ethics. E.W. is still in her life: 'I have been thinking a good deal about E.W. and am beginning to like him but that will only last till I see him.' She is anxious that he may ask her to marry him again when her spirits are low:

> It is just because I often meet men for whom I have a strong attraction that makes me like them in spite of faults, that I feel sure that if in a moment of depression I imagined I liked him because he was worthy of being loved for his virtues and married him I should grow to hate him & perhaps even fall wildly in love with some one else or feel that I really & truly liked a dozen other men better than I did him. It is much better to live an old maid and get a little honey from the short real

friendships I can have with men for whom I really care myself, than to be bound for life to a man just because he thinks he cares for me.

By October 1885 Clara was living in College Hall, Gordon Square, and studying for an MA in Political Economy at University College London. She was supporting herself on her savings from Leicester. After what appears to have been a long gap, she meets Tussy Marx again.[14] During that gap both the Marx parents have died (though Clara, oddly, makes no mention of the fact) and Tussy is now living with the Dr Edward Aveling with whom Clara once did classes in statistics. It is possible that his still being married to someone else explains Clara's mysterious refusal to go home with her old friend – possible, but uncharacteristic of the woman who became the close friend of George Gissing some years later. It seems more likely that Clara is referring back to the original cause of the rift when she writes:

> Today I spoke to Tussy and we made friends; she asked me to go and see her & I explained why I could not; she flushed a little but she knew that I was not blaming her and that I cared for her as much as ever. She promised that if ever I could help her she would ask me. I hope she will if she needs help & that no cowardice of mine will ever prevent me from giving help when she asks for it for herself or anyone she cares for.

V

The Collet family had been Unitarians since the early eighteenth century and, as I have already pointed out, Collet Dobson Collet and his sister Sophia returned to Unitarianism in the face of some family lapses: one of their brothers even became an Anglican clergyman. There are several respects in which Unitarianism is important to an understanding of Clara's development.[15] The universities were closed to Nonconformists until University College London opened in 1826, with a unique charter to admit (male) students of all religious denominations. Clara's father attended classes there in the 1830s, but did not have a degree. It appears, however, that this history of exclusion from the universities contributed to Unitarians' particular interest in women's education. Fathers took pains to educate their daughters so that perhaps, as mothers, they might at least be enabled to remedy some gaps in their sons' early education.[16] Young men wishing to enter business or the professions often spent several years abroad, learning the business or acquiring a professional training. Clara and her brothers and sisters had all spent a year or so in France or Germany as part of their schooling, and this seems to have been quite common in Unitarian families. Clara undoubtedly grew up in a tradition which encouraged women to be knowledgeable and hard-working and to participate either voluntarily or professionally in public life. It was a tradition of which Clara was always aware, stretching as it did from the somewhat older Harriet Martineau to include the work of women like Octavia Hill, Helen Bosanquet and Beatrice Webb.

For much of her life Clara thought of herself as an agnostic. Yet her involvement with Unitarianism and with Unitarians' particular concern for forms of social improvement was an intrinsic element in both her intellectual and professional life, and in her classically Liberal and liberal beliefs. She was proud of the 'rationality', the 'fairness', of Unitarianism and exasperated by all forms of religious intolerance or 'enthusiasm'. Towards the end of her life she became interested in the so-called Liberal Jewish movement for these reasons.

Clara's religious and political inheritance articulated with her developing sense of her destiny as a woman. Common sense, rationality, categories of knowledge and thought which she straightforwardly thought of as male, and even the imperialist and expansionist energies of a male and liberal hegemony, would need to accommodate her as a woman participating in those traditions. This seems to have entailed a proud refusal on her part to dwell on the constraints she experienced herself as a woman (in fact, 'not complaining' belonged for her with other necessary and unheroic 'male' virtues) and a determined concentration on those organisa-tions and outlets which welcomed her participation and her contri-bution. She attended – and on occasion gave – lectures at the South Place Ethical Society, for instance[17]. Her surprisingly long involve-ment with the Charity Organisation Society (from 1884 to at least 1906), to whose *Reporter* and later *Review* she regularly contributed articles and book reviews, may also be partly explained by her willingness to make use of those channels which were hospitable to women writers.

The COS had attracted many intelligent Unitarian women during the seventies and eighties. Most of them – particularly Beatrice Webb – abandoned the organisation and its principles much earlier than Clara did. Her continuing adherence to an organisation which Beatrice Webb had already, by the late 1880s, characterised as neither seeking the causes of poverty nor having any cure for it, is extremely difficult to explain. The COS emphasis on social investiga-tion and on forms of self-help connects with, and could be seen to have developed out of, the kinds of work she did with Charles Booth, and it even consorts in some respects with aspects of government policy she worked with at the Board of Trade. Yet that does not account for her supporting this position on poverty for so long when alternative analyses and approaches were undoubtedly available to her.

Meanwhile, Clara's own education had served her well, and one of the first chapters she contributed to Booth's *Labour and Life of the People. London*[18] charts the growth of high schools for girls in London. The North London Collegiate School had been the first of these in 1850. During the seventies and eighties several thousand places became available in schools, many on scholarships; though, as Clara tartly put it, 'for all practical purposes the scholarships might as well be awarded at once to the cleanest and healthiest-looking children'. This growth in educational provision for middle-class girls was significant, but limited. As Clara showed in her survey, very few poor working-class girls benefited from these new possibilities, though there was an increase in the numbers of better-off working-class girls going first to Middle Schools, then to High Schools on scholarships, and afterwards to Teacher Training Colleges. The majority of middle-class girls were still poorly educated, however, and it is worth noting, for instance, that Marx did not bother to educate or train his daughters seriously, and he did not expect them to work. Upper-class girls still went to private schools or stayed at home with governesses.

Having taken her MA[19] after two happy years spent mostly in the British Museum Reading Room, Clara returned, reluctantly, to teaching for a little over a year at her old school. By 1887, however, she was working for Charles Booth, as was Beatrice Webb, with whom Clara corresponded intermittently throughout their lives. Since the work Clara did for Booth laid the foundation for her new career it may be useful to refer to Gareth Stedman Jones's account of the origins of Booth's project:

Booth first became interested in the condition of the poor after a visit to [Samuel] Barnett in Whitechapel in 1878. Unlike Barnett, however, he envisaged his role as a social investigator rather than as a philanthropist or a charity worker. Booth's ideas on poverty were initially very close to those of the COS Like the leaders of the Society, he considered that the extent of chronic poverty had been wildly exaggerated by agitators and the sensational writers of the popular press. Significantly, Booth finally committed himself to the task of concrete investigation in response to the crisis of February 1886. His decision to embark upon an extensive enquiry was provoked by Hyndman's claim that 25 per cent of the London population lived in conditions of extreme poverty. Booth intended to refute Hyndman's claim for very much the same reasons that the COS had refuted similar claims about the extent of distress in the previous seven years.[20]

Stedman Jones goes on to describe how Booth's discovery that 35 per cent of the population of Tower Hamlets were almost always in serious need worked to separate him henceforth from the COS. He could no longer support its 'administering' of charity in ways thought likely to promote individual independence and self-help. The COS regarded the dispensing of relief as deliberate pauperisation.

Between 1887 and 1901 Clara built up an expertise in interviewing women workers, principally within various sectors of the clothing industry, and turning her findings into statistical evidence and descriptive reports. Both this work for Booth and the 'case-study' investigations fostered by the COS have been seen by some as prefiguring sociology as an academic study, but also social work as a practice.[21] Clara's enthusiasm for her new calling fluctuated. There were times when she disliked interviewing. It left 'no roots behind'. She often felt dispersed by the sheer range of her interests at this time and had, she wrote, 'no longer any vague dreams of success in something or other or even desires'.[22] Occasionally, she was able to bring her interests together. In an article called 'Maria Edgeworth and Charity'[23] she combined an expression of her enthusiasm for Edgeworth's novels with her own views on charity. Recommending Edgeworth as a model COS writer, she also asserted:

> To give their children the necessaries of life is the duty of all parents; to give them to adults is to pauperise them ... All charity must then have as its primary object the good of the recipient; and, if no good can be done, charity must not be expended merely to indulge one's own sentiment of compassion.

She often used the opportunities of reviewing novels and other books at this time to bring out the economic realities as she saw them, and their potential effect on fictional lives.

During these years Clara came face to face with permanent and temporary poverty in its most extreme forms, as it was experienced by more than 30 per cent of London's population and in ways which were peculiar to the capital's reliance on multiple forms of casual and seasonal labour. There is no doubt that at this stage of her career she put her faith in, first, the need for detailed and accurate information about people's conditions and needs and, second, a carefully orchestrated response to need in the form of programmes of improvement sponsored by both government and charity. Clara's work for Booth must have earned her her place as one of the four Assistant

Commissioners (the others were the Misses Orme, Abraham and Irwin) who reported on women's Home Work to the Royal Commission on Labour set up in 1891. Hilda Martindale notes that 'the report presented by these first official women investigators of industrial conditions received high praise'.[24] The year when she was first appointed a civil servant also marked the beginning of her friendship with George Gissing.

VI

In March 1892 George Gissing noted in his diary that a lecture had been 'delivered . . . by a Miss Clara E. Collet M.A . . . can't make out what the lecture really was – except that she maintained the "healthiness" of my mind.'[25] She also, according to another report, opposed the idea that Gissing was a fatalist and defended his novels for their combination of idealism and realism.[26] Almost a year later Clara wrote to him, asking if she might call. He refused. She sent copies of her articles, and then an invitation to him and to his wife Edith. He still refused. Then, on 18 July 1893, Gissing wrote in his diary:

> Richmond by arrangement, I called on Miss Collet at 34 Hill St. We at once went out on to the river, and rowed to Kingston and back. Home by the 8.45 train. Miss Collet younger than I had expected. She wishes to come and call on E., but I fear.[27]

This was the year when Gissing's eleventh novel, *The Odd Women*, was published: too late, it might be said, for Clara to have inspired its account of the lives of educated unmarried women, as she is sometimes supposed to have done. Coincidentally, it was the novel of Gissing's she liked least. Indeed, she disliked it 'so much that I nearly did not make George Gissing's acquaintance because of it'.[28] Gissing was thirty-six when he met Clara. He was married for the second time, to a 'respectable' working-class girl whom he had, by his own admission, picked up in Camden Town three years earlier. Indeed, there are ways in which *The Odd Women* has far more to say about his marriage with Edith than about his friendship with Clara. At this point there was one child, Walter.

Almost as soon as they met Gissing started to confide in Clara both his despair with his current marriage and, not very long afterwards, the dark and guilty secret of his youth (which she was to become instrumental in keeping just as dark for many more years). As a poor scholarship student at Owens College in Manchester he had stolen small sums of money in order to support an alcoholic young prostitute called Nell, with whom he had become sexually obsessed.

After a year of exile in America, where he survived by selling stories to newspapers and magazines, he returned and instantly – and with characteristic perversity – married Nell. The marriage was a nightmare for them both, though it took some time to end. As she speedily drank herself to death, Gissing paid fifteen shillings a week for her to board in a nursing home in Battersea until she died there in 1888.[29]

As his friend, Clara became bizarrely implicated in Gissing's living out of a dilemma which might well be thought of as entirely alien to her, though it was one with which she seems always to have sympathised. His snobbery and fastidiousness, added to his sense of his own social inferiority, made him seek out as sexual partners – and wives – women he regarded as *his* social inferiors. His dream of a life's partner who would share his intellectual interests while gracing his home remained a dream unfulfillable within a view of his own sexual nature as both importunate and squalid.

Other writers of the time – Wells, Meredith and Hardy, for instance – were also concerned with the appeal as well as the problem of having sexual relations with women who might be intellectually a man's equal, possibly even his superior. What came to be called 'The Woman Question', with its decoratively 'new' or 'emancipated' woman, was translated by some male novelists into an exploration of what these newly critical and independent women might offer men as sexual partners or wives. The political, economic and educational aspirations of women were acknowledged, but dwelled on finally for this potential especially. In Wells's *Ann Veronica*, for instance, the domesticating of a clever, educated woman becomes a heightened form of seduction with, as its reward for success, a capable wife who is also appreciative and supportive of her husband and his work. Men have everything to gain, the novel appears to be saying, from the freely given submission of intelligent, well-educated women.

Fifteen years earlier, in *The Odd Women*, Gissing explored the possibility that the truly emancipated woman might not after all be 'asexual', as he had asserted in *Born in Exile*, but sexually promising precisely for the spirited resistance she would be likely to put up and the intelligent discourse such titillating resistance would produce. Everard Barfoot 'can't live without intelligent female society'. For him 'nothing female was alien: woman, merely as woman, interested him profoundly'. The excitement for the seducer is in awakening in a woman who initially 'had no sensual attraction for him'[30] a passionate need and responsiveness. Neither the character of this strenuously awakened sexuality nor its satisfactions is explored, it should be said.

The lines of the friendship between Gissing and Clara Collet were set early on, and by him. He told her about his domestic tribulations.

It seems likely that he even told her something of his sexual history and his sexual relations with his wife. Certainly, his announcement that his wife is pregnant again arrives in the midst of a spate of letters complaining about her sluttishness, shrewishness and stupidity. Alongside these confessions go congratulations. Miss Collet is congratulated on her intelligence and strength, on her good sense, good fortune and good health. He thanks her for her kindness to him, to his wife, to his child. Within a few months of their first meeting she has offered to pay for Walter's schooling and has taken Edith on outings, which it is not altogether clear that Edith enjoyed. Somewhat unflatteringly, Gissing reassures her that his wife 'does not now misinterpret your position'. Less than a year later he writes to her:

> A strange thing that, but for our having come to know each other, these struggles & gaspings of mine would have been unspoken of to anyone. I suppose my reason for telling you of such miseries is the assurance I have that you cannot be depressed by them; you are the sole & single person of my acquaintance who is living a healthy, active life, of large intercourse with men and women . . . you are unassociated & unassociable with gloom.[31]

Edith does not misinterpret her position because Gissing has rendered Clara untroubling and untroubled, a person removed from and immune to sexual feeling and its dangerous consequences.

Clara gets him to read Maria Edgeworth and a Life of Adam Smith (whom Gissing refers to as her 'ideal man'). She rebukes him tiresomely for using 'like' in the place of 'as' and for occasional affectations of style. A title is reprehensibly 'prettyish' and he is too often given to exaggeration: for instance, in suggesting that women generally have come to dislike domestic life. He is 'always glad when you feel able to praise my writing'. He is not so glad when she criticises his behaviour, and it seems that she did sometimes rebuke him for unkindness and impatience towards his wife and child. Many of his complaints are about the impossibility of inviting friends to his home. He is ashamed of his wife and of the acrimony and chaos of his household. Clara appears to have taken this in her stride and simply to have insisted on visiting him.

By 1897 things had come to a head, and Gissing left his wife, sending Walter to live with his family in Wakefield while the younger son, Alfred, remained with Edith. Amongst other things, a new friendship with H.G. Wells may have helped to fuel his decision. For a few months the correspondence between Gissing and Clara expressed more of their feelings for one another. She received a fevered letter from him in Rome in January 1898. He is ill and unhappy:

> We are now pretty old friends, & yet I find that I am only just beginning really to know you. I have always inclined to think of you as very self-reliant, rather scornful of weaker people & especially impatient of anything like sentimental troubles. There is no harm in saying that your last two or three letters have pleased me just because they differed in some respects from those of a year or two ago. I used to feel that, however friendly, you regarded me with a good deal of dis-approbation & perhaps a little lurking contempt. Well, I know that a certain amount of contempt you must feel for me, & always will; but you are gentler than of old. And rightly so. One who suffers incessantly – even though as the result of his own folly – should not be sternly treated.

The letter then slides – somewhat typically – into a rehearsal of his woes, ailments and deserts, and a rejection of her offer to come and look after him should he need her to. He makes her his executor and begs her to use her 'strong brain and pure woman's heart to guard my boys against the accursed temptations of early life'. Since Clara then noted both that Gissing met Gabrielle Fleury on 10 February 1898, and that she, Clara, destroyed Gissing's letters to her between that date and 22 July 1899, it seems likely that there is a connection between the two events. She also notes without comment that Gissing has written to her of Gabrielle as 'a French woman of the finest type and infinitely graceful', and that 'my letters to G.G. were much more formal from this time forward'.

Such evidence as there is of this time has been read as suggesting that Clara made some kind of declaration to Gissing after his separation from Edith, which he elaborately (and perhaps even tactfully) turned down.[32] Amongst Clara's papers there exists a story called 'Undercurrents', written in her handwriting and signed Clover King.[33] It is not possible to date it, but its plot, characters and theme suggest that Clara, as its author, drew on her knowledge of Gissing's early life, as well as on her own inadmissible and contradictory feelings about him. It is the story of a romance between a professional woman and a brilliant scientist with a murky past.

The heroine is Marian, a woman in her late twenties who enjoys considerable freedom, mixes with men, does men's work and is happy. She is charged with being 'a time server and a trimmer' by some of her professional and unmarried women friends, because she defends the decision of one of them, a doctor, to marry, of all people, a stockbroker. Marian has staying with her a teacher called Maggie, who is pretty, while Marian has 'no looks to speak of'. They are together when they first meet Frank Rust, a scientific 'genius' and a contemporary of Maggie's from Cambridge. The older Marian instantly distrusts him, while Maggie encourages his interest in herself. But when he proposes to her, while hinting at the same time at something dark and disgraceful in his past, she is suddenly overcome by revulsion. Marian still distrusts him, but she is oddly touched by his lack of belief in himself as a person who might at all plausibly be loved.

Two years later Marian and Maggie are at a 'brilliant' lecture given by Frank. It is interrupted by the drunken shouting of a girl: 'That's my 'usband, that is. My! aint he a toff. Three cheers for Frankie.' Frank shamefully disowns her and resigns from his post at University College at the same time.

Marian is moved to help Frank. She discovers that his wife Mollie is terminally ill with an inherited disease as well as being alcoholic and pregnant. Marian grows fond of her, particularly for so unswervingly loving her husband. Maggie, meanwhile, has married a dull barrister, amusingly encountered on the Metropolitan Line in a scene which might have provided a rare comic moment in a Gissing novel.[34] Mollie dies, and before long Marian's deep-blue eyes are startling Frank with their unexpected gleams. After a solemn kiss, likened to a sacrament, and difficulties in coming clean about their emotions, Frank and Marian agree to marry. ' "It is no sacrifice," said Marian, with glowing eyes, "I love you".'

This is – and it must be apparent – a poor story in a number of respects. It is significant, though, that Clara, the scourge of sentimentality, found this an appropriate form in which to express something of the facts and feelings of her friendship with Gissing. There were few, if any, obviously available models for such a story and such a relationship, and telling it as a Romance made it to some extent both recognisable and controllable, while putting it firmly and ironically in its place. It is interesting in this context to consider how many lesbian novels also use the conventions of the Romance, and how central many of these conventions come to seem to women's representations of female sexual desire, especially when these deviate markedly from traditional male accounts. Though the outcome of this story *is* the conventional and perfunctory one of a million Romances, with the heroine made briefly beautiful by love and an evening out, the plot makes its way circuitously. The scenes and settings allow for Marian's and the other women's complex and uncertain views about marriage to be aired and tried out. A central concern for each of them, which the story addresses with considerable frankness, is male sexuality and female views of it.

Frank the genius, with his shameful shame, his murky past, his refined aspirations, is there for Marian to take on sexually. Maggie's barrister, on the other hand, found on the train, possessed of tastes similar to Maggie's and ordinarily respectable, is offered as 'asexual' and undesirable. Frank's sexuality, by contrast, is aberrant, out of control, not to be tidily accommodated. Where it is to be feared in relation to Marian's daughter/protégée Maggie, it is to be received as a challenge by the maturer and more direct Marian. Frank's sexuality and genius both explain and exonerate him. In taking on this sexuality and this genius, however, Marian is doing what Ann Veronica did and what the doctor at the beginning of the story did in marrying her stockbroker. She is sacrificing her life, deliberately relinquishing her own hard-won power, skills and independence in exchange for this offer of male sexuality, and she is not even looking for a partnership in which her own strengths might be usable.

Marian's dilemma – and it may well have been Clara's – is that she wants to possess male genius, male sexuality, doubly: for themselves and for herself. Marian's identification with Frank is with the unlovable, the aberrant man. His shame corresponds to her reticence and his awkwardness to her sexual inexperience. The Romance form works here to express female desire for male power as well as male love, and pleasure in fantasies of capitulation to them.

It is no wonder that Clara disliked *The Odd Women*. The passionately reiterated question of her own story, 'How many men are satisfied with merely intellectual life?', is trivialised and teasingly reversed in Gissing's novel to cast doubt on whether women would bother with the intellectual life at all if they had a man to do it for them.

Gabrielle Fleury began living with Gissing in 1899. Her family insisted on a pseudo-wedding ceremony, but they were never married. Gabrielle called herself Madame Gissing to the day she died and was always desperately uncomfortable with the irregularity of their union, for which she never quite forgave Gissing. Earlier that year Gissing wrote to Gabrielle:

> A day or two ago I wrote to Miss Collet, telling her how glad I should be if any way could be found for a legitimate marriage, but that I feared. – To-day she replies: 'Can you not impress upon Gabrielle that, here in England, the best men and women recognize love and loyalty and courage?'[35]

She reminded him about George Eliot and George Lewes.

When Gissing died on 28 December 1903 Gabrielle and he had spent four years together, often in France with her mother (whom he greatly disliked and accused of starving him) and punctuated by long and bitter separations. Clara was kept informed of the pleasures and the pains of it all by Gissing and, before long, by Gabrielle too. As the executor, with Gissing's brother, of a will which left what little there was to Edith and their sons, and nothing to Gabrielle, communication between the two women became necessary. They met on the first anniversary of Gissing's death in St. Jean-de-Luz, where he had died. When Gabrielle left after a visit in the summer, Clara wrote in her diary: 'I miss her more than I have missed anyone.'

VII

Between Gissing's death and the beginning of the war in 1914, when Clara was fifty-four, friendships she had found difficult to realise in her youth became easier. Her work at the Board of Trade took her more directly into policy-making and the 'corridors of power' during these years. Her brother Wilfred would by now leave his wife and sons in London for his sisters to keep an eye on while he did his overseas stints in what were then called British Guiana and British Honduras. Clara assumed almost total responsibility for Gissing's affairs, in relation both to his books and to his family. She struggled for a time to agree with H.G. Wells on plans to reissue out-of-print novels and a mooted biography by Morley Roberts, an old friend. In the end it was Wells who backed off, exasperated by Clara almost as much as by the Gissing family and Gabrielle. Clara negotiated reissues on her own, even of her least favourite, *The Odd Women*, and she appears single-handedly to have arranged with Number 10 Downing Street for a Civil List pension to be granted to Gissing's sons 'in recognition of the literary services of their father and of his straitened circumstances'.

Gabrielle assumed many of Gissing's dependent habits in her friendship with Clara. She wrote to her regularly, plangently and on a restricted number of topics, each of which would swarm across a year or more in unstoppable prose. Her furniture had been stored by Maples, whose inventory mysteriously failed to match the objects it claimed to account for. What could Clara do about it? Gabrielle's health was of a kind to require the attention always of 'doctors' rather than a doctor; and these were always obligingly and unanimously ready to forbid her doing things she clearly did not wish to do: travel, move flats, see people, attend to others. Clara was expected to confirm the wisdom of such choral advice. Like many an evolved hypochondriac, Gabrielle lived to a great age. I was introduced to her as she sat bolt upright in her Paris apartment in the early fifties, and I had been firmly reminded to address her clearly and often as Madame Gissing. Clara loved her and was entirely loyal to her though their friendship cooled with time; and it was probably not until about 1914 that she received a letter from Gabrielle which was neither grossly self-absorbed nor hectoring. They eventually became able to discuss Gissing's early life and misdemeanours when they met, and Clara appears always to have defended him.[36]

It is easy to detect in Clara's diary, and even through Gabrielle's letters to her, a confidence and pleasure in her life which were not there in the past. She knows herself to be trusted, relied on, immensely capable and responsible. She trusts her own instincts. Her diary reveals, for instance, that Morley Roberts confided in her as early as 1908 that he meant to write a novel, *The Private Life of Henry Maitland*, rather than the biography of Gissing which had been discussed. When the novel came out in 1912 it was generally despised by Gissing's family and friends, and execrated by Gabrielle, because it revealed that she had been either bigamously married to Gissing or not married at all. Yet Clara had known about the projected novel and had obviously thought fit to keep out of it.[37]

She became friendly during these years with the French novelist Romain Rolland, and with his sister Madeleine. She made friends with some of the men she worked with and would dine with them, sometimes alone, sometimes with their wives. There was Ramsay MacDonald, Edward Worthington, Edward Spencer – who did, it is true, turn out to be disappointingly married – and Mr Ibry from Russia, who was looking for his ideal wife. There were official social engagements, some to do with University College, and parties and meetings and holidays and theatres. She met people at the house of Miss Toynbee, who produced copies of Turner which could be bought for a fiver and given as wedding presents. Her sisters, meanwhile, were still living with their mother, and Carrie was often ill with the strain of it. Clara swooped down on them from time to time to sort out the servant problem and give advice. She refers to her 'masterfulness' ironically on this score and admits to a tendency to 'tactlessness and general overbearingness'. It is interesting to compare the scope of her responsibilities outside her job with her position within it.

VIII

In 1909 Clara recorded 'a complete change in my official work'. This meant attending meetings in the office of the President of the Board of Trade (who was Winston Churchill) with a group of politicians, civil servants and invited advisers, including Sidney Webb and William Beveridge, who were working at speed to draft a new Trade Boards Bill. Clara already had some experience of giving evidence to the Select Committee of the House of Commons on 'Home Work'. This time she is stopped as she makes her way to Sir Edward Grey's room by the police, 'who were nervous about me but took my word for my being authorised to go in'. Of Churchill she writes:

> I don't think the Board of Trade loves Mr Churchill; but I confess that he interests me as a human being whatever his faults may be. It is partly because I only know 'intellectuals' or 'thoughtful men' that this type of person governing them appeals to a side of me which might belong to a respectable Bohemian.

Lord Robert Cecil, however, appeals to her even more. He 'is like a gentle highly intelligent monk'. She notes the way they all treat her:

> Mr Churchill 'damned that fellow Carlile' and then apologised to me for doing so. It is very amusing to contrast the different ways in which they treat me. Mr Askwith [a colleague she disliked] aims at treating me like a man with no more respect than a man in the same place; all the others treat me with a little more consideration because I am a woman, but quite rightly don't put themselves out for me, and treat me as a colleague. Lord Hamilton, not being a colleague, is especially polite to me.[38]

Churchill and Lord Robert Cecil disagree over a clause intended to prevent employers using a surrogate, who would covertly organise sweated labour and be prepared to go to prison in the place of his employer. Between 1901 and 1918 a series of Trade Boards Acts were passed in attempts to extend the powers of such boards to supervise the paying of minimum wages to all workers in particular low-paid trades and industries. Clara's contribution to the discussions she described covered a vast range of women's employment – particularly, however, the work done by married women at home. This, of all categories of work, was the least susceptible to wage control and the most likely to be performed by women in desperate straits. It still is, of course.

In her days with Booth and the *Survey* she had reported on the conditions of women who took home, amongst other things, parts of shirts, umbrellas, ties, trousers, vests, corsets and stays, furs, boxes, brushes, matches and artificial flowers and curled ostrich feathers for the hats of the rich. Her work for the *Survey* is a model for its detail, coherence and clarity. Her cool command of the facts and the issues gives emphasis to moments of passion and rage, even if that rage seems almost to be directed at the women themselves rather than at the society which thrives on their exploitation:

On the whole, the home-workers are the first to point out that as they have their children to attend to and the meals to prepare, and the washing and mending and cleaning to do, they cannot give very long hours to their work. But unskilled working women – shirtmakers, match-box makers, trouser-makers – do undoubtedly work very long hours when they have others to support. Life to large numbers of married women in the East End is nothing more than procrastination of death. They bear children and bury them. Their minds have been starved and their senses dulled. 'Abandon hope, all ye who enter here' might well be inscribed above the entrance to the Red Church. For these women but little can be done. The position of the married woman can only be affected through the better education of the child, the training of the girl, and through everything that tends to raise the man morally and industrially.[39]

Her account of this work on drafting a new Bill illustrates the more usual distance assumed by Clara in her role as a civil servant and statistician who knew a great deal about women's conditions and pay, from the major political debates of the day on poverty and unemployment. Beveridge, who was also involved in the drafting, had been publishing papers attributing unemployment to the disorganisation of the labour market rather than to the unemployable character of the unemployed. It may well have been from him that Churchill developed his belief in Labour Exchanges as the cure for the capital's and the country's poverty.[40] And in 1909, both majority and minority reports were published from the Royal Commission on the Poor Law, on which – besides Octavia Hill and Helen Bosanquet – Beatrice Webb had served as a commissioner.

It is instructive to set Webb's account of the three years spent on the Commission and of its public reception[41] alongside Clara's initial pleasure at working with politicians, which so rapidly turned to an impatience which was to explode in 1910 with her abortive resignation. There is not much doubt that this impatience was provoked as much by political solutions themselves as by politicians. Finally, her exasperation with 'the way in which the women's side of the Labour Exchanges is being organised' was such that she felt compelled to resign and to recommend, with considerable bitterness, that she could anyway be easily replaced by some 'first class university woman upper division clerk'.[42]

The saga of her threatened resignation fills many pages of her diary and contains a good deal of the ambiguity of her position. She records formal and decorous conversations about it all with the Knights and other gentlemen with whom she worked. Yet her exasperation is finally with them, the very men who confer on her such power and influence as she would ever have. And while all this is going on, 'very important questio is come up' which require someone of her experience to deal with them. She is 'having a good many qualms of conscience'. Quite apart from the substantive issues of the case there are questions about her life, her estimate of her work and its achievements, her pension, questions about who might be appointed in her place.

Her troubles erupt into one of her few outbursts of resentment against Gabrielle, who has made so many demands on her, several of them financial. Then the crisis is over, and she agrees to stay. But it is time, as she sees, to think about the future, money, retirement, perhaps a cottage somewhere in the country. The incident reminds us of the anomalous predicament of professional women at a time when no woman might vote or stand for Parliament and when women's 'expertise' was understood to emerge from their natures and to be similarly expendable. The full history of the predicament is alluded to with the most fastidious irony in Hilda Martindale's dedication of her book on women civil servants: 'To those men who have encouraged women in rendering service to the state'.[43]

In 1902 Clara had published a book of essays called *Educated Working Women*[44] and dedicated it to the memory of Frances Mary Buss. She starts from the differences between such women and 'the great majority of women, [who] belong to the working classes and spend their youth as wage-earners, in many cases under conditions injurious to mind and body, although the real work of their lives is eventually to be found in their homes'. Middle-class women face different dilemmas. Many of them will need to become self-supporting, since the imbalance between men and women in the middle classes is such that 'to expect a hundred women to devote their energies to attracting fifty men seems slightly ridiculous'.[45] The question then is how 'the lives of educated women may be made of more value to themselves and others'.[46] Her focus will be a civil servant's, on the 'cost and reward of efficiency' in relation to these questions. The book is characterised by critical good sense, considerable knowledge and some views about women's 'nature' which bear the imprint of her times, but are important for her argument.

She exquisitely picks out the contradictions inherent in the refusal of the ancient universities to admit women to degrees, even as they maintain that women are by nature incapable of studying to this level:

> The futility of forbidding women to do what they were incapable of doing was never perceived by the opponents of the

movement for the higher education of women, who based their opposition on this ground.[47]

Yet she also goes on to write that 'it is now at least admitted that the rather-above-the-average woman is quite on a level with the average man',[48] without spelling out the historical and cultural assumptions underlying the adoption of even that position. In some ways, of course, Clara accepted many of the nature/culture oppositions of her own day, because she had lived them. She did believe that women differed from men in their 'nervous organisation' and in their 'emotional nature'. She also had enormous faith in the power of education and literature to reinforce prejudice, but also potentially to attack it. In one passage she puts some of the blame both for the poor education of girls and for the reluctance of men to promote or encourage higher education for women on a long tradition of appalling literature for children. She characterises *Mrs Teachum and the Little Academy* as

> a delightful account of the training received by Mrs Teachum for the post of Schoolmistress [which] shows the prevalence of a humble deference to men's superior judgment, which may help to explain the absence of enthusiasm on their part for the higher education of women.[49]

But in satirising such literature and its effects, she remembers too that:

> We are all of us apt to imagine that the writers of children's books in the last century had so little artistic faculty as to be constantly writing a language which no human being could ever have indulged in in real life. But, in fact these prematurely grown-up girls were never called on to exercise their intelligence on any subject except morals.[50]

She was fully aware of the intricate interconnections between history and culture, and human development and identity. She believed, for instance, 'that women come to intellectual maturity later than men',[51] and though she may have attributed this to their 'nature' she was scathing about the uses to which such a 'truth' might be put. She writes of teachers: 'Their youth and inexperience are facts constantly brought before them up to the age of thirty or thereabouts, and then with hardly an interval they find themselves confronted by this theory of sudden decay of faculties in women.'[52] The answer lay in first establishing the ways in which career traditions failed to take women's experience into account, and then in challenging those traditions.

IX

It is not easy to characterise Clara's position on women in relation to contemporary argument. She defended many of the political and professional constraints on women – those which she experienced herself as well as others which she knew a good deal about – on absolutely traditional and masculine grounds. Too few women were well enough educated or trained, in her view, to be entrusted with major public responsibilities and decisions. She had, as she put it, no 'objection to pecuniary dependence on the husband'[53] in principle. This was in a long and disparaging review of a book by an American writer, a Mrs Stetson, based specifically on that objection. 'The charm of the book' (*Women and Economics*), Clara writes sourly, 'is its excessive femininity', and:

> while declining, therefore, to follow Mrs Stetson in her wonderful flights of fancy with regard to unknown times and races of mankind, and acknowledging myself incapable of judging whether women have become more or less feminine as compared with prehistoric times, I agree with Mrs Stetson, so far as regards a section of American and English society, when she says that 'women are growing honester, braver, stronger, more healthful and skilful and able and free – more human in all ways', and that this improvement has been at least coincident with, and to some extent due to, the effort to become at least *capable* of economic independence.[54]

This catches some of the substance as well as some of the ambiguity of Clara's views and feelings. She found 'femininity' as an idea both inescapable and mortifying. It seems that in her own life she struggled to ensure her prospects in a world which might well be expected to find her wanting in 'femininity', though she also saw this same 'femininity' as a condition of human weakness, which bizarrely attracted to itself the undeniably valuable reward of supportive and even occasionally stimulating male company. Human strengths were, by and large, male strengths, to be sought by women as by men. She may never have been able to accept – and who would blame her? – that contempt, or at least neglect, might be visited on any woman who took it upon herself to aspire to men's vaunted standards of intelligence and moral behaviour.

By 1910 the campaign for women's suffrage had exploded into occasional violence. There were demonstrations, arson attacks and picture slashing. Another relative of mine chained herself and her sisters to the railings of Holborn Post Office, and they were carried off to jail. It is always claimed in the family that their mother joined them there in order to keep her eye on the girls. This family was much richer than the Collet family, and though the girls were brought up to have accomplishments and intellectual interests they were neither educated nor trained to earn their living.

Clara, by contrast, lived by her own labours. She also voted for the Liberal Party until nearly the end of her life, when she voted for the Labour Party. She would certainly not have called herself a Socialist, and despite her childhood friendship with the Marx family appears not to have read Marx in either German or English and apparently thought him 'uninteresting' as an economist. Her formation was Liberal, rationalist, Utilitarian, reformist: traditions, it might be said, which were neither more nor less hospitable to efforts to improve women's lives than many socialist traditions. In retrospect it may – perhaps too easily – be thought that Clara *was* in some ways seduced by an aristocratic and male liberal tradition, and that her spasmodic resistances to that tradition could be said to have been made, perhaps inevitably, on its own terms.

Her expressed view of the relation between men and women was that 'it is on this difference between men and women, amidst much which is common to both, that I build my hopes of women's success in the future. I do not urge women to compete with men because they can do what men can, but because I believe they can do what men cannot.'[55] Her sense of women's disadvantages – and particularly of working-class women's disadvantages – was that their manifestations could neither be conceived of nor tackled in isolation. She had on most issues the pragmatism of the civil servant, and she continued to believe in the general usefulness of detailed investigation of social problems of the sort she had first practised for Booth's survey. It is interesting, if finally fruitless, to speculate as to how she might have reacted to Gareth Stedman Jones's claim that 'once decent and regular employment was made available, "the unemployables" proved impossible to find. In fact they had never existed, except as a phantom army called up by late Victorian and Edwardian social science to legitimize its practice.'[56]

In many ways Clara was a woman bounded by common sense and by a perhaps excessive faith in fairness, rationality and knowledge. This made her an eminently balanced and reliable person, but reduced her speculative capacities. So it is odd to read her notes on 'Reconstruction', prepared after the war for the consideration of the Chairman of the Employment of Women Committee, with their two somewhat divergent proposals for reform. The first of these would be 'to nationalise ground rents and mining royalties and ration the income at so much per head per week to the whole population', and the second that 'instead of State services, the ideal would be the growth of co-operative enterprise, of societies run by the people for the people'.[57] Perhaps this odd combination of nationalisation and almost anarchistic collectivism constituted her utopian expression of the need in 1918 for a brand new world.

X

I have wanted to show, in these fragments and glimpses of a life, how a particular woman both accepted and resisted the accounts of femininity which influenced her growing up and her adult life. And as I have explored aspects of her life from the vantage point of my own in its specific historical point in time and space – the late 1980s in London – I have tried to heed her scepticism, and what I have read as her wan hope, that I would neither pretend to knowledge I hadn't got nor exaggerate the significance of her life or the significance of my reading of it. This adjuring voice is an odd one: wavering in pitch, slightly lisping, contemptuous, but also modest and proud. Clara lived out clusters of contradictions in her education, in her work and in her private life. The very beliefs and values to which she felt most loyal also required her to denigrate aspects of herself and her sex, so that she could function effectively and with dignity. The sexual seduction she avoided – and often regretted – in one part of her life returned in another guise to influence her work and her politics. For what marks her out particularly from many of her contemporaries (though not altogether from mine) is that her working life, which figured prominently in these contradictions, required her to collect and describe facts and figures about other women's experiences, particularly working-class women's experiences. This meant mastering a language and a discipline of distance, impersonality and authority, which inevitably shaped the ways in which women's experiences of the kind she was researching might be discussed or treated. She was simultaneously expected to sympathise in a particularly womanly way and to disengage from those she investigated. So that social investigation of the sort she and other women virtually pioneered was to be seen (as in many ways it still is) as especially appropriate work for women, and especially appropriate as a way of finding out about and regulating women. The anomalies of her position as a worker, *vis-à-vis* male authority and female experience, also affected her own life and its more public privacies. For none of her relations with other people were quite of a kind to match or fit the stories that could be told about them.

In an essay she wrote on the economic progress of women, she defined the minimum requirement for a woman like her:

Most women, on the other hand, who look forward to a long

working career must have an occupation to which they can give both heart and mind. The reason is simple. The woman is living an isolated life; unless her work involves the exercise of what may be termed her maternal faculties, she is living an unnatural life.[58]

Perhaps, of course, we all live 'unnatural' lives, and knowing that we do so is simply better than not knowing. There are questions to be asked, after all, about the naturalness of 'maternal faculties'. I am left with an image and an enigma. Clara, as I have already mentioned, had a breast removed because of cancer when she was already in her seventies. How might we read that event? The family memory retains the name of the surgeon, Geoffrey Keynes, but does not speculate about Clara's feelings. Did this distinguished and interesting surgeon, with his books on Blake and his connections with Bloomsbury, whom she must have liked, mutilate her? Or did he restore her to herself, mark her out as an Amazon? These are questions from which Clara herself would have flinched, and to which I expect no answers.

4

Imperial Seductions

Woman's voice is not one voice to be added to the orchestra; *every* voice is inhabited by the sexual differential.

Gayatri Chakravorty Spivak, *In Other Worlds*

I

Isn't there something suspicious about the censorious voice in the passage that follows?

> It represented a woman, considerably larger, I thought, than the life. I calculated that this lady, put into a scale of magnitude suitable for the reception of a commodity of bulk, would infallibly turn from fourteen to sixteen stone. She was, indeed, extremely well fed: very much butcher's meat – to say nothing of bread, vegetables, and liquids – must she have consumed to attain that breadth and height, that wealth of muscle, that affluence of flesh. She lay half-reclined on a couch: why, it would be difficult to say; broad daylight blazed round her: she appeared in hearty health, strong enough to do the work of two plain cooks; she could not plead a weak spine; she ought to have been standing, or at least sitting bolt upright. She had no business to lounge away the noon on a sofa. She ought likewise to have worn decent garments; a gown covering her properly, which was not the case: out of abundance of material – seven-and-twenty yards, I should say, of drapery – she managed to make inefficient raiment. Then, for the wretched untidiness surrounding her, there could be no excuse. Pots and pans – perhaps I ought to say vases and goblets – were rolled here and there on the foreground; a perfect rubbish of flowers was mixed amongst them, and an absurd and disorderly mass of curtain upholstery smothered the couch and cumbered the floor. On referring to the catalogue, I found that this notable production bore name 'Cleopatra'.
>
> Well, I was sitting wondering at it (as the bench was there, I thought I might as well take advantage of its accommodation), and thinking that while some of the details – as roses, gold cups, jewels, etc., were very prettily painted, it was on the whole an enormous piece of claptrap; the room, almost vacant when I entered, began to fill. Scarcely noticing this circumstance (as,

indeed, it did not matter to me) I retained my seat; rather to rest myself than with a view to studying this huge, dark-complexioned gipsy-queen; of whom, indeed, I soon tired, and betook myself for refreshment to the contemplation of some exquisite little pictures of still life: wild-flowers, wild fruit, mossy wood-nests, casketing eggs that looked like pearls seen through clear green sea-water; all hung modestly beneath that coarse and preposterous canvas.[1]

What has provoked such censure? Is it the painting and its painter? Or is the spectacle of an untidy and indolent woman enough to arouse such disapproval in itself? Does the voice belong to an art critic, to a disappointed sensualist, to a puritan or to an ironist? Is the distaste primarily that of a fastidious classicist or of an exasperated administrator? And is all that exasperation genuine? Are we convinced by the insistence on how boring all that excess and exotic ebullience really are? Is the voice a man's or a woman's? Does it matter? Do our expectations of who more usually censures whom and for what incline us to believe it is one rather than the other? And if we recollect that the voice is in fact Lucy Snowe's, and the moment extracted from the middle of Charlotte Brontë's last novel, *Villette*, are we instantly soothed by the knowledge or further perplexed? And who are *we* anyway?

And have I emphasised censure at the expense of the humour with which Lucy addresses this painting of a woman, whose material and sexual power may well be felt (by Brontë and by Lucy and by me) as a reproof but also as a disproof of women's more commonly anticipated economic weakness and sexual invisibility? Lucy's dismissal of the painting as 'on the whole an enormous piece of claptrap' – with its tone of ironic and surely male superiority towards painter and model – could be read as a strategy for coping publicly with the impossibility for women of settling themselves at all easily into male perceptions of female beauty and sexuality. Lucy's boredom with the painting may not ring true. Yet she manages to convey its coarseness and preposterousness (and its dangerous vitality), not least by comparing the painting with the small, inoffensive and pretty *still* lives beneath it. Surprisingly, they manage – if only just – to survive its exuberance. In such a reading the passage comes to enact an encounter between a male view of the sexual feeling produced by a desirable woman, and a woman watcher's (or reader's) sense of her own ambiguous presence and absence within such a view and in relation to such an image. Lucy Snowe scrutinises a man-made image of female voluptuousness and adopts a man's voice (could she have done otherwise?) as she wrestles with the problems it poses for her as a woman who writes.

Brontë reproduces the peering we need to perform as readers into the framing and the perspectives of the painting by placing her convalescent Lucy helplessly before the picture she has been determined to ignore until now. We peer too. It is, after all, a famous painting of the most famous of all black women, a woman who has been much written about and painted and considerably whitened in both processes. Cleopatra, Queen of Egypt, seductress, sorceress, and possessed of Eastern wiles and magic, reduces Mark Antony, 'grand captain' and 'crown o' th' earth', to a 'womanly' shadow of himself.[2] The lure and the impossibility of the painting lie for Lucy somewhere within its blurrings and overlappings of sex and race and class. If we are now inclined to hear the censoriousness as a man's, we have also to concede that Lucy Snowe's male impersonation enables her to displace on to a painting a life's constraints and a history of imperialism, in which she is implicated.

Powerless and poor and ill, Lucy Snowe is none the less briefly privileged: at liberty to look at and to criticise a queen, a woman beloved — as *she* is not — by men; a woman who is, in this case, the creation (or the recreation) of a man. For a moment she is even in a position to give Rubens, a male artist, a proper debunking: deflating with a word all that Great Master over-excitement with imaginary feasts of female flesh. And then, with the merest narrowing of the eyes, she can transform that oriental wealth (or bric-à-brac) into the pots and pans of a sluttish housewife or a servant, or into the profligate and legitimate disorder of a male artist's studio or study. Cleopatra, whose person 'beggared all description', becomes a painter's model, a servant and, later, 'a mulatto'. The strain is temporarily resolved, assuaged, and Lucy moves on to the contemplation of a series of four paintings called 'La vie d'une femme'. Their women are angels, 'grim and grey as burglars, and cold and vapid as ghosts'. They are 'as bad in their way as the indolent gipsy-giantess, the Cleopatra, in hers'.

Faced with the necessity for silence about sexual love and with women's consequent distrust of one another in a society which patrols the terrain and the boundaries of women's activity and thought, Lucy takes refuge in male impersonation, as Charlotte Brontë did. With an amused male eye she may peer into territory forbidden to her, where female identity is watched and measured against men's dreams of what it offers. And in those dreams, class and race embargoes may seem momentarily (if dubiously) relaxed. It is in relation to race that Lucy's impersonation stumbles, for Cleopatra, whether as 'queen' or as 'mulatto', promises unimaginable sexual pleasures. They are unimaginable because they are men's pleasures and because they are located — and deliberately — beyond the vision of the small, passionate and sexually innocent English woman, whose purity, it could be said, is preserved precisely by endowing Cleopatra with everything that is (literally) outlandish and foreign and necessarily repugnant to a decent young woman like Lucy.

Expressing her contempt for the class, the race, even the incompetence of the woman in the picture can only partly compensate Lucy, however, for the riches and the pleasure she is so specifically denied. Charlotte Brontë, Lucy Snowe, the reader – even, if differently, Rubens – are caught within the two-way determinations of what has come to be called Orientalism. The delights and disarray of the seraglio interior (which is available to Lucy as an image) stand for the Eastern woman's promise of infinite submissiveness, for the Eastern man's unworthy and brutishly unappreciative self-indulgence, and for the secret pleasures made available by the one and justified by the other to the white male traveller from the West. It is a hidden place to which entry is expressly denied European women. Yet historically women of Charlotte Brontë's class could not avoid being implicated (if indirectly) in imperialism, colonialism and in those exploitations of a class society which were nearer home, any more than Clara Collet could at the end of the nineteenth century. I am intent for the moment on neither exoneration nor exculpation, but on considering women's – and feminism's – relation to particular and significant *critical* accounts of imperialism and racism. There seem to me to be a number of reasons for attempting to interrogate these critiques from a feminist point of view.

First, women as half the world have participated in colonised as well as in colonising societies, and in both they have experienced diverse and multiple forms of dependency. They have, simultaneously, been excluded from the very modes of critical analysis which have addressed their own and others' oppression. Second, since many arguments about imperialism and racism tackle the relation of historical and material oppression to cultural and psychological oppression – that is, oppression that is learned, internalised, even self-administered – such arguments must necessarily interest those who are endeavouring to develop a feminist analysis and a feminist politics. Third, many anti-imperialist arguments show how peoples and places which have been conquered and marginalised are frequently seen and spoken of in terms of their otherness, their difference, as both lesser and female. Finally – and crucially – few arguments, theories or analyses in this area address their own suppression of female experience and testimony, nor do they associate their own critical positions with those which have been elaborated within feminism. It is essential, moreover, to keep these reasons for investigating women's relation to imperialism and feminism's relation to anti-imperialist discourses together. Historical and political experience should not be separated from the language and the imagery which both delimit and deny that experience.

In an article about Bangladeshi women, Naila Kabeer illustrates in an aside how we all (women too) accept the category of women as concurrently separate, subsumed and subordinate. 'The Mujib regime', she writes, 'was preoccupied with attempts to cope with the ravages of war, deteriorating law and order and the disastrous famine of 1974. It had little scope to deal specifically with the situation of women.'[3] It is as though women were mysteriously protected from war and famine and the breakdown of law and order – as though, too, the seriousness of the national crisis would be somehow trivialised by a focus on women. I am reminded of the gravel-voiced Studs Terkel and his bizarre characterisation of the 1988 American presidential election as 'trivial' because everybody talked about 'food and babies'.[4] It is hard for the moment to think of what issues could have been talked about which are in themselves less trivial.

In some of the work I shall be looking at in this chapter, women are not merely left out or tagged on or expected to wait until more serious and central groups within a population have been attended to; they may also be blamed. Anna Davin[5] has shown how women at the turn of the century were blamed simultaneously for the high infant mortality, for a general deterioration of health in the population, and for failing to produce enough sons to replace those killed in wars or sent to the colonies. Blaming women for national deficiences amounts to an admission that nothing can or need be done to improve the situation. Women have also been blamed by the colonised as arch-collaborators as well as the occasion and the repository for the self-hatred of the colonised. It is as if the overheated sexual imagery so characteristic of writing and painting about the East fuels at least some of the language of retaliation. As Frantz Fanon – whose isolating and blaming of women I shall go on to discuss – puts it in *Toward the African Revolution*: 'Having judged, condemned, abandoned his cultural forms, his language, his food habits, his sexual behaviour, his way of sitting down; of resting, of laughing, of enjoying himself, the oppressed *flings himself* upon the imposed culture with the desperation of a drowning man.'[6] To blame women for the value they may come to acquire for the invaders and for the use women may be obliged to make of this anomalous value is rather like blaming women for being raped *and* for the public account of the rape as no more, finally, than a seduction. If women are to be picked off as collaborators, the pressures on them to collaborate must, at the very least, be entered in any analysis of colonialism, not left to the mercy of natural explanations.

II

Recent studies of aspects of colonialism – and most particularly Edward Said's book *Orientalism* – have concentrated on the cultural and ideological thrust within the West's imperialist history, which has contributed to the systematic construction of an 'East' as irreducibly different and inferior. Such studies owe a good deal to Gramsci's insistence that:

> Obviously East and West are arbitrary and conventional, that is historical, constructions, since outside of real history every point on the earth is East and West at the same time. This can be seen more clearly from the fact that these terms have crystallised not from the point of view of a hypothetical melancholic man in general but from the point of view of the European cultured classes who, as a result of their world-wide hegemony, have caused them to be accepted everywhere . . . So because of the historical content that has become attached to the geographical terms, the expressions East and West have finished up indicating specific relations between different cultural complexes.[7]

Said focuses on English and French scholarly texts – and on some of the novels which they inspired – from the end of the eighteenth century, in order, as he puts it, to get 'a better understanding of the way cultural domination has operated'.[8] Within his analysis, Orientalism is 'itself a product of certain political forces and activities . . . a school of interpretation whose material happens to be the Orient, its civilizations, peoples, and localities'.[9] Said draws on the work of the historian and philosopher Foucault to define Orientalism as a field simultaneously independent of and parasitic upon the actual lives which people have lived in the East. This is not, as Said says,

> an airy European fantasy about the Orient, but a created body of theory and practice in which, for many generations, there has been a considerable material investment. Continued investment made Orientalism, as a system of knowledge about the Orient, an accepted grid for filtering through the Orient into Western consciousness, just as that same investment multiplied – indeed, made truly productive – the statements proliferating out from Orientalism into the general culture.[10]

His book tracks a network of interwoven forms of language and tradition which, collectively, have defined and produced an 'East' which might justifiably be discovered, taken over, controlled and exploited and, finally, instructed about itself.

In an article which anathematises the novelist William Golding for his distortions and omissions when writing about his travels in Egypt, the Egyptian writer Ahdaf Soueif remarks that 'the trouble with travel books is that their subjects/victims don't normally get to read them, much less to give their version of what things were like.'[11] Said, as a Palestinian who now lives and works in America, puts that stricture within its complex political history. He does not undertake to speak for those who are silenced by Orientalism (though his political engagement and his writings on the Palestinian question do,[12] and eloquently). Rather, by denaturalising, as it were, many strongly held Western beliefs about the East, he demonstrates how pervasive and vigorously proliferating such ideas can be, and how exactly their effect has been to defuse threats of mutiny and to maintain order. Said demonstrates how the cultural manifestations of imperialism are produced by, and also productive of, a politics which facilitates and bolsters Western domination. *Orientalism* also develops, at quite a general level, a theory of cultural interpretation as depending on a history which has seen absolutely unequal distributions of power between West and East. There is no doubt of the potential in such an undertaking for an analysis of culture which takes as its focus the relation of culture to class and gender as well as to race, geography and nationality.

Said asks how and whether it is possible to envisage another culture at all; what, in fact, another culture might be thought to be; and whether, indeed, 'the notion of a distinct culture'[13] is a useful one. For we are all bound to enter the strangeness of another culture via precisely those features of it which we recognise as familiar. We move sideways, as it were, through metaphor and analogy and oversimplification. Said then goes on to outline certain ways in which cumulatively 'the modern Orient . . . participates in its own Orientalizing'.[14] He assembles a dynamic and complex sense of the apparatus and practices of political and cultural domination and, significantly, of the processes involved for those who are dominated as they internalise the rationale for, and even the justice of, others' domination of them.

This, then, is an immensely seductive theory about seduction. Said introduces us to texts, traditions and ideas which have interested and delighted their readers. Stories of strange customs and secret pleasures, of the unknowable and the inexplicable, have been found simultaneously exciting and consoling for Western readers. Travellers' tales, discoveries, explorations, archaeological digs and anthropological investigations have together composed a world which may be construed as utterly strange and as entirely reassuring as well, for its confirmation of Western competence, enterprise, straightforwardness, progress and overall superiority. The seduction has also served to distract from the rape, from the barbarous history of invasion, theft and violence, whilst buttressing that history's maintenance and continuation against all possible threats to its survival.

The cultural takeover is comprehensive in this account, for resistance is blocked by all those ways in which the East has been seduced into an acceptance of the rightness of the West's version of things. As Said put it elsewhere, in a later work:

> ... in the transmission and persistence of a culture there is a continual process of reinforcement, by which the hegemonic culture will add to itself the prerogatives given it by its sense of national identity, its power as an implement, ally, or branch of the state, its rightness, its exterior forms and assertions of itself: and, most important, by its vindicated power as a victor over everything not itself.[15]

So a variant of Gramsci's hegemony is enacted within the imperialist relation, and the oppressed are thereby enlisted as participants, colluding agents of their own oppression.

From the beginning of *Orientalism* Said gives examples of the sexual imagery which has been central to the West's interpretation and articulation of the East. He refers to Flaubert's description of an

> encounter with an Egyptian courtesan [which] produced a widely influential model of the Oriental woman; she never spoke of herself, she never represented her emotions, presence, or history. *He* spoke for and represented her. He was foreign, comparatively wealthy, male, and these were historical facts of domination that allowed him not only to possess Kuchuk Hanem physically but to speak for her and tell his readers in what way she was 'typically Oriental'.[16]

Said is doing more here than associating the East with both the colonised and women. Power, whiteness, wealth and maleness are threaded into each term of his guiding metaphor. The East offers easy access to women (actually, of course, it only offers some white men access, and to a small number of women). The East also *is* a woman, however: a womb, female in its vulnerability and weakness and otherness and in its seductiveness, fertility and profitability. The East, then, is a playground for chosen and powerful white men (some of whom may even have acquired power by virtue of their activities in this playground) and it is also – and as if coincidentally – productive.

Later in the book, Said returns to Kuchuk and to Flaubert's ambiguous passion for her:

> The Oriental woman is an occasion and an opportunity for Flaubert's musings; he is entranced by her self-sufficiency, by her emotional carelessness, and also by what, lying next to him, she allows him to think.[17]

Kuchuk's passivity and unresponsiveness add to her charm for him; his recognition of her lack of interest in him is only partly rueful.

In her *Europe's Myths of Orient* (a book which owes a considerable debt to *Orientalism*), the Syrian writer Rana Kabbani does none the less add an essential element to Said's account in her treatment of the sexual relations enjoyed by white men with Eastern women. She quotes the Orientalist Richard Burton's remark that 'while thousands of Europeans have cohabited for years with and have had families by native women, they are never loved by them – at least I have never heard of a single case.' Kabbani tells us that Burton attributed

> this lack of romantic attachment on the part of the native woman to the European's clumsy sexual techniques. The Westerner could not meet the demands imposed upon him by the native woman's body (who could not be satisfied, as Burton had calculated, with less than twenty minutes), and could therefore never win her affections.[18]

Kabbani usefully reminds us that there may be more complex reasons for this:

> The European, after all, had occupied her land, oppressed her people, and imposed his personal will upon her. Her emotional detachment was her only defence – feeble as it was – against total victimisation. He had the power to enslave her, but he could not *make* her love him.[19]

Kabbani's reasons are not only more complex than Burton's. They instantly prise the supine Eastern woman out of those views which reduce her to no more than a collection of predictable (and racially specific) sexual needs and tricks and restore her to something resembling autonomous, if oppressed, humanity. It is startling in this context to hear of 'her land', for instance.

Women figure in Said's analysis in a number of ways, but he appears not to see that their presumed sexual availability is itself produced by the transformation already performed on it and on the countries which it then comes to represent. Women and colonies and invaded territories generally become available *because* they are undeveloped, uncultivated, swathed in their natural vulnerability and therefore weak, passive, receptive and intuitive. Their value to the coloniser is for their natural resources. They are likely to be blessed with a crude and unadulterated beauty, which is likely, in its turn, to be marred by a certain coarseness and by an inability to appreciate the finer gifts of their rescuing conquerors. A prevailing imagery of penetration, of stamina and of the eventual discovery of the strange and the hidden at the end of a journey requiring courage and cunning serves to merge the colonising adventure definitively with the sexual adventure.

Towards the end of Said's assembling of Orientalists' lavish denigrations of Arabs and the Arab world, he introduces the idea of 'an undifferentiated sexual drive'[20] as the underlying defect bestowed by the Orientalist tradition on Arab men. It is undifferentiated in every sense: overactive, misdirected, violent, unconsidered, and simultaneously vitiated by a kind of passivity and even by a capacity to lapse into that 'womanliness' which seeps contagiously into the language whenever colonisation is likened to the sexual act. The very circuitousness of these slippages and connections mimics the ineffectual character of all sexual activity undertaken by people who have been colonised and have therefore been seduced by something outside themselves. To have been seduced is to have let yourself be seduced, to have been seducible. Said writes:

> If Arab society is represented in almost completely negative and generally passive terms, to be ravished and won by the Orientalist hero, we can assume that such a representation is a way of dealing with the great variety and potency of Arab diversity, whose source is, if not intellectual and social, then sexual and biological. Yet the absolutely inviolable taboo in Orientalist discourse is that that very sexuality must never be taken seriously.[21]

In an impressive finale to his book, Said demonstrates how recent Orientalists have left this contradiction unexamined and have assimilated the notion of an ubiquitous and deficient sexuality in the racially inferior to fruitless revolutionary spasms, or even equated the two, so that all sexual and all political effort becomes useless against the twin energies of imperialism and Orientalism. The book ends with a summary of its message:

> If the knowledge of Orientalism has any meaning, it is in being a reminder of the seductive degradation of knowledge, of any knowledge, anywhere, at any time. Now perhaps more than before.[22]

There is no doubt, I think, that Said's analysis has a general usefulness and relevance for cultural, historical and political understandings on a broad front, so that the absence of any recognition of connections between his work and some forms of feminist analysis is disappointing. This is, first, because his theory of cultural hegemony within imperialist history in the Middle East suggests powerful analogies with forms of patriarchal oppression within that history and, of course, within other histories. But there is also the question of how women's perceptions are affected by imagery doing at least double duty in its mediation of class, race and sexual relations. Finally, there is the difficulty of somehow invoking, or seeming to realise, a material history through particular and carefully selected cultural manifestations, which certainly derive from that history, just as they participate in its construction, but which are also separate, not the same thing.

Said sets out with care and delicacy the parallels and analogies developed in this field between colonial relations and sexual relations, and he shows how illuminating of the reality of the imperial adventure those parallels have been for both West and East. What he does not confront are the sexual meanings on which those illuminating parallels depend. It is possible to feel that within his analysis it is with the distortions of male sexuality produced by the language of Orientalism that he is chiefly concerned. To undermine the economy, the sovereignty and the culture of another people is, above all, to undermine the identity and integrity of its male citizens. That has often involved the theft of their women, as part of a process which is to be thought of as infantilisation or, ultimately, as feminisation. The question remains: why does such an analysis not entail a concern for women's loss of political and economic status, in itself? The possibility that women had little or no political or economic status to lose does not become part of the history which is being rewritten.

There is no doubt that there would have been immense difficulties in pursuing the implications of the colonial/sexual parallel beyond its reference to the humiliations of men. To do that Said would have needed to follow it through in relation to the control, the exploitation, the marginalising and the exclusion of women in quite different societies. The apparently complaisant, or alternatively unbridled, woman of the seraglio would have to be understood in relation to other constructions of womanhood: the frigid Victorian wife, perhaps; the unmarried or barren woman in Europe or in the East; and so on.

Perhaps most vitally, the deliberate confusion with brothels of the seraglio and the harem — that is, the female quarters of certain polygamous households — would need untangling. For the harems of rich men were by no means forbidden territory for all upper-class European women, but even a kind of tourist attraction and refuge for some.[23] Indeed, for over two centuries a few upper-class English women have travelled in the East, sometimes alone, and have both set and broken standards of what was allowable for women. Much closer attention would have to be paid to the material histories of women in particular countries of the East, for there is certainly some difficulty in tracing the transmission of salient ideas independently of such a history. It is not only feminism which gets lost, but women and their history, when ideology becomes, retrospectively, untethered and virtually autonomous, therefore, as a level of activity.

It has also to be said that an adequate history of women's relations to even a fraction of the eighteenth- and nineteenth-century Western expansionist undertaking would be an immensely difficult history to write. Such a history could not be written without dissolving the category 'women' into groups and classes of women, whose interests were most frequently in conflict. There were ways in which women were (most often through their fathers and husbands) actively engaged in the founding and maintaining of empires. A history which included working-class women, however, would need to take account of the mostly devastating effects on them and on their children of the military and trade projects within imperialist expansion. And this would not even touch on the vitally significant economic, cultural, caste and religious differences and divisions between women in colonised countries. To list such obstacles is not to admit that an adequate history of imperialism is entitled to skirt women, on the grounds that they always live at one remove from the central political structures and struggles of societies and that a consideration of their relation to such struggles simply muddies the waters of an otherwise hard-nosed theory of power dynamics.

III

I shall return for a moment to Charlotte Brontë's portrait of a young middle-class Englishwoman of the 1840s looking at and thinking about a male painter's representation of the most powerful and sexually celebrated black woman in perhaps the whole of Western history. It would not be quite true to say that I see myself as a woman reading Said's *Orientalism* in Lucy Snowe's more straightforwardly mutinous scrutiny of Rubens's painting in the National Gallery of *Villette*. My reading may not, in fact, be nearly mutinous enough. I have almost certainly been seduced by this masterly dissection of the imperialists' capacity for thought control into accepting a powerful discourse which excludes women while articulating itself on the basis of a perception of their vulnerabilities. I use the word 'discourse' advisedly here: for its suggestions of a difficult and scholarly tradition, for its association with Foucault, and for its sense of a specialised kind of male speech. The irony is that within these anti-imperialist discourses it is women's vulnerabilities and the injuries they attract to themselves which become metaphors for the injuries suffered by whole societies and for the consequent humiliations of their men.

The question I have to ask myself is whether, by listening to this argument, I am colluding with those who would ignore what is done to – and said about – women's bodies, whether they are Eastern or Western women, until more important matters have been attended to. Have I too allowed women's bodies to disappear into metaphor or flourish as exemplarily natural? Have I been reading (and writing) over the heads and bodies, as it were, of women like these, women whose economic dependence on men is total, in parts of contemporary Bangladesh, for instance?

> A daughter is likely to be regarded as a burden by her own family. She has to be supported during her least productive years and kept under constant surveillance so that she can be handed over to her husband with her chastity intact. Her membership of her father's household is truncated at the very point at which she is entering the productive and reproductive stage of her life. Physical care of the daughter has been compared to 'watering the neighbour's tree; you take all the trouble to nurture the plant, but the fruit goes to someone else.[24]

Or like these wives of British soldiers in India in the mid nineteenth century, who were grateful to be allowed to follow their husbands there, since staying at home could mean a separation of ten years or more without any financial support whatever:

> The women struggled behind the regiments with their children as best they might since no concessions were made for them at all, sleeping in tents with the men and their families, head to the wall, feet to the central pole. They gave birth unattended, often had to search battlefields alone for their dead, and frequently died pathetically neglected and exhausted in a regiment's wake.[25]

Neither Charlotte Brontë nor Lucy Snowe could have known about the lives of women like these at first hand, and their ignorance has to be understood in the context of constraints on middle-class women's lives and on what could be known by many people about such experiences. Lucy Snowe may be railing in part at the painting's hints at what she did not and could not know, its silences and embargoes. But in the end it is probably the case that her reading of Cleopatra is no more straightforwardly mutinous than mine is of *Orientalism*.

Indeed, at the end of the novel she characterises and affirms her love for her teacher, Paul Emanuel, with the words: 'For the moment of utmost mutiny, he reserved the one deep spell of peace.'[26] All Brontë's novels enact this double need: for mutiny and for a man's stilling and containing of that mutiny. So that her mutiny, like mine, can be made to seem not much more than a revolutionary spasm, doggishly responsive to a little male head-patting.

That is not all, though. The difficulty I am grappling with has something else in common with the problems with which Brontë presents Lucy in *Villette*. The dilemma is this: how do I find a language which will enable me to enter a powerful and male tradition of cultural criticism addressing concerns that I share? For on the one hand that tradition will block all entry to itself so long as my intrusion is represented as sectional in its interests and intent, therefore, only on disturbing and distracting from the truth and universality of these ideas, from the altogether grander history which they illuminate. On the other, a tradition so barbed and fortified against women's appropriation of any of it can hardly, after all, offer an ideal entry into the debate.

Somewhere within Said's history of Orientalism are lives, consciousnesses; and women have, for instance, made decisions either to accept or to reject men's economic support on conditions which could mean life or death for them and for their children. The character of those dependencies within capitalism and imperialism (and within other forms of government) is addressed only in principle by Foucault, for instance, and it sits awkwardly, if at all, within almost all Marxist analysis. Nor can it simply be a matter of adjusting such analyses to accommodate women and feminism in the nick of time. Writing of Wayne Booth's 'look, no hands' foray of this kind into the implications of feminism for literary interpretation, Gayatri Spivak points out that 'if the "she" is seriously introduced into these essays, the argument might need to change its shape'. What she calls 'the quick fix of a mandatory "he or she"'[27] will do little more than reveal how entirely absent women have always been from such discussions.

I am left with another, subsidiary, question: does Rubens, does Said, assume that women are amongst the viewers and the readers of their work? If the answer to that question is yes, do they also assume that we shelve, suspend our gender, our difference from men, in the process, or that we become temporary – perhaps honorary – men, or even androgynous? Women's banishment from the making of theory and from its subsequent articulations is historical, after all, not a matter of principle. The fact that a very few women have participated in developing significant ideas and putting them to use does not affect my argument, since such women were required to suppress their difference in order to do so. For ideas which claim for themselves a 'human', even a 'universal', usefulness include women precisely by excluding the historically differentiated people women have actually been.

The painting confronting Lucy Snowe is Rubens's representation of a woman, and a loved woman. Women may look at the painting or refuse to look at it. They may consider it solely as a man's representation of female desirability, or as a formal arrangement of planes and colour tones. In many cases one or a combination of those ways of viewing it will do quite well. I am suggesting, though, that such approaches require the suppression of the potentially problematic relations between the woman spectator, the painting, the painter and his model. Similarly, white Western women – variously implicated, as we cannot avoid being, in the racism and the depredations of the imperial past and present – cannot unequivocally contemplate the sexual imagery of either colonialism or anti-colonialism. Nor can we accept without demur any proposal that anti-imperialism or anti-racism, as a politics and an analysis, should unquestionably enjoy supremacy over a politics and an analysis which start from women and from a society's organisation and regulation of sexuality.

In accepting the power and the usefulness of an analysis like Said's there is an essential proviso of this sort to be made. If women are ambiguously present within the discourses of Orientalism, they are just as ambiguously present within the discourses developed to expose and to oppose Orientalism. Their presence in both is as forms of coinage, exchange value offered or stolen or forbidden, tokens of men's power and wealth or lack of them. The sexual use and productiveness of women are allowed to seem equivalent to their actual presence and their consciousness. They are, finally, 'Orientalised' within Said's terms into the perceptions and the language which express, but also elaborate on, the uses men have for women within exploitative societies.

IV

I was in my early twenties when I first read Simone de Beauvoir's *The Second Sex*. I found it upsetting, and I remember clearly that after reading about fifty pages I nearly gave up. I had never before encountered (let alone admitted to) women's contempt for themselves, nor had it spelled out so simply why such contempt might, after all, be perfectly justified.

The superiority of the male is, indeed, overwhelming: Perseus,

Hercules, David, Achilles, Lancelot, the old French warriors Du Guesclin and Bayard, Napoleon – so many men for one Joan of Arc; and behind her one decries the great male figure of the archangel Michael! Nothing could be more tiresome than the biographies of famous women; they are but pallid figures compared with great men; and most of them bask in the glory of some masculine hero. Eve was not created for her own sake but as a companion for Adam, and she was made from his rib.[28]

The irony did something to mitigate the pain and the truth; but twenty pages on came this assertion:

In a sexually egalitarian society, woman would regard menstruation simply as her special way of reaching adult life; the human body in both men and women has other and more disagreeable needs to be taken care of, but they are easily adjusted to because, being common to all, they do not represent blemishes for anyone; the menses inspire horror in the adolescent girl because they throw her into an inferior and defective category.[29]

I was reminded by this of an episode I had wanted to forget and had not understood. It was something like a sense of being no longer human, of belonging to 'an inferior and defective category' – no longer, in fact, a potential boy – that made me at twelve, when my periods began, lock myself into my room for two days and refuse to confess to anyone that I had started bleeding. It was not the learning of something even as simple as difference which was so horrifying. It was the abrupt recognition that I was after all, and inescapably, exactly what I had grown up to despise: a girl.

Frantz Fanon describes the moment when a young black boy recognises that his own blackness is the very same blackness he has learned to regard as inferior:

In the Antilles, the young Negro identifies himself *de facto* with Tarzan against the Negroes. This is much more difficult for him in a European theatre, for the rest of the audience, which is white, automatically identifies him with the savages on the screen. It is a conclusive experience. The Negro learns that one is not black without problems.[30]

Fanon was born in Martinique in 1925 and studied first medicine and then psychiatry in France. His first book, *Black Skin White Masks*, begins from a furious, anguished exploration of *négritude*, a word for black consciousness developed by Fanon's compatriot, the poet and statesman Aimé Césaire. It is a word Fanon himself loaded with the particular self-hatred produced by colonialism: a self-hatred which was itself hateful and shameful. *Négritude* in this sense is something like blackness as it is learned and lived within colonial oppression.

Fanon is outraged in the book by Sartre's neatly appropriating the idea in *Orphée Noir* in order to drift off into optimistic contemplation of its revolutionary potential – so that for Sartre *négritude* contains 'the root of its own destruction, it is a transition and not a conclusion, a means and not an ultimate end.'[31] Fanon rejects this. He is determined to find full expression for the living through of learned blackness in colonialism, the experiencing of contradiction, of the possibility and the impossibility of an injunction to accept oneself as opposite, other, negative, inferior. Assimilation has, of course, been on offer, and Fanon movingly remembers the hunger with which he and other young men approached mainland France, French culture, as theirs. There was even, they found, a kind of welcome:

> Oh, certainly, I will be told, now and then when we are worn out by our lives in big buildings, we will turn to you as we do to our children – to the innocent, the ingenuous, the spontaneous . . . Thus my unreason was countered with reason, my reason with 'real reason'.[32]

The terms of the welcome are unacceptable. Fanon realises that even his efforts to reclaim *négritude* for himself may be overwhelmed, swamped by a white interpretation of it as no more, in the end, than 'a term in the dialectic' as it was for Sartre.

Two chapters of Fanon's book concentrate on sexual relations within racist, colonial societies. One chapter is called 'The Woman of Colour and the White Man', the other 'The Man of Colour and the White Woman'. Fanon's contempt for black women who sleep with or even marry white men is limitless, and he explains the white woman who dreams of a black lover on Freudian lines as living out a fantasy of rape by a Negro, which enacts 'the phenomenon of turning against self, it is the woman who rapes herself'.[33] Black and white women are understood as motivated by impulses deriving from causes quite other than the social and economic ones which produce *négritude*. Indeed, black women fall outside Fanon's account of the internalising of racism, and become uncomplicatedly agents for its perpetuation:

> I know a great number of girls from Martinique, students in France, who admitted to me with complete candour – completely white candour – that they would find it impossible to marry black men. (Get out of that and then deliberately go back to it? Thank you, no.) Besides, they added, it is not that we deny

that blacks have any good qualities, but you know it is so much better to be white. I was talking only recently to one such woman. Breathless with anger, she stormed at me, 'If Césaire makes so much display about accepting his race, it is because he really feels it as a curse. Do the whites boast like that about theirs? Every one of us has a white potential, but some try to ignore it and others simply reverse it. As far as I am concerned, I wouldn't marry a Negro for anything in the world.' Such attitudes are not rare, and I must confess that they disturb me, for in a few years this young woman will have finished her examinations and gone off to teach in some school in the Antilles. It is not hard to guess what will come of that.[34]

The dismissive anger of this passage could be said to have a long history and its own reasons, and it may be read as expressing fear of female resistance at least as much as habits of contempt and exclusion. It is interesting, moreover, that Fanon should refer in a note to the work of Lacan and, particularly, to Lacan's essay outlining his theory of the 'mirror stage',[35] for this is an essay much turned to by feminists too.

During the first year of life, according to this theory, the child confronts the illusion or myth of itself as a coherent and separate identity. It is significant for Lacan that the mirrored reflection in which as children we may first recognise ourselves is, in fact, a misrecognition. This 'moment' is echoed by a parallel finding from linguistics, in which the child's discovery and use of 'I' in relation to herself is accompanied by the concomitant discovery that every other human being has access to 'I' within a system of contrasts which allows 'I' its meaning. So that its promise of uniqueness, wholeness, singleness of meaning, is illusory. Lacan's theory was developed out of a rereading of Freud and in relation to work by de Saussure and his followers in structural linguistics. This may explain the highly abstract character of his account of learning and the somewhat idealist and universalist cast of his thought. For instance, cultural differences may be assumed to figure in it, but they are not specified.

Lacan's interpretation of the mirror stage has been important to feminist theory in ways which are not entirely easy to account for. The schematic and formulaic character of the work, and the obdurately impenetrable language in which it is formulated, offer a notable example of the barbed temptation for feminists of language and modes of thought which might have been designed to impede all communication with other women. Yet it is also possible to see why Lacan's work has been useful. It has, first, allowed for an understanding of identity as constructed rather than revealed and as necessarily fractured, fragmented and unstable. This has constituted a major challenge to traditional notions of a unified self or subjectivity; and in requiring a return to and a reworking of the relation of language to the activities of the subconscious has been helpful in considering how gender, for instance, might be learned. It is also possible that Lacan's work has short-circuited other important questions for feminist thinking by encouraging too structuralist and too ahistorical a paradigm of human development.

It is no coincidence, however, that Fanon was asserting in the early fifties that:

> When one has grasped the mechanism described by Lacan, one can have no further doubt that the real Other for the white man is and will continue to be the black man. And conversely. Only for the white man The Other is perceived on the level of the body image, absolutely as the not-self – that is, the unidentifiable, the unassimilable. For the black man, as we have shown, historical and economic realities come into the picture.[36]

Within Fanon's perhaps idiosyncratic reading of Lacan (which, given Lacan's opaque style and unanchored abstractions, is certainly no more idiosyncratic than a feminist reading), women, whether black or white, are, it seems, denied entry to this realm of 'realities'. They remain, in his argument, timelessly and helplessly at the mercy of their individual and natural characters – which are defined and circumscribed biologically – and ontologically and morally autonomous within a seemingly total and bizarrely asocial solitude.

It is clear from Fanon's skirmishes with Lacan – and from feminism's – that a psychology which could explain the learning of difference would need to be yoked to a theory of culture and of society complex enough to register the dynamics of unequal access to power, to modes of representation and to meaning. The Russian psychologist, Vygotsky, outlined a theory of learning[37] which entailed a ceaseless struggle for meaning. The individual's struggle progresses by establishing, in communication with other speakers of the same language, what a word *does not* mean. The current meanings of the word 'dog' are learned not by assembling the characteristics of 'dog' which distinguish it from, say, 'sheep', but by winnowing 'dog' out of the clusters of overlapping concepts within the language which are not regarded by adult speakers as essential components of the meaning of 'dog'. Such a theory – developed in opposition to behaviourist explanations of learning and to structuralist theories of mind and language – makes learning, and particularly the learning of self, a process of strenuous and intention-directed activity, mediated by language and performed always within specific social and cultural relations. So that the learning of 'I', like the learning of 'dog', has always entailed the learning of 'not I' and 'not dog'. And it follows from this that the learning of identity is also the learning of 'the other' and the 'not-self' as well. The striking difference between such an account and the structuralist one of Lacan is that these are not the arbitrary terms of a binary system, but words learned within a specific material history and saturated with social uses.

The relatively recent rediscovery of Vygotsky's work and of the theory of language developed by the Russian writers Vološinov[38] and Bakhtin[39] allows us to think of the learning of identity through language as brought about in history and within social relations which position the person in relation to specific, though always changing, cultural contexts and practices. Blackness, femaleness, class are not learned as separate abstractions, but together and shiftingly, within settings which mark difference and value inconsistently in relation to those settings. Bakhtin's 'dialogic' view of language (to which I shall return in the next chapter) reminds us that language is learned within actual conversations rather than as a system abstractable from its primary oral uses, and it is a rare conversation which is not internally unsettled by the inequality of its participants. Age, size, gender, class, authority: these are not the context of conversation, they are its organising principles.

Learning the self and learning the parameters of a life are never achieved once and for all, nor are they ever simply a matter of assimilating to one set of models while rejecting another. Growing up within the materially overwhelming oppression and poverty of certain communities which have been corroded by colonialism undoubtedly exacerbates the confusions of this learning, for it will take place within stark contrasts and contradictions between positive and negative values, and also amidst infinitely more uncertain, protean and dangerous constraints and possibilities. And it is with those uncertainties, with conflicting allegiances, with the manoeuvres developed by individuals and communities in order to survive, that I am concerned here, and with a black woman writer's narrative, grounded in a history which is reorganised by its vision and its voice.

V

Women do more than participate in the communities they inhabit: they are their foundation and *raison d'être*. For in all but the most sophisticated societies, communities are constructed round the bearing and rearing of children, round marriages and families and homes and the economy which supports them.[40] Women's absence from the

histories and the analyses of communities tells us a good deal about
traditions of political and scholarly discourse, about institutional
power structures and about the effects of these on the capacity or
willingness of women to challenge or reverse such structures. There is
a developing tradition of research and debate amongst feminists from
the Arab world[41] on questions to do with women's lives now and in
the past in a variety of Muslim societies. There have been some
centrally contentious questions: is men's controlling of women an
unchanging condition of Islam, for instance, or, on the contrary,
crucially produced by different economic conditions, different histories, different societies and geographies within the Arab world? Has
the influence of the West been liberating for women, or has its
presence as colonising force and capitalist entrepreneur exacerbated
women's economic dependence? Can 'women' remain an undifferentiated category in such discussion, permeable to neither class nor
cultural difference? What constitutes 'resistance' by women? And
what, finally and perhaps most importantly, constitutes valid testimony from women, given that many women in vast areas of the
colonised world will have had little or no schooling, may not be
literate and will certainly have had no access to a language likely to
be listened to with respect either in their own countries or in the
West?

Much Western women's writing, now and in the past, has
accepted, with varying amounts of frustration, that the terrains
marked out for women as their own – their reservations, as it were –
were at least theirs. Families, relations between women and between
women and men, the development of creative practical intelligence
and the cultivation of small-scale beauties and comforts, of well-
being: these were known areas. And, above all, there was the
bringing up of children. Many Western women writers have felt these
things as values – values which were often neglected, denigrated or
eclipsed by men, but which were undeniably worth preserving and
writing about. Jane Austen's well-known comment in a letter to her
nephew perfectly illustrates the tension out of which her best work
emerged:

> By the bye, my dear Edward, I am quite concerned for the loss
> your Mother mentions in her Letter; two Chapters & a half to
> be missing is monstrous! It is well that *I* have not been at
> Steventon lately, & therefore cannot be suspected of purloining
> them; two strong twigs & a half towards a Nest of my own,
> would have been something. I do not think however that any
> theft of that sort would be really very useful to me. What should
> I do with your strong, manly spirited Sketches, full of Variety

and Glow? How could I possibly join them on to the little bit
(two Inches wide) of Ivory on which I work with so fine a Brush,
as produces little effect after much labour?[42]

Spirited social confidence may serve to disguise (even to heal) the
split Jane Austen registers here between the world of men and the
separated and reduced world of women's lives. Yet even as Austen
tells us of what must often have been an exiguous and monotonous
experience, she is also telling us that what she made of it – her nest –
was a refuge.

For many women, however, there is not – could never have been –
such a refuge; and the split between men's and women's lives and the
scope of their activities will have been quite differently experienced.
A writer like Toni Morrison, for instance, would have had little
inducement to write about women's lives as proceeding somewhere
within a protected enclave beyond politics. For her, women are not
only as centrally implicated in a social history as men are; men and
women are inevitably implicated together, in relations with each
other which are not given, but are themselves produced by a
particular history. Sahar Khalifeh's novel *Wild Thorns*[43] is a
woman's novel in the same sense. It tells a story from the Palestinian
struggle in Nablus in the Israeli-occupied West Bank during the early
seventies, and is necessarily as much about men as it is about women.
What it shares with Morrison's work is the sense of political struggle
growing out of the intimate relations lived within an oppressed
community, and the effects on those relations and on that community of a politics of resistance.

In turning now to Morrison's most recent novel, *Beloved*, I hope to
do two things. The first is to look at a novel about slavery: a novel,
that is, about the original episode and the informing metaphor of all
histories of oppression founded on race. The second is to suggest
how a woman's vision of slavery may – by starting from sexual
relations – enable us to grasp certain vital aspects of the economic
and cultural character of the history of slavery in the United States.
Beloved is a novel created out of what Morrison has elsewhere
described as 'a survivalist intention to forget certain things'.[44]
Indeed, all her novels have been constructed, and are magically
unsettled, by the unique character of historical memory for African
Americans. That is to say, she has wanted to account for black
experience that has been ignored or quite inadequately narrated by
white historians and novelists; and, even more significantly, in order
to do that she has needed to confront precisely those aspects of the
experience which have blocked memory, made remembering intolerable and memories inexpressible, literally unspeakable. Indeed, the

very word 'rememory' is invented in *Beloved* to stand for something like a willed remembering which includes its own strenuous reluctance to return to the past.

The people of the novel are rooted in a known physical world, shared and chorally spoken for. In such a world even the hardest daily tasks may be welcomed, for there is 'nothing better than that to start the day's serious work of beating back the past'.[45] It is with the sudden and inescapable eruptions of the past into the present, however, and with the capacities of people to live with and rework the impossibly painful and humiliating, that her fiction is concerned. White guilt and breast-beating drop away to become a backcloth, an incomprehensible cause prompting the terrifying question: 'What *are* these people?'[46]

Toni Morrison's language enacts the conflicting movements of memory within the cultural history of those who were slaves and their descendants, people who have wrestled with that past and with its endlessly destructive consequences. Some of the richest and most finely controlled writing of the twentieth century re-creates a culture and a history characterised by illiteracy and by a speech spun out of resistance and inhumanly controlled. Illiteracy is experienced here not as a deprivation in itself, but as a symptom and symbol of the ultimate deprivations of a slave's life. When Paul D, an ex-slave, is shown an old newspaper cutting with a drawing of a black woman he tries not to recognise, he is whipped by fear, 'because there was no way in hell a black face could appear in a newspaper if the story was about something anybody wanted to hear'.[47]

With each of her earlier novels, Toni Morrison was inching her way back beyond twentieth-century experiencing of racism, poverty and injustice towards its origins in the history of slavery – a history which Morrison has likened to 'having World War Two for two hundred years'.[48] *Beloved* is set in Ohio, on the edges of Cincinnati. It begins in 1873, with Sethe and her adolescent daughter, Denver, alone in No. 124 Bluestone Road, a house haunted by a dead baby. Remembering starts at once, gingerly backing away from the present to repopulate the house and recover its past as a refuge for escaping slaves and its brief apparent heyday, when Sethe's mother-in-law, Baby Suggs, seemed able to hold together the remnants of her family and preached powerfully to the members of a black community so damaged by their lives as slaves that they must learn from scratch to attend to their own bodies:

'Here,' she said, 'in this here place, we flesh; flesh that weeps, laughs; flesh that dances on bare feet in grass. Love it. Love it hard. Yonder they do not love your flesh. They despise it. They don't love your eyes; they'd just as soon pick em out. No more do they love the skin on your back. Yonder they flay it. And O my people they do not love your hands. Those they only use, tie, bind, chop off and leave empty. Love your hands! Love them.'[49]

Slowly, delicately and shockingly the narrative picks its way backwards to Sethe's girlhood as a slave, to her escape, to her isolation within a shared past, which Morrison never allows to be more appalling for those who suffered it than the subsequent mutilations they were to commit on themselves in its wake. Time and time again the narrative appears to recoil from its own destination. The novel tells us about implements of torture, imaginatively designed to cause the greatest pain, to curb movement and speech and sleep. It alludes to the viciousness, the unending and inhuman cruelty of white slave-owners in cold, brilliantly lit asides. It does not forget that there were kinder white people, that there are pleasures for Sethe to remember too. But the story of slavery it tells is always from within the heads of those who were slaves.

Paul D, the only survivor of the male slaves Sethe knew years ago on Sweet Home Farm, arrives at No. 124. It is eighteen years since he last saw Sethe, whom he loved and generously relinquished to his friend Halle. Now he becomes her lover and they begin to be happy. They do not discuss the past very much, but we learn that Sethe herself arrived at this same house in 1855 with four small children, the youngest only just delivered with the help of a runaway white girl in a boat during her flight north. Sethe's back had been suppurating then from the beating she was given, during which she was also raped. Her back, with its branch-like weals and blossoming pus, has since become an elaborate tree of scarred flesh, made bizarrely beautiful by Paul D's loving her, and standing for the secrets her body contains and emits in a gradual gathering of voices.

Then Beloved appears: a young woman fully and strangely dressed walks out of the water and waits for Sethe and Denver. Her skin is unlined except for three minute vertical scratches on her forehead. Her simplicity and unworldliness are disconcerting, blandly and mysteriously malevolent. Sethe and Denver are drawn to this needy young woman. Paul D is on his guard. We have no difficulty in recognising Beloved as the baby's ghost which has haunted the house for so long, now grown up. We learn that Sethe's two sons left the house, unable to bear the manifestations of the ghost baby. We learn, too, that Sethe had a baby daughter – not the youngest – who died. Her gravestone bears only the word 'Beloved', for Sethe could not afford to have 'Dearly' carved on it as well. By the time we are told the truth, harshly and as seen through the eyes of hostile outsiders, we have experienced Sethe's choice, her decision, the life she has made for herself for the last eighteen years. We see the scene which greets Sethe's sadistic old master, known as 'schoolteacher', as he arrives on horseback to reclaim his runaway slave and her children, who are legally his:

> Inside, two boys bled in the sawdust and dirt at the feet of a nigger woman holding a blood-soaked child to her chest with one hand and an infant by the heels in the other. She did not look at them; she simply swung the baby toward the wall planks, missed and tried to connect a second time, when out of nowhere – in the ticking time the men spent staring at what there was to stare at – the old nigger boy, still mewing, ran through the door behind them and snatched the baby from the arch of its mother's swing.
>
> Right off it was clear, to schoolteacher especially, that there was nothing there to claim.[50]

Beloved has come back to punish her mother, but also to elicit her love. She is on the point of strangling Sethe when her stroking hands are stopped by tenderness, by her delight in her mother's neck, 'the damp skin that felt like chamois and looked like taffeta'.[51] Toni Morrison has based Sethe's story on a true one of an ex-slave who killed her children to prevent their recapture. The experience of slavery which the novel so extraordinarily gives us begins from this act and from the compelling need to understand it. The lives of people who are denied their own names, denied the marriage ceremony and denied the right to love their children as parents is explosively compressed within that image. When Paul D learns that Sethe, 'this sweet sturdy woman', has murdered her own child, he is moved to leave and is only eventually drawn back by love. He recalls a dead friend saying of the woman he loved: 'She is a friend of my mind. She gather me, man. The pieces I am, she gather them and give them back to me in all the right order.'[52] Finally, Sethe explains her murderous actions:

> That anybody white could take your whole self for anything that came to mind. Not just work, kill, or maim you, but dirty you. Dirty you so bad you couldn't like yourself anymore. Dirty you so bad you forgot who you were and couldn't think it up. And though she and others lived through and got over it, she could never let it happen to her own. The best thing she was, was her children. Whites might dirty *her* all right, but not her best thing, her beautiful, magical best thing – the part of her that was clean.[53]

And finally Paul D gently says to her: 'You your best thing, Sethe. You are.'[54]

Beloved is dispersed by love. She disappears and is gradually forgotten. Her need to understand her own death, to know for certain that her mother killed her because she loved her, is met. That painful, paradoxical love is matched by the discovery Paul D makes during his eighteen years of desperate escapes and recaptures – that 'he could not help being astonished by the beauty of this land that was not his'.[55] Love combines a capacity to be moved by beauty and pleasure and a recognition that human beings are always human.

VI

I have wanted in this chapter to characterise the seductiveness of certain critical accounts of imperialism and colonialism and, at the same time, to challenge the tendency they share with other 'grand' social theories to omit women and feminist analysis from their field of attention and their mode of interpretation. Such an omission simultaneously separates, subsumes and subordinates the category of women. It also takes women for granted –paternalistically, no doubt – as undifferentiated elements of a collective humanity: a view which would be easier to accept were that collective humanity not itself, within such theories, under perpetual scrutiny for its splits and conflicts especially. Yet pleas for the inclusion of women within such political theories are likely to be met by objections that they are sectional, sectarian and certainly distracting pleas. The very notion of a testable hypothesis, after all, or of a theory with real explanatory power and usefulness, depends on intellectual traditions which prioritise qualities of thought like coherence or generalisability. So that the invoking of women as absent from such theory and from its making – or as misrepresented by it – can appear to disturb the very foundation and character of serious and valuable academic work.

Possible solutions to this impasse can seem to recede irrevocably when we find that even accounts of oppression which emphasise the policing of language and representation omit women and feminism in this way. It becomes clear soon enough that tacking women on to such accounts, or attempting to make a bit of room for them, simply fails. Turning to a writer like Toni Morrison may at least enable us to understand something of this failure.

Divorced from the specificity of experience of those who were slaves as well as those who were involved in other ways, slavery becomes an abstraction, a moveable structure – with, it is true, a history and certain causative and institutional features which can be studied. There are several academic disciplines which may, singly or collaboratively, enable the pursuit of such study: history, economics, law, philosophy, psychology, sociology, and so on. If, however, the validity of knowledge about slavery arrived at in these ways is allowed to pre-empt the validity of the particular and the individual, more will be lost, I think, than particular case histories, or scraps of rare autobiographical or documentary testimony. Slavery as a complex history will be simplified and distorted and our understanding of it impoverished. An inevitable consequence of that will be the suppression of female experience wherever that experience cannot straightforwardly be thought of as 'human' experience.

There is nothing in Toni Morrison's work which smacks of redressing the balance or of a focus on women's experience at the expense of men's: the reverse. Her books begin from a community clinging to survival under the intolerable conditions of slavery and then against the most crushing racism and poverty. Since her novels engage with the history of such communities and with their internal and external social relations, women will be at the centre of these imagined worlds, because there is nowhere else where they could be. Morrison begins by assuming quite simply that communities *are* women, just as they are men, and that they are also produced and maintained by the connections which are possible between women and men. A feminism which would abstract women from community in order to isolate an alternative tradition for them only mimics those modes of thought which have made it so easy to suppress or marginalise women's demands for inclusion.

I began with *Villette* and I have ended with *Beloved*: two wonderful novels by women. I could be charged, I suppose, with having done no more than pitted women's novels against men's arguments – and taking unfair advantage by doing so – in an attempt to upstage male discourses of scholarship and revolutionary incitement by listening to the beguiling rhythms of narrative. I have also shifted ground, moving without warning from my difficulties with a critique of Orientalist scholarship and an analysis of the cultural and psychological effects of colonial oppression to a fictional account of slavery; and from arguments within feminism about learning and identity to questions about how fictional constructions of experience get read. Once the category 'women' is understood to be crossed by the categories of class and race, it becomes possible to challenge those modes of thought and language which have made that connection almost unimaginable and almost impossible, therefore, to articulate. A high price is exacted for obedience to standards of intellectual coherence and cohesion, consistency of theoretical level, method of analysis, and so on. Elsewhere I have likened women's dealings with language to a bilingual's, and in doing so I was suggesting that there were strengths as well as drawbacks implied by the analogy.[56] Among the strengths was an awareness possessed by bilinguals that form and meaning in language stand in a tricky relation to one another, a relation which emerges from the material and historical world in which language is used and which language articulates for us. That awareness – which is harder for monolinguals to come by – extends to an understanding of the struggles for power and for powerful meanings, which language enacts.

It will not be possible to persuade most scholars and intellectuals to reconsider, let alone redescribe, their research and their arguments in the light of a dawning realisation that half the world has been systematically ignored or traduced by their accounts of it. What does begin to look like a possibility, though, is that they might learn to hear hitherto suppressed voices as potentially oppositional and different, not simply as alternative. Cora Kaplan puts this question about reading Alice Walker's *The Color Purple*:

> How can we then, in Britain, 'read' *The Color Purple* so that its cultural and political conditions of production are not deracinated, so that its narrative retains its rich, polychromatic texture, its provocative politics? How can we keep it from being bleached into a pallid progressive homily, an uncontentious, sentimental, harmless piece of international libertarianism?[57]

Feminist readings are inevitably critical readings: readings, that is, which expose in texts what is suppressed by them as well as what is visibly contestable in them.

5

Feasters and Spoilsports

I wish there was no such thing as jokes.

Four-year-old boy

I

I can feel the elegiac warmth of late September, when at the beginning of my third year at Cambridge, in 1954, I went back early, before term. There was a small commotion in my college, I remember. A handsome American woman, from Vassar or Bryn Mawr, had sent her car and jewels ahead and they hadn't arrived. The few of us in the building were called to the library and sleepily questioned by the police. Back in my new room, strewn with cups and books and a kettle retrieved from summer storage, I muttered to myself about cars and jewels and what did she think she'd do with such things here anyway. My room was graced by six high barred windows. One bar had been neatly sawn through, so that the room provided the best way into college for anyone who came back late. It was a pretty room, none the less, and popular with mice. Having moved my desk to a rakish slant across one corner of the room and casually settled a full bottle of rum on the ledge above the gas fire, I left for town.

G2, in one of the men's colleges, a cluttered pair of rooms facing inward to a mean wisteria-covered courtyard, was shared by two friends. One, for most of the time elegantly prone, was later and with some ignominy diagnosed as suffering from too much sleep, not too much sin. The other, his slight squint trained on next year and London, arose each day at six to get started on his letters of apology and application. The dull blue curtains were drawn against the sun. A typewriter clattered in the bedroom and light groans issued from my friend on his back as he gauged the temperature of the day outside from the sounds of footsteps. Three more friends came in. Someone had brought a bottle of wine, someone else some beer. This year was to be a special one for us all, it was agreed; a year when pleasure would prevail, when wit, laughter and many varieties of bad behaviour would reach new heights of creative refinement. We would be Falstaffian. Might we not indeed constitute ourselves as the Falstaffian society, dedicated to excess and friendship and literature and, above all, to sexual intercourse? There would be no more restraint, no cowardice, no inhibitions. We would have no time for the drearily authoritarian, the pettily anxious, the abjectly obedient. Someone read aloud from Henry IV Part I:

> Marry then, sweet wag, when thou art king let not us that are squires of the night's body be called thieves of the day's beauty; let us be Diana's foresters, gentlemen of the shade, minions of the moon, and let men say we be men of good government, being governed as the sea is by our noble and chaste mistress the moon, under whose countenance we steal.

And unwisely I asked if I was to be Diana in all this, or just another of her foresters, a wag.

'Oh, there are parts for you,' someone airily replied, 'Mistress Quickly, Doll Tearsheet.'

My question, easily read from here as spoilsport, spoiled nothing. The society would need more women, and others who would be back in a week were considered. I blushed at my uneasiness, hoped I'd got the joke and that I'd be able to make one or two myself in time: for a sense of humour was as mandatory for mothers as for playmates. The euphoria of that day evaporated, of course, though its memory conjures up other times. 'Panache' was a favourite word, and 'clad only in his panache' was how a friend's scaling of King's College in the dead of night came to be told.

It is not by any means that memories like these are miserable ones; nor do I feel in the least inclined to relinquish or disown them. They are as much a part of my youth as they are part of the youth of those young men who were, admittedly, more likely than I was to figure heroically in them. But I am taunted by their ambiguity, and I write of them as dilemmas. There is, especially, my uncertain membership of a group which was already so adept at its own narrative and so clear about the traditions impinging on that narrative. A few of my male contemporaries have, in fact, written of that time, of 'backs' and bikes, of Mill Lane and the Eagle pub, of friends and supervisors and even of girls.[1] Their reminiscences are full of jokes and revelations of a kind which are to be understood as presaging later achievements or surprises.

It may well be thought instructive that I should fix on a moment before term began, when, as it happened, I was the only woman in this group of men. I think I need to separate myself like this to avoid seeming to speak for other – let alone all – women. Certainly my sense of difference and isolation was not at all straightforwardly shared by my women friends, for our relations with men could characteristically cut us off from one another in this world remembered so unequivocally as golden by so many of the men in it. The young woman with whom I have to identify in a whole sequence of scenes is hard to fathom. I think of her cringing from her own duplicity, ashamed of the sheer accomplishment represented by her quizzical glance, running from invitations and from the impossible demands they threatened to make on wit and wardrobe. And I recoil now at the thought that this young woman was in some way desired by one or more of the men in the group, that she knew this, that her head and senses were flushed with the thought. And though, of course, she'd have wanted to claim an additional history and purpose to her presence there, an awkward but compelling honesty would have made both quite difficult to pinpoint.

Now I am not so sure that I am not missing even from my own memories. Can I hope to watch, let alone to inhabit, the body of that young woman more than thirty-five years ago, within a narrative which has always found it so easy to dispose of her testimony? And what would that testimony have contained anyway? Pleasure? Desire? Whose pleasure and desire? A sense of time, perhaps, of a moment holding what might become of us all? Was it ever *not* the pleasure and desire of others that she knew about? And what *was* the pleasure in the strange chance of knowing herself only as the object of others' intentions or momentary covetousness? Her eyes seem too open and shining. She will learn to guard against displays of ignorance, innocence. What could she say in defence of her essay about *Anna Karenina* to the brusque military man who obliged his male students to get to their feet when she arrived? A city of men. She was welcome here so long as she laughed and danced for them in the ways literature told them women could and did. Let her beware, though, of asking for quarter in the examinations hall or of asserting her difference from them in ways which embarrassed them.

If women are not always sure how they stand in relation to traditions of knowledge and study and rationality, how infinitely and ludicrously harder still is it for them to ascertain what their position might be within traditions of criticism and – more interestingly still – of heresy and subversiveness. For men can seem to have appropriated the management of misrule as well as the imposition of order, so that women's voicing of their objections may get as niggardly a look-in as their assertions of what is worth knowing. Yet it is also true that women's recent discovery, or recovery, of their marginality has increased feminism's critical scope and its leverage, and there are male critics now who are envious, it seems, of this surprising and belated gift of outsiderdom to those they like to regard – though only when it suits them, of course – as their equals in privilege.

There are, then, a number of reasons for starting from this characteristically frivolous moment in my own life, and its frivolity is one of them. For though – as I shall go on to show – my concern is with girls learning to be readers and with what that entails, I am also concerned with women's relation to jokes, to criticism and to subversiveness. Carlo Ginzburg, whose study of a sixteenth-century reader (and miller) will come into this later on, starts from the assertion that

> only knowledge of the historical and social variability of the person of the reader will really lay the foundations for a history of ideas that is also *qualitatively* different.[2]

So that my readings in this chapter of Bakhtin, Vološinov, Ginzburg and Atwood, which will be viewed (I assume) as tendentious and idiosyncratic, will come flanked by some sense of how this reader, at least, came to read as she does.

II

When, in his wonderful book about Rabelais, the Russian critic Bakhtin writes that

> the woman of Gallic tradition is the bodily grave of man. She represents in person the undoing of pretentiousness, of all that is finished, completed, and exhausted. She is the inexhaustible vessel of conception, which dooms all that is old and terminated[3]

it is possible to feel, if only for a split second, that this might indeed prefigure some kind of confidence amongst feminists in the efficacy of their point of view and of their puncturing and mockery. And there are most certainly some ways in which that is so; as Julia Kristeva, whose work is intimately developed out of Bakhtin's, has shown.[4] The theories of language and literature worked on by Bakhtin and his friend and colleague, Vološinov, from the early thirties, which build so creatively on doubleness and ambivalence as essential aspects of human beings' use of language, do chime very strikingly with the forms of doubleness and ambivalence I have wanted to associate with female experience. Yet neither Bakhtin nor Vološinov appears to have recognised the implications of their ideas for women; and in Bakhtin's work – most particularly in *Rabelais and His World* (which was written in the late thirties, completed in 1940 and first published in the Soviet Union in the early sixties) – women's presence within culture is slippery indeed, and entirely untheorised.

Bakhtin's Rabelais is, above all, a Renaissance writer, whose work connected a medieval folk culture with an especially high point in a developing and sophisticated literature and in a number

of European languages which were becoming increasingly differentiated:

> In the Renaissance, laughter in its most radical, universal, and at
> the same time gay form emerged from the depths of folk culture;
> it emerged but once in the course of history, over a period of
> some fifty or sixty years (in various countries and at various
> times) and entered with its popular (vulgar) language the sphere
> of great literature and high ideology. It appeared to play an
> essential role in the creation of such masterpieces of world
> literature as Boccaccio's *Decameron*, the novels of Rabelais and
> Cervantes, Shakespeare's dramas and comedies, and others. The
> walls between official and nonofficial literature were inevitably
> to crumble, especially because in the most important ideological
> sectors these walls also served to separate languages – Latin
> from the vernacular. The adoption of the vernacular by litera-
> ture and by certain ideological spheres was to sweep away or at
> least weaken these boundaries.[5]

Bakhtin's book marks out the character of this explosive encounter
between the Middle Ages and the Renaissance, and between a largely
oral folk culture and the beginnings of a finely aware and controlled
literature. A central theme of the book is his tracking of the
persistence of carnival, of forms of what Bakhtin calls 'unofficial'
culture, forms which appear to threaten the 'official' culture, denying, undermining, and also acting out a violent destruction of that
culture's most fundamental structures within an endless dramati-
sation of change, renewal, rebirth.

The substance of carnival is laughter, characterised here as the
quintessentially shared human experience, a vital collective capacity,
simultaneously allowed for and ruled out by the legitimate social
order. And as Julia Kristeva puts it, 'a carnival participant is both
actor and spectator; he loses his sense of individuality'.[6] So carnival
is playing and travesty and even, by extension, a 'free and critical
historical consciousness',[7] occupying the places and times of ordinary life, but standing also as 'the true feast of time'.[8] It requires no
roped-off stage or occasion for itself, however, and is always, as
Bakhtin puts it, 'saturated with actuality'.[9] The official/unofficial
relation, unceasingly protean in its manifestations, delivers itself of
stories and imagery which bear out and proliferate ambivalence,
contrast, contradiction. The grotesque, the exaggerated, the violent
and the abusive create an alternative but recognisable cosmos, which
is also the outlandish, freakish underside of a world of order and
light.

Bakhtin was intent on signalling precisely those elements of this tradition which fed Rabelais, and those which had by the beginning of the eighteenth century already become attenuated, vitiated by individualism: so that in Bakhtin's view, Rabelais was generally misread in the eighteenth century and by 1776 an expurgated edition of his novel could be published 'especially for the ladies'.[10] This shift to individualism, to what Bakhtin calls the 'monologic', utterly disrupted the force of a folk culture which relied on its 'dialogic', conversational, interactive character, on what it drew uncomplicatedly from the shared — indeed, universal — physical truths of human life. Individualism reduces the playful to the obscene, in Bakhtin's account, and the robustly physical and sexual to the scatological. The body, with its orifices and emissions, the sexual act itself, pregnancy, childbirth — these are elements of an imagery of freedom and fearlessness in the medieval world of carnival, in which the celebration of life entails a confrontation with the body's absurdities as well as its vulnerabilities.

Essentially, carnival laughter challenges categories by blurring or reversing them, so that male and female, old and young, even high and low become interchangeable terms within a humour which exploits and ignores their difference and makes each oddly parasitic upon the other. In this almost infinitely reversible and remakeable world, human life is sustained by uproarious and therapeutic disrespect, and human activity becomes an animated version of Mr Venus's shop for replaceable human parts in Dickens's *Our Mutual Friend*. Sorting women out from all this, even winnowing out the bits which belong especially to them, is no easy task, therefore; for though Bakhtin lovingly accounts for human genitalia and their multiple functions, sexual differentiation is virtually forbidden. Cavities, protuberances, emptyings and swellings, even pregnancy and childbirth are envisaged as simply human functions, exemplary in their tussles with death and decay and prized as assertions of the more ungovernable of human energies.

But this is not quite true. Women are sometimes distinguishable amidst this seething mass of limbs as it heaves with laughter. There are prostitutes, for instance, and noble ladies, and there are old hags with pregnant bellies, whose grotesque and anomalous bodies merge birth with death in an image which is both monstrous and hilarious. The female body generally serves as a metaphor for kinds of degradation, but also for an equally death-dealing gentility.

A difficulty in all this is disentangling Bakhtin, the Soviet literary historian and theorist, from Rabelais, the sixteenth-century 'runaway Franciscan friar'[11] and misogynist, and both from Bakhtin's celebration of a rebellious popular tradition and a humanist culture on the one hand, and Rabelais's extraordinary subversive novel on the other. Yet entanglement could be said to impregnate Bakhtin's sense both of culture and of language, and of the literary theorist's relation to the books he (in this case) undertakes to untangle. For what Bakhtin took from Formalist accounts of literature was enriched by his insistence on historical specificity and on the communicative character of language. His reading of Rabelais, and the reading he wishes his readers to take from him, insists on the absolute connectedness of a text with a history and a tradition. An example may help me to penetrate this. Bakhtin quotes a scene from the second half of Rabelais's novel in which a bride is violently assaulted:

> The bride crying laughed, and laughing cried, because the catchpole was not satisfied with drubbing her without choice or distinction of members, but had also rudely roused and toused her; pulled off her topping, and not having the fear of her husband before his eyes, treacherously trepignemanpenillorifrizonoufresterfumbledtumbled and squeezed her lower parts . . . The steward held his left arm in a scarf, as if it had been rent and torn in twain. I think it was the devil, said he, that moved me to assist at these nuptials; shame on ill luck; I must needs be meddling with a pox, and now see what I have got by the bargain, both my arms are wretchedly engoulevezinemassed and bruised. Do you call this a wedding? . . . This is, on my word, even just such another feast as was that of the Lapithae described by the philosopher of Samosata.[12]

Bakhtin turns to this moment within an argument about thrashings and other kinds of ritual violence which, if we are to make sense of them in Rabelais's novel, must be read in the context of the carnival tradition. Bakhtin accepts the thrashing of the bride as 'erotic rather than simply harsh [bridal beating]' and it is also, through his choice of quotation and omission, relegated to a position of secondary concern within a sequence of thrashings of the catchpoles, who are, after all, officers of the law. This whole episode, says Bakhtin,

> presents no ordinary fight, no commonplace blows administered in everyday life. The blows have here a broadened, symbolic, ambivalent meaning; they at once kill and regenerate, put an end to the old life and start the new. The entire episode is filled with a bacchic atmosphere.[13]

The sleight of hand is a familiar one. Violence against a woman is conceded as sexual and is mitigated first by its playful character and second for being a mere by-product of examples of equal (and equally playful) violence between men, which in this case acquires broader social significance because it consists of fisticuffs between the people and the law. The particular tradition of 'bridal beating' is made to disappear, almost unremarked, into the general 'humanity' of the protagonists and the character of the ritual in which they participate. So that even 'the erotic' becomes desexed, the feelings and sensations to which it might refer displaced from the individual men or women to a generalised sexuality. The fact that male violence towards a woman cannot quite be subsumed into the rough-and-tumble of male fisticuffs or the playing out of social rebelliousness is met only by this offhand allusion to 'the erotic' and by gathering into a general ambivalence the bride's uncertainty as to whether to laugh or cry.

Women have often enough been thought to be bad at 'getting' jokes and worse at telling them. So many jokes are, after all, about women. Nor is it clear that women's problems with jokes are in the least eased by claims for their (therapeutic) seriousness and for the general healthiness of humour and a good laugh. In fact, women's insecure relation to jokes could hardly be better illustrated than by Rabelais's one about the young Gargantua's triumphant arrival in Paris, which Bakhtin treats to a considerable fanfare *qua* joke:

> Then smiling, he untied his fair braguette, and drawing out his mentul into the open air, he so bitterly all-to-be-pissed them, that he drowned two hundred and sixty thousand four hundred and eighteen, besides the women and little children.[14]

Comparisons with, for instance, the one about a pint, a pie and a woman all for the price of a beer ('Hang on a minute, whose pies are they?') don't need labouring. The issue is simpler even than the mode of disparagement: are women able to laugh at such jokes, and if they don't laugh, can they explain why they don't without crying?

Of course, women are present in Bakhtin as they are present in Rabelais. The American critic Wayne Booth[15] discovered a kind of feminism for himself through his reading of Bakhtin's exegesis on that incident in Rabelais's novel where '600,014 dogs . . . follow the lady and besmirch her dress, Panurge having sprinkled it with the diced genital organs of a bitch'.[16] Booth found himself able to imagine and even empathise with the female reader of such a passage, and while deploring its multiple discourtesies, drew attention to the more important question of the absence of women's voices speaking on their own behalf in Bakhtin's account of Rabelais. This, as Booth pointed out, is unsurprising but also peculiarly noticeable in a book which adumbrates a theory of polyphony, of multivoiced language.

Women are physically present in Bakhtin's world. They are also topics of conversation and debate. They become the split, polarised 'woman' of the '*querelle des femmes*', a dispute which, as Bakhtin tells us, 'stirred France, especially in 1542–1550'. This dispute about the nature of women and of wedlock engaged 'nearly all French poets, writers, and philosophers'.[17] It appears not to have particularly engaged women, let alone wives, those experts on both subjects. Two lines, Bakhtin tells us, run through this debate:

> The first one is usually called 'the Gallic tradition' [*tradition gauloise*]: this is the medieval concept, a negative attitude toward women. The second line, which Abel Lefranc calls the 'idealizing tradition', exalts womanhood. At the time of Rabelais, this second line was supported by the 'Platonizing' poets and was based in part on the tradition of chivalry of the Middle Ages.[18]

Having admitted that Rabelais undoubtedly took the first, 'negative' attitude to women, Bakhtin goes on to make another distinction within this first, Gallic tradition: between a popular comic view of women and the ascetic tendency of medieval Christianity. It is to this distinction that Bakhtin holds particularly: for the comic view of women invested them with an admirable (if unfocused) human energy and with a potential for criticism, rebellion and 'the undoing of pretentiousness'.[19] Women, then, are redeemed by the jokes that may be made about them. What about the jokes they may make themselves?

In a chapter of his book in which Bakhtin explains how the popular cultural forms which so enriched Rabelais's novel came to degenerate during the seventeenth century, he singles out a particular literary form consisting of short pieces, known as *Caquets* (Cackles), which were most often written as dialogues between women. Bakhtin introduces these as examples of 'the traditions of grotesque realism [which] are even more feeble and narrow in seventeenth-century literature, with its dialogue'. He tells us that these pieces were probably 'composed by several authors',[20] and we are to assume, I think, that these authors were men. We are to assume this because *Caquets* took the form of conversations between women which were being overheard by an eavesdropper. Bakhtin gives examples: women talking round the bed of a woman who has just had a baby is one; the chatter of market women, of servants, of fisherwomen, are others. His scorn for these literary works is withering:

> The entire work is based on eavesdropping and voyeurism and frank discussion of what was heard and seen. Compared to the dialogue-containing literature of the sixteenth century, this work shows the complete degeneracy of marketplace frankness: it is nothing but the washing of personal unclean underwear.[21]

The importance of this historical moment and its marking of change and contrast for Bakhtin's argument transcends for him, predictably, the kinds of question I want to raise about women's voices and our access as readers to accounts they might give of their own experience:

> The seventeenth-century dialogues are interesting historical documents reflecting this degeneracy; the frank talk of marketplace and banquet hall was transformed into the novel of private manners of modern times. And yet a tiny spark of the carnival flame was still alive in these writings.[22]

These are virtually the only references Bakhtin makes to women talking, either in Rabelais's novel or in other works of the period which he mentions. In fact, of course, these were not anyway the unmediated voices of women, but artefacts embodying kinds of mimicry and ventriloquism. Though Bakhtin does concede their vestigial relation to carnival, he recoils from their emphasis on the private, the personal, the secret, the withdrawn and unshared (or unwillingly shared) character of the language. And the physical and sexual world to which these conversations allude is unclean, associated with women's *private* parts, their soiled underwear. Yet this is also the only moment in all this celebration of sexual appetite and profligacy which allows that women are different from men; that they are human beings who bleed and may become pregnant as a consequence of participating in the sexual act, and who go through labour to give birth; and that these are functions they do not share with the whole of the human race.

So to some extent women's participation in all this fun and feasting, this celebratory death-defying sex, this fearless rebellion, is an illusion. Women are easier to pick out in the imagery of the backcloth than in the performance in the foreground. As Bakhtin puts it in a passage which sings the praises of overeating and of excretion to Rabelais's refrain, '*O belle matière fécale*', 'the limits between the devouring and the devoured body are erased'.[23] Bakhtin envisages women's devouring orifices, gaping and hellish openings in so much of Rabelais's novel, as dangerous entries to the underworld, to disaster and death. Yet women are also devoured; and one is bound to recall the hunting and eating of women in Richardson's *Clarissa*. The comedy will contain the doubleness of pleasure and hell for men in all this. It is not clear that the same comic sense will make room for an equivalent account of the grim hazards in store for women; for their lives, like their bodies, are melted down into a generalised human existence, where men squeamishly repudiate all those pains and leakages which are not common to both sexes.

III

The ways in which women may be simultaneously present in and absent from Bakhtin's reading of a popular cultural tradition, and an elaborate literary work which derives from that tradition, are significant in the light of the theory of language and literature which Bakhtin and Vološinov developed. An insistence on the irreducibly social character of language and on its essentially 'dialogic' substance has to be understood in relation to Bakhtin's quarrel with Saussurian structural linguistics and his break with the Formalist work on literary forms carried out in the Soviet Union during the twenties.

An account of language which would include questions about style as something more than individual idiosyncrasy would need, Bakhtin believed, to start from the conversational and interactive, communicative character of language, as it is learned (although he did not focus on this as his compatriot and contemporary Vygotsky did) and used. In the essay 'The Problem of Speech Genres',[24] written towards the end of his life, Bakhtin spells out this reorientation or revision as a theory of language which would have to be able to explain that though 'each separate utterance is individual . . . each sphere in which language is used develops its own *relatively stable types* of these utterances'.[25] These types he calls 'speech genres', and they pre-exist individual utterances as normative forms within language communities.

An utterance, then, is quite different from a sentence, being defined neither by its content nor by its linguistic composition, but in terms of its boundaries:

> The boundaries of each concrete utterance as a unit of speech communication are determined by a *change of speaking subjects,* that is, a change of speakers.[26]

For there is always another speaker; not only because no speaker is ever 'the first speaker, the one who disturbs the eternal silence of the universe',[27] but because all utterance — and Bakhtin includes everything from a single word to a three-volume novel in this idea — presupposes, and indeed requires, another speaker, hearer, reader, interlocutor. And this is so even when the other speaker is absent or silent, for other speakers are implied by the character of language itself.

To some extent this is what is meant by 'dialogism', the 'dialogic': an idea at once central to Bakhtin's theory of language and something like a critical and discriminating principle in his work on literature. Even within Bakhtin's own work the term has incompatible faces to it and presents problems. Ken Hirschkop, to whose excellent critique of Bakhtin I shall return, puts it like this: 'dialogism, the common term, is both an essential feature of all discourse and a specific oppositional practice within it.'[28] Can dialogism stand simultaneously for the social and conversational base of language and for those uses of language (and particularly literary uses) which challenge what Bakhtin characterises as the monologic forms of public, official language and the inflexible and authoritarian forces articulated by such language? At the very least this ambiguity makes one wonder whose alternative, rebellious and critical voices Bakhtin is hearing in novels, and just what sort of range is encompassed by the chorus of dissonant voices a novel may rehearse or enact.

Vološinov, in his *Marxism and the Philosophy of Language*, inserts into Bakhtin's account of language as the battleground for oppositions to an otherwise monologic and impermeable official culture a more recognisably Marxist flavour. In a much-quoted passage, to which several feminist writers have turned, Vološinov introduces class, conflict and ideology into Bakhtin's somewhat undifferentiated voices of unruly popular objection:

> Existence reflected in sign is not merely reflected but *refracted*. How is this refraction of existence in the ideological sign determined? By an intersecting of differently oriented social interests within one and the same sign community, i.e. *by the class struggle*.
>
> Class does not coincide with the sign community, i.e. with the community which is the totality of users of the same set of signs for ideological communication. Thus various different classes will use one and the same language. As a result, differently oriented accents intersect in every ideological sign. Sign becomes an arena of the class struggle.[29]

For 'class' we may read 'gender' – at least in principle. It is in fact difficult to find in Bakhtin either class oppression or class conflict, let alone the ideological consequences and hegemonic tensions of such conflict. Instead, the dialogic expresses a perpetual social and individual tussle between those who rule and those who are ruled; between the power of those who maintain order and the potential of those who disrupt it. And that potential is to be found within a collective and popular creativity and within art forms which may shape that creativity towards specific purposes.

Novels – and amongst novels those of Rabelais and then of Dostoevsky – were for Bakhtin exemplars of literary works whose form encourages the expression of a collective resistance to manifestations of singleness and authority, even and indeed especially, the author's. We have seen how Bakhtin argues this for Rabelais and

Rabelais's use of popular cultural models. A different, though similar, case is made for the novels of Dostoevky:

> Dostoevsky's particular gift for hearing and understanding all voices immediately and simultaneously, a gift whose equal we find only in Dante, also permitted him to create the polyphonic novel. The objective complexity, contradictoriness and multi-voicedness of Dostoevsky's epoch, the position of the déclassé intellectual and the social wanderer, his deep biographical and inner participation in the objective multi-leveledness of life and finally his gift for seeing the world in terms of interaction and coexistence – all this prepared the soil in which Dostoevsky's polyphonic novel was to grow.[30]

We should probably take from this a somewhat reduced set of meanings for polyphony and for the dialogic. Indeed, accepting that this is so may begin to suggest reasons for the largely unheard voices of women within Bakhtin's analysis. For the voices Bakhtin adjures his solitary writer or intellectual to let in, to incorporate into and set against his own, are ultimately undifferentiated and unspecific. They present an almost metaphysical notion of multiplicity, collaboration and diversity, and they have no clear material or group existence in a class society. From his Marxist perspective, Hirschkop puts it like this:

> . . . a social theory unable to conceive of social connection in terms other than the interaction of consciousnesses cannot explain how social institutions can work to limit or occlude consciousness.[31]

It must be the case that a social theory of language can only be as effectively explanatory as the theory of society on which it depends. Battle is undeniably joined in Bakhtin's theory, though it may be more of a 'rhetorical battle between groups of intellectuals',[32] as Hirschkop says, than a struggle between groups with absolutely hostile economic interests and commitments to change. The corrupt and 'monologic' society of Bakhtin's theoretical universe will have all too little trouble maintaining itself against mere novels, for all their mockery and laughter. For power and control are acquired and kept precisely through understanding and exploiting the differences between the canonical and the subversive, between standard languages and dialects, between literacy and oral culture. Bakhtin undoubtedly offers us too easy and too optimistic a portrait of those in power. It is as if, as Hirschkop expresses it, 'political domination issues from the ignorance and pretensions of a deluded ruling class . . . and the deflation of these pretences should lead directly to the crumbling of the political edifice'.[33] There is a connection between this underestimating of power and Bakhtin's idealising of the popular, for in the end these abstractions come close to locking his argument into a kind of Romanticism which can specify neither difference nor similarity.

Yet Bakhtin was writing during some of the darkest and most troubled years of Soviet history. His work, in its extraordinary scale and scope, its learning and its analytical inventiveness, was produced under the least promising circumstances. To discover Bakhtin through his writing on the novel, on Rabelais, on Dostoevsky, and Vološinov through his book on language and his critique of Freud, is to be unusually moved and excited by such passionate intelligence, vast reading, humanity. Bakhtin's tenacity in relation to his intellectual project survived his work going unpublished, undistributed, often therefore almost unread. One story about him goes like this:

> Sovetsky pisatel [Soviet Writer], the publishing house that was to bring out Bakhtin's book *The Novel of Education and Its Significance in the History of Realism*, was blown up in the early months of the German invasion, with the loss of the manuscript on which he had worked for at least two years (1936–38). Bakhtin retained only certain preparatory materials and a prospectus of the book; due to the paper shortage, he had torn them up page by page during the war to make wrappers for his endless chain of cigarettes. He began smoking pages from the conclusion of the manuscript, so what we have is a small portion of its opening section, primarily about Goethe.[34]

What is also remarkable is the general level of theoretical productivity in the Soviet Union during these years, which are so often characterised in the West as years in which culturally and intellectually the Soviet Union existed in sealed-off isolation from the nourishing influence of Western ideas. Bakhtin's interest in and knowledge of European literatures would be hard to match anywhere at any time. Only a writer like Erich Auerbach begins to do so.

It is not surprising that certain feminist writers have turned to Bakhtin's and Vološinov's work on language, given its emphasis on speakers of language rather than on language as an abstraction and on literature's place within such a view of language. Vološinov's insistence that 'meaning belongs to a word in its position between speakers'[35] can seem to encourage the idea that gender, amongst other class allegiances and interests, affects – and at times may even determine – meaning. Yet within the theoretical work itself women's voices remain subsumed within male ones, spoken for, unmarked, inaudible. Two questions remain: is this to be understood as an inevitable condition of certain kinds and levels of theorising? Or is the inability of even these writers to make gender difference and sexual relations central to their work produced by a particular history and their own place in it?

IV

I shall return to that smudged glimpse of a young woman who was, in 1954, starting her final year as a student at an ancient British university. Just six years earlier, in 1948, the women's colleges had been granted full membership of that university, though women had studied there since 1869. When I was at Cambridge women were still in a ratio of one to ten male students, so that, as a history of my old college drily puts it, young women 'were in constant demand to sing, act, or simply be escorted to parties and dances'.[36] We were also in some demand as possible members of a dreamed-up Falstaffian society bent above all on continuous sexual intercourse.

These anomalies were not, of course, intolerable, nor were they much discussed, I think. We knew that most of our contemporaries (male and female) still left school at fourteen to start work. A few girls stayed on beyond fourteen to study art or domestic science subjects – in preparation for marriage, some would have said. A majority of the girls I knew stayed at school until they were seventeen or eighteen and then trained as nurses or secretaries. Most young women of my age in 1954 had far more to complain about than I had, and such were the times, I expect they complained far less. The contradictions inherent in my position as a young woman student in an ancient and originally monastic institution are only one aspect of contradictions which have persistently dogged the education of girls during the last one hundred and fifty years. And these contradictions are ones which can only be met in the end by the most radical reordering of social and economic relations between men and women. We may be helped, none the less, by going a little further into these central issues of education, of literacy and of intellectual work generally.

I believe that the education on offer at Cambridge when I was there relied on the assumption that whereas men were always and everywhere simply men, women were women for only some of the time. For in our reading, our writing, in lectures and seminars and examinations, we were expected to drop whatever being a woman might mean to us or to others and to become as like men as we could – or at least flexibly androgynous. Such a division of ourselves often felt quite comfortable, since even those of us whose schooling had been in all-female institutions (as most of mine, in fact, had not) were accustomed to the uneasy settlement entailed in joining the 'we' of science textbook writers, historical researchers, critics or philosophers. We had learned to perform this trick during the last years of our schooling, and we learned it as boys did alongside all those other tricks which potential university students master in order to announce their worldliness, omniscience and detachment.

Inevitably, there were difficulties. It was not only the fact of our bodies, our biological difference from men, which was cancelled out by such manoeuvres. A great many of our past and current preoccupations were also ruled irrelevant. And then these separated parts of ourselves refused at times to stay separate, particularly if the work we were doing was in history or literature. History and literature are, after all, crammed with women. The dilemma there is with who has undertaken to tell us about them and how we, as serious students, might ourselves think and talk about women. Sweet girl graduate or '*Was will das Weib*?', playmate or arcane subject matter requiring the most rigorous of methodologies? For some of us there were one or two writers on the syllabus who were women: not many, but some; and we were quite often taught by women as well. But if women writers and scholars were to be worthy of our most serious attention, it became all the more necessary to shed our own gender and theirs in any evaluations we might make of their work.

What I am remembering, I suppose, is a particular form of induction into the way things were done in universities in Britain in particular subject areas and at a particular time. We have learned from writers like Bourdieu and Foucault about how institutions maintain their hierarchical and self-fulfilling arrangements against those who would invade or undermine them from without, and anthropologists like Shirley Brice Heath in America or Brian Street in this country have explored the specialist and differentiating literacies developed in particular communities.[37] For young people in universities the modes of teaching and learning and the accepted styles of written and spoken language constitute an induction into forms of knowledge, but also forms of knowing and showing that you know. The examination validates the rightness of these procedures against any single student's objections to them.

Many feminist writers have recalled the devastating loss of confidence dealt them by these traditions, from which not only women but sexual difference had, by definition, been excluded. In remembering that time in my own life I realise that I accepted without demur what seemed like a requirement to read and write and think in at least two entirely different ways. For many years, I have to admit, I believed that you should not include anything you actually thought or felt in an essay. It is possible that when I wrote about *Anna*

Karenina I let some cat out of the bag, which accounts for my memory of having somehow discomfited my soldierly Russian supervisor. I think now that I too naively took to heart a diffuse set of injunctions to be sophisticated at all costs and never to make too much of my own predilections. I don't mean to dwell on this experience as an especially debilitating one or as the consequence of unusually insensitive teaching. I do, though, want to explore some of its implications. For it may be that in different degrees many children experience schooling like this: as requiring a dropping or suspending of aspects of themselves, when those aspects may in fact be essential to the processes of successful learning.

A central feature of learning is the compatibility of new knowledge with old and the kinds of mental effort required to accommodate to the new. Vygotsky elaborated for psychology and for education the term 'the zone of proximal development', in order to give particular emphasis to the processes and to the elements of those processes entailed in achieving that compatibility. He defined this 'zone' as

> the distance between the actual developmental level as determined by independent problem solving and the level of potential development as determined through problem solving under adult guidance or in collaboration with more capable peers.[38]

The usefulness of this formulation clearly lies in its focus on what it really is necessary for teachers to know about children's capabilities: their teachability. This is far from being some timeless and abstracted measurement of intelligence, but is more like the progress a child is able to make when well taught. Just as important, however, and intimately connected, is Vygotsky's way of including in his account of children's learning the surrounding culture's specific modes of doing things and of teaching others to do them. Learning is no longer a matter of individual heads and minds grappling in isolation with concepts, skills and, in their wake, the full armoury of Western 'rationality'. Instead, Vygotsky directs our attention to the individual child's development within the culture through induction into a whole range of specialised practices. In the West these will be learned in school for the most part, though the school and its more evolved practices do not, of course, function in a vacuum. Learning to read, for instance, requires children to make conscious use of their knowledge and experience of literacy at home and in the community. This is especially important where there are serious divergences between home, community and school and where the methods developed by teachers in school are intended to deliver the range of literacies which modern life demands.

Let us consider one example of the kind of specialised literacy I mean. Jemila, whose parents came to Britain from Jamaica, is one of a small group of black seventeen-year-old girls in an A level literature class in a London school.[39] Their teacher is white and male, and the class is working on the poetry of the St Lucian poet Derek Walcott. Jemila has just read her essay out to the class. It ends with the words, 'Walcott is left with the task of trying to make sense of what the carnival means in relation to Caribbean history', to which she adds this quotation from Walcott: 'some hand must crawl and recollect your rubbish,/someone must write your poems.'[40]

The teacher moves her on from there, in order to initiate a group discussion and in order to lead Jemila towards setting her reading alongside others which may be developed collectively by the class: 'Could we just stop there,' he says. 'Is . . . Are we happy with Walcott's conclusion?' To which Jemila responds with a telling question: 'You mean personally?'

The teacher's 'we' and then Jemila's question to him, which asks in effect whether he wants to know what she actually thinks herself rather than what she, as an A level literature student, might be expected to agree to, marks out a new terrain for her. Entering, surveying and occupying this terrain with confidence is probably the most important thing Jemila is learning to do at this moment; and the fact that she can ask this question in a classroom and of her teacher bodes well, it seems to me. She already knows that there are several ways of reading a poem by Walcott, that some of them involve her own particular experience and knowledge and interest: what she knows, for instance, directly or through her family, about life and language in the Caribbean; perhaps something about Walcott's language and its relation to Creole speech and to the language of English poetry. But her teacher is also leading her towards ways of thinking and talking and writing about poetry which are required by an examination and which derive, tenuously at times, it is true, from activities like scholarship, criticism, book reviewing, and so on. Jemila is also likely to learn, if she hasn't already, that Walcott's poetry, and even her own reading of it in this classroom, stand in a relation to these institutions and traditions which is marked by racism and exclusion. Walcott's place in the syllabus has been a contested one, and it has been fought for by teachers in the context of increasing numbers of black students staying on at school to study literature for A level.[41]

And I have not even mentioned gender. Besides being young and black, however, Jemila is a girl reading a greatly admired black, male contemporary poet and taught by an immensely gifted male teacher. The discourses to which he is introducing her are, it is true, discourses to which many young women are yearly introduced, and by no means always by men or always in terms of male writers. Yet the division between her own reading and the reading she rightly thinks her teacher wants to hear about – and which her 'personally?' signals – is a reminder that the agreement her teacher looks for in her answer to his question undeniably excludes the difference of gender. To assert her reading as a woman's reading would be to personalise and therefore fracture the level of discussion teacher and class are aiming for. The authoritative voice these young women are learning to use must not come out as falsetto.

The problem is not that I – as a young woman in the early fifties – or Jemila now, have failed to assume or adopt that voice. Rather, the danger has been that in assuming it we become safe, adaptable students, performing adequately, but damaged (almost imperceptibly) by disowning the sources of our potentially most illuminating critical starting point. Clearly, Jemila needs to understand Walcott's poem and she also needs to know how to write essays in answer to formulaic questions designed to elicit selected kinds of knowledge about it and about other texts. But she also needs to understand her own history as a reader and the relation of her history to Walcott's and to the processes of cultural change which have kept them apart and now bring them together in this London classroom. But even if she does all those things, and does them well, she will need to know that she is doing them as a woman and that that means, amongst other things, that she must recognise these specialised literacy practices in which she is beginning to participate as practices whch have been developed historically, with no thought for the changing possibilities of a girl like her.

V

So a reader is a person in history, a person with a history. Like literature itself, readers have been idealised, and this idealisation has depended on a peculiar privileging and therefore unsexing of reading as one version of the aesthetic encounter, which is essentially available to anyone who makes a certain sort of effort. We will recall the assertion made by the Italian historian Carlo Ginzburg, at the beginning of his book about a reader, *The Cheese and the Worms*:

> Only knowledge of the historical and social variability of the person of the reader will really lay the foundations for a history of ideas that is also *qualitatively* different.[42]

Menocchio, the hero of the book, was a miller who lived in a large Friulian village in Northern Italy in the sixteenth century. His life, his thoughts, his reading and even his speech are available to us, because he was interrogated twice at great length by the Inquisition as a heretic. Finally, they put him to death. He was unusual in his village because he was literate, and since as a miller he played a pivotal role in village life, he seems to have exploited all this by talking unstoppably about his ideas and his reading. In ways which owe a good deal to Bakhtin, Ginzburg offers a historian's reconstruction of the oral and the literate cultures which could be said to have contributed to Menocchio's development and to his heretical ideas. Ginzburg lists eleven books which were mentioned at Menocchio's first trial. Amongst them were the Bible in the vernacular, an odd medieval Catalan anthology of apocryphal gospels and later commentary, an edition of the lives of the saints, an anonymous fifteenth-century poem called *Historia del Giudicio*, Mandeville's *Travels* (in Italian), *The Decameron* of Boccaccio in an unexpurgated edition, and an unidentified book thought by a contemporary witness to be the Koran in an Italian translation.

What is even more revealing for us is that the Inquisition has left clues as to *how* Menocchio read these texts, how his readings sat with other kinds of experience and knowledge, how he expressed these connections and discrepancies and how he discussed them and conversed with people more powerful than himself as well as less. It is this that Ginzburg interprets for us:

When we compare, one by one, passages from the books mentioned by Menocchio with the conclusions that he drew from them (if not with the manner in which he reported them to the judges), we invariably find gaps and discrepancies of serious proportions. Any attempt to consider these books as 'sources' in the mechanical sense of the term collapses before the aggressive originality of Menocchio's reading. More than the text, then, what is important is the key to his reading, a screen that he unconsciously placed between himself and the printed page: a filter that emphasized certain words while obscuring others, that stretched the meaning of a word, taking it out of its context, that acted on Menocchio's memory and distorted the very words of the text. And this screen, this key to his reading, continually leads us back to a culture that is very different from the one expressed on the printed page – one based on an oral tradition . . . We have seen how Menocchio read his books: isolating words and phrases, sometimes distorting them, juxtaposing different passages, firing off rapid analogies. Each time, a comparison between the texts and Menocchio's responses to them has led us to suggest a hidden key to his reading that possible relations with one heretical group or another aren't sufficient to explain. Menocchio mulled over and elaborated on his readings outside any pre-existent framework. And his most extraordinary declarations originated from contact with such innocuous texts as Mandeville's *Travels* or the *Historia del Giudicio*. It was not the book as such, but the encounter between the printed page and oral culture that formed an explosive mixture in Menocchio's head.[43]

Menocchio is not, in Ginzburg's account, simply poised between or straddling two cultures. We are able to watch him making sense of the ideas he met in his reading as an individual who is clear about his own position and his own knowledge, and about the culture of his own world. The title of Ginzburg's book is drawn from the everyday explanation, analogy or fable which Menocchio constructed as his account of God's creation of the world:

> I have said that, in my opinion, all was chaos . . . and out of that bulk a mass formed – just as cheese is made out of milk – and worms appeared in it, and these were the angels. The most holy majesty decreed that these should be God and the angels, and among that number of angels, there was also God, *he too having been created out of that mass at the same time* . . .[44]

And from this vantage point there is nothing intrinsically less plausible about this explanation than Genesis. The stream of testimony to the Inquisition shows too how Menocchio's explanation changed in its retelling by other villagers. It is easy to pick up from Ginzburg's analysis a sense only of Menocchio's reading as undisciplined, wayward. What seems at least as important, however, is Menocchio's confident *using* of texts to build theories and narratives of his own, and his constant and confident moves between all the books he knows and what he knows from his experience outside books.

What Ginzburg also demonstrates is how difficult it may be for *us* to read Menocchio, because we're used to the testimony and the interpretation of confident readers, who 'know how to' read and what it is permissible under different kinds of circumstance to reveal about our readings. Menocchio's culture – his use of metaphor and analogy, for instance – had not developed in isolation or independently of the dominant culture, but in particular (yet always unfixed) relations to it, and in absolutely specific engagements with, for instance, priests, landowners, writers of books.

It can seem now, and must often have seemed then, that Menocchio's culture was submerged by the dominant culture. Yet the argument between Menocchio and the Inquisition belies such a simple view of it. Ginzburg allows us to watch the loquacious miller struggling to account in his own way for the oppositions within the society he inhabited. Those oppositions were revealed to him in new ways by the process of reading himself into discourses which discounted him or positioned him as inaudibly included within them, or as helplessly outside them. But also, most importantly of all, his particular experiences of power and of subordination to power told him how to read. God, for Menocchio, had many of the traits of the Lord of his particular manor.

Menocchio is defeated in the end. He miscalculates what his inquisitors want to hear from him, which of his ideas are considered heretical and which innocent. He ignores the advice of a more worldly friend: 'Tell them what they want to know, and try not to talk too much; do not go out of your way to discuss these things. Answer only their questions.'[45] Ginzburg describes Menocchio as caught within a circularity of cultural power. He is released, but also destroyed, by reading, because he does not fully recognise his own exclusion from the texts he reads and the literacy he enters. His confidence as a reader is aggressive and original, as Ginzburg describes it, but he is also mistaken in thinking that the sheer strength of his beliefs and the apparent coherence of his knowledge are enough to overwhelm the convictions and the power of his opponents.

Enthusiastic teachers sometimes speak of literacy as 'empowering' for children. The story of Menocchio illustrates the ambiguity of such empowering. For his ignorance of the interests invested in certain texts and certain readings of them, his hazardous disobedience of the regulations which literacy both enjoined and accompanied in his society, actually brought about his death. And the question I take from his story is this: is Jemila similarly 'empowered' by what she is learning to do, and is she therefore similarly threatened? For it seems to me that I recognise her grappling with apparently twin but actually opposite forces. There is a seductive invitation to join those who can seem to have earned the right to take part in certain kinds of discussion of literature and of their own experiences of it. There is, simultaneously, a realisation that her own voice has historically been excluded from that discussion. Because Jemila has learned to read in school, however, and may therefore be more aware of literacy's pitfalls than was Menocchio, the autodidact, these contradictions may often – paradoxically – be disguised.

The practices, the skills and the behaviours of reading and writing are offered to children in school as themselves controlling and even dictating of the uses to which they may be put. Reading matter will always be divided into the acceptable and the unacceptable on a variety of grounds. Children learn to write neatly, clearly, accurately, to spell conventionally, to punctuate. They learn that these skills are not uncomplicatedly transferable. They are not, for instance, meant for graffiti or pornography; nor, I suppose, in order to write poison-pen letters. Jokes will be a problem; for although adults quite often find children's writing funny, they are also apt to use words like 'derivative' or even 'childish' about exactly those efforts which children may themselves regard as adult in form or subject matter.

And as children learn what writing is *not* meant for, they also learn about what it *is* meant for. Many children tell us, if asked, that they need to be good at reading and writing in order to get a decent job. In the mid seventies, when Paul Willis questioned a group of teenage working-class boys at school in the Midlands, many of them were absolutely clear that literacy was unnecessary for the kinds of low-paid manufacturing jobs they expected to get.[46] Employment possibilities changed in the eighties – in many cases for the worse – for children like these; but the relevance of most forms of literacy learned at school remains as confused as ever. Word-processing, for instance, can now assist literacy, but it also depends on some level of literacy. It can also offer kinds of substitute for reading and writing. Young people usually know, from their knowledge of their own families and communities, that there are quite serious discrepancies between how the adults they know use written language and the claims made for literacy by schools and employers. The values of literacy are not anyway, and have never been, equivalent to its usefulness or its relevance.

Indeed, children have never just learned how to read and write and then looked round for uses to which they might put these skills. As they learn to do these things they are also learning to engage with the culture and with specific and specialised practices in that culture. They are also learning about being children in this culture, and especially children who may be black, girls, working-class, poor. Literacy does not in itself deliver any kind of liberation from these conditions, any more than reading literature provides either escape from social problems or solutions to them. And by and large young people see through and reject claims for literacy which exceed their experiences of who goes in for reading and writing, and why.

So, far from advocating either some sort of enriched literacy as an answer to social inequalities, or a sanctioned liberality of readings, which leaves meaning and pleasure and value to individual readers spinning in eccentric isolation, I want the constraints, the differences, the social relations of reading and of the production of texts to become the curriculum, so that reading is seen as engagement and as continuous with – as well as at odds with – the social practices and alliances of people's lives. Children need to know, as adult readers do too, that it is very difficult to make sense of texts which reject our questions and our replies. Texts which exclude our readings exclude us. Context, particularity, relationships, speech: these drench language in its own concurrent metalanguage, perpetually furthering, impeding, commenting on and questioning the efficacy of conversational communication. Within that process, differences of age, race, gender, class, will not speak or be spoken in separate languages. Rather, to return to Vološinov and his claim, 'various different classes will use one and the same language. As a result, differently oriented accents intersect in every ideological sign. Sign becomes an arena of the class struggle.'[47]

No reading can happen without misreading, multiple readings. Difference has seemed to allow only for individual readings. But individuals are formed by groups, classes, within conflict. So readings must also be assertions, and if they are disputed, they are also shared. What it is always necessary to remember is that our readings are driven by more than a need for coherence, wholeness, completion. Because they are powered by the dynamics of conversation, they are characteristically produced by disagreement as well as agreement.

VI

Fifty-year-old Elaine Risley, painter, narrator and eye of Margaret Atwood's *Cat's Eye*, has a past which is at once inaccessible to her and revealed to us in language of profuse and baffling candour. Revisiting Toronto, where she lived as a child and a young woman before escaping to Vancouver and a new life, she is intent now on reaching some mature settlement of her life's disparities. Her paintings, catalogued for us (and hideously taken off by the book's dust jacket) are triumphantly and retrospectively on show here, hailed and reviled for their feminist vision. As she waits for her Private View to start, she thinks:

> This is like birthday parties, with streamers and balloons at the ready and the hotdogs waiting in the kitchen, but what if nobody comes? Which will be worse: if they don't come, or if they do? Soon the door will open, and in will crowd a horde of snide and treacherous little girls, whispering and pointing, and I will be servile, grateful.[48]

Her past is populated by treacherous little girls, but it is their mothers, damaged and damaging, who gaze grimly out of her paintings. The novel accounts, sourly as well as exuberantly, for the infinite seductiveness of men in a world where women are left to itemise their own and each other's multiple imperfections and to undertake to effect improvements on the widest possible front.

Elaine and her 'brilliant' older brother grow up between journeys to the northernmost parts of Canada – where their father scrutinises insect infestations and their mother cheerfully manages warm clothes and baked beans – and the constraints of a Toronto suburb, to which the family more or less permanently move once the children need to go to school and their father takes up a professorship at the university.

The Toronto of the novel is all houses: houses which are continuously built and rebuilt, adorned, stuffed, made impregnable, cramped, consuming of their occupants. Elaine's mother is the only mother who comes near to resisting the terrible temptations of houses: neatness, hygiene, taste and all those invitations to spend energy, talent, whole lifetimes on their surfaces. Against this is the wild country of the north, where the family travel lightly, camping and lodging, impermanent. That double life fades to a trace, a bare, enticing memory for Elaine, as the travelling part of the family's life shrinks and the Toronto part swells in its place.

Even as a small girl it occurs to her that 'in the daily life of houses, fathers are largely invisible'.[49] Her evidence for this is drawn from the homes of her three friends, Carol, Grace and Cordelia, as well as from her own. Cordelia's father is the most absent of them all, and Elaine reels from 'the full force of his ponderous, ironic, terrifying charm'.[50] Grace's father 'is a squat, balding, flabby man, but still a man. He does not judge me.'[51] Her loyalty to this father is like her loyalty to her own brother. In the end, 'both are on the side of ox eyeballs, toe-jam under the microscope, the outrageous, the subversive'. And when she wonders to herself, 'outrageous to whom, subversive of what?' her answer comes pat: 'Of Grace and Mrs Smeath, of tidy paper ladies pasted into scrapbooks.'[52]

The central – and forgotten – events of Elaine's life happen when she is about to be nine. They are the culmination of long, torturing rituals prepared for her by her three friends in furious mimicry of the controlling and correcting functions they have already learned to think of as exclusively women's and the source of their own leverage and power. They have learned this from mothers and sisters and school and each other. And as they rehearse all the ways they know of for regulating other women and girls, the self-hatred which powers them is momentarily obscured. Elaine becomes ill, spending days in bed to avoid her friends' cruelty but also so that she may indulge in versions of the same thing. It is her identification with her friends which is so horrifying to her, not her difference from them:

Sometimes I cut things out of magazines and paste them into a scrapbook with LePage mucilage, from the bottle that looks like a chess bishop. I cut out pictures of women, from *Good Housekeeping, The Ladies' Home Journal, Chatelaine*. If I don't like their faces I cut off the heads and glue other heads on. These women have dresses with puffed sleeves and full skirts, and white aprons that tie very tightly around their waists. They put germ-killers onto germs, in toilet bowls; they polish windows, or clean their spotty complexions with bars of soap, or shampoo their oily hair; they get rid of their unwanted odours, rub hand lotion onto their rough wrinkly hands, hug rolls of toilet paper against their cheeks.

Other pictures show women doing things they aren't supposed to do. Some of them gossip too much, some are sloppy, others bossy. Some of them knit too much. 'Walking, riding, standing, sitting, Where she goes, there goes her knitting,' says one. The picture shows a woman knitting on a streetcar, with the ends of her knitting needles poking into the people beside her and her ball of wool unrolling down the aisle. Some of the women have a Watchbird beside them, a red and black bird like a child's drawing, with big eyes and stick feet. 'This is a Watchbird watching a Busybody,' it says. 'This is a Watchbird watching YOU.'

I see that there will be no end to imperfection, or to doing things the wrong way. Even if you grow up, no matter how hard you scrub, whatever you do, there will always be some other stain or spot on your face or stupid act, somebody frowning. But it pleases me somehow to cut out all these imperfect women, with their forehead wrinkles that show how worried they are, and fix them into my scrapbook.[53]

In contrast to this, the world of boys spells freedom, humour. Boys, and even her superior brother, become Elaine's 'secret allies', and her relations with them are 'effortless' compared with the shameful miseries she endures at the hands of her three little friends. Even after a series of débâcles with men, when she is living alone with a child and first joins a women's group, sisterhood remains difficult for her as 'brotherhood' does not. She senses always that other women detect her inauthenticity and will point this out. She continues to find that 'forgiving men is so much easier than forgiving women'[54] – perhaps, one is tempted to say, because like the rest of us she gets so much practice.

The novel is finally even-handed in its mutilations. Her brother is murdered by plane hijackers. Cordelia is submitted to a series of damaging transformations: becoming fat, mad, depressed, and so on. Elaine flies home to Vancouver and is amazed by the two old women sitting by her:

> . . . each with a knitted cardigan, each with yellowy-white hair and thick-lensed glasses with a chain for around the neck, each with a desiccated mouth lipsticked bright red with bravado. They have their trays lowered and are drinking tea and playing Snap, fumbling the slippery cards, laughing like cars on gravel when they cheat or make mistakes. From time to time they get up, unbuckling themselves laboriously, and hobble to the back of the plane, to smoke cigarettes and line up for the washroom. When they return they make bathroom jokes, quips about wetting your pants and running out of toilet paper, eyeing me cunningly while they do so. I wonder how old they think they are, underneath the disguise of their bodies; or how old they think I am. Perhaps, to them, I look like their mother.
>
> They seem to me amazingly carefree. They have saved up for this trip and they are damn well going to enjoy it, despite the arthritis of one, the swollen legs of the other. They're rambunctious, they're full of beans; they're tough as thirteen, they're innocent and dirty, they don't give a hoot. Responsibilities have fallen away from them, obligations, old hates and grievances; now for a short while they can play again like children, but this time without pain.[55]

The painless childhood Atwood has conferred on her two old women is a boys' childhood and a Rabelaisian one. At last they are 'innocent and dirty' and at last 'they don't give a hoot'. This second childhood will have none of the disabling dualities of being girls, the bitter learning of inadequacy, control, need for improvement or subterfuge. They will be free at last of all their stored-up guilt at the put-downs, the send-ups, the retaliatory moves they have administered to other girls and other women as well as to themselves. This time they will say what they mean, whether it is trivial or not: no muzzling, no gagging. At last, and late as ever – and only because their sexuality may be discounted now and their physical powers are so drastically reduced – they may permit themselves a few minor infringements, some feathery disobediences. And if they are more likely to be thought mad than creatively rambunctious, so be it, for an advantage of failing faculties is that other people's views of you are finally so much less influential.

VII

We should all know by now, of course, that it is *our* seductive charms that have been our downfall, not men's. Marina Warner, in her book *Alone of All Her Sex. The Myth and the Cult of the Virgin Mary*, reminds us of this in a chapter which sets Eve alongside Mary as her *alter ego*:

> The fury unleashed against Eve and all her kind is almost flattering, so exaggerated is the picture of women's fatal and all-powerful charms and men's incapacity to resist.[56]

And typically, Eve's seductions have been advanced in a language of passionate denial and disgust, with injunctions to men to resist them:

> Eve, cursed to bear children rather than blessed with motherhood, was identified with nature, a form of low matter that drags man's soul down the spiritual ladder. In the faeces and urine – Augustine's phrase – of childbirth, the closeness of woman to all that is vile, lowly, corruptible, and material was epitomized; in the 'curse' of menstruation, she lay closer to the beasts; the lure of her beauty was nothing but an aspect of the death brought about by her seduction of Adam in the garden. St. John Chrysostom warned: 'The whole of her bodily beauty is nothing less than phlegm, blood, bile, rheum, and the fluid of digested food ... If you consider what is stored up behind those lovely eyes, the angle of the nose, the mouth and cheeks, you will agree that the well-proportioned body is merely a whited sepulchre.'[57]

Augustine's disgust is the underside of Bakhtin's squeamish evasions; and Eve herself is as tempting and as troubling for women as for men. Her endlessly transforming manifestations measure out a history of rationales for controlling and oppressing women. Yet the opprobrium she attracts to herself is precisely for the disobedience, the anarchy, the criticism which all forms of radical rethinking have relied on and admired. Feminism itself may be said to have had high hopes of Eve. Would she not boldly have her way with men and settle down afterwards with her feet up and a good Romance? Would she not bear children (in every sense) and ask nobody's blessing for doing so? And would she not delight in the exertion of her own coarse energies and her uncomfortable intelligence, and have the last laugh?

VIII

My purpose in these chapters has been to enact as well as to argue for and demonstrate the very many ways in which women are, and have been, seduced into agreements and alliances with men. These seductions have not been deplored – far from it. Rather, I have wanted to understand the pressures and the enticements to which women are susceptible. I have also wanted to explore the character and scope of women's resistances and the blockades, the escape routes, the bypasses they have built like some maze of burrowing tunnels, which disappear from view at times, then surface, surreptitiously at first, then more boldly, only to merge invisibly into the main arterial thoroughfares. The critiques I have offered of certain exemplarily seductive male writers are punctuated by moments from women's lives and examples from their writing, which simultaneously acknowledge the seduction and elude it. So that Willoughby, the seducer of Jane Austen's *Sense and Sensibility*, is both heir to Samuel Richardson's Lovelace and critical counter. Similarly, Carolyn Steedman's narratives of working-class girlhood have learned from Raymond Williams and his understandings about class in history, but they also challenge his analysis to its roots. My Great-Aunt Clara bore the disparagements and injustices meted out to women at the end of the nineteenth century with aplomb, but her life and her view of the world were constrained and damaged by them.

In the subtle and seductive studies of racism, colonialism and Orientalism to be found in the writing of Frantz Fanon and Edward Said, women are apt to dissolve into metaphor: a condition from which they are redeemed in a novel like Toni Morrison's *Beloved*, where comprehension of the historical experience of slavery in North America starts from the physical suffering of men, women and children. And finally, I set the brave, funny, self-lacerating *Cat's Eye* by Margaret Atwood against those critical traditions which look askance at women's laughter and disobedience and ignore the impact on girls of epistemological and educational traditions within which gender is judged an irrelevance.

Women have not been helped much by what have been called 'positive images'. Most of us find it hard to recognise ourselves in models of assured and unambiguous womanhood, and such simplicities are anyway welcomed and exploited by all those who want to keep women in their place. Women must allow themselves complexity, doubleness, the strength of uncertainty, insights afforded by confronting the unequal historical relations between women and men and between women of different classes, nationalities, races, ages. Only truthfulness to the diversity of women's experience and to the problems of thinking and talking and writing about these things will bring real change.

NOTES

Introduction

1   This view of the philosopher is developed by the American philosopher Richard Rorty in his book *Contingency, Irony and Solidarity* (Cambridge University Press, 1989). I am making a somewhat unfair elision between this writer's work and the works of critics like the American Michael Walzer or the Irish Denis Donaghue. It is not that these writers straightforwardly share a politics, but rather that for them the issues raised by feminism can be appropriately handled by a combination of courteous disapproval and some light massaging of habitual English usage.

2   Claire Tomalin in 'The Sage of Polygon Road', a review of *The Works of Mary Wollstonecraft, Vols 1–V11,* ed. Janet Todd and Marilyn Butler (Pickering & Chatto, 1989), *London Review of Books,* vol. 11, no. 18, September 1989.

3   'The one great silent area' is a phrase used by Raymond Williams's interlocutors in Raymond Williams: *Politics and Letters. Interviews with New Left Review* (Verso, 1981).

4   There has been a long-running debate about the nature of the collaboration between Bakhtin, Vološinov and, indeed, Pavel Medvedev. There are those who believe that Bakhtin was in some sense the author of all the works that have been attributed to his colleagues; others go so far as to doubt whether the three writers can be distinguished usefully at all. The debate is unresolved. My decision to regard Bakhtin and Vološinov as separate writers rests on my sense that there are important philosophical and thematic differences in the works currently attributed to each of them, despite the evidence that they shared central concerns and worked together to develop their ideas within similar traditions of thought. I have relied on the somewhat ambiguous version of Bakhtin's 'ventriloquist's' relation to Vološinov's work to be found in Katerina Clark and Michael Holquist's biography of Bakhtin and Tzvetan Todorov's *Mikhail Bakhtin: The Dialogical Principle,* transl. Wlad Godzich, University of Minnesota Press, 1984.

5   Antonio Gramsci: *Selections from Cultural Writings,* ed. David Forgacs and Geoffrey Nowell-Smith (Lawrence & Wishart, 1985): 'Art and Culture', p.98.

6   Gayatri Chakravorty Spivak uses the word in the context of recent Indian historical studies. See her 'Subaltern Studies: Deconstructing

Historiography', in *In Other Worlds. Essays in Cultural Politics* (Methuen, 1987). Spivak's work has consistently approached feminism, Marxism and anti-colonialism in conjunction.

7 The field is too large to cover here. Useful and available texts are Juliet Mitchell and Jacqueline Rose, *Feminine Sexuality. Jacques Lacan and the École Freudienne* (Macmillan, 1982); and *In Dora's Case: Freud. Hysteria. Feminism,* ed. Charles Bernheimer and Claire Kahane (Virago, 1985).

8 Juliet Mitchell: *Psychoanalysis and Feminism* (Penguin, 1975).

9 Jane Gallop: *Feminism and Psychoanalysis. The Daughter's Seduction* (Macmillan, 1982), p. 35.

10 ibid., p. 120. Gallop castigates Kristeva for having 'the cheek to constitute herself in the privileged position by which she alone might be able to bridge the abyss of otherness, to contact and report the heterogeneous'. This is an ironic warning delivered in some sense to all feminists.

11 ibid., p. 38.

12 Seyla Benhabib and Drucilla Cornell (eds): *Feminism as Critique* (Polity Press, 1987).

13 Kate Soper: '*Feminism as Critique*', a reveiw of the collection of essays with that title, *New Left Review*, no. 176, July/August 1989, p. 95.

14 A most interesting collection of essays by women working in higher education and confronted daily and practically, therefore, with the implications of that dilemma, is Ann Thompson and Helen Wilcox (eds): *Teaching Women. Feminism and English Studies* (Manchester University Press, 1989).

15 Nicky Hart: 'Gender and the Rise and Fall of Class Politics', *New Left Review*, no. 175, May/June 1989, p. 21.

16 ibid. p. 27.

17 ibid. p. 45.

18 Catherine Clément: *Opera or the Undoing of Women* (Virago, 1989), p. 75.

1 Seduction and Hegemony

1 Betty Miller: 'Amazons and Afterwards', *The Twentieth Century, Special Number on Women*, vol. 164. no. 978, August 1958.

2 Hannah Gavron: *The Captive Wife* (Routledge & Kegan Paul, 1966).

3 Juliet Mitchell and Ann Oakley (eds): *What is Feminism?* (Blackwell, 1986).

4 Toril Moi (ed.): *The Kristeva Reader* (Blackwell, 1986).

5 Juliet Mitchell and Ann Oakley (eds): *The Rights and Wrongs of Women* (Penguin, 1976).

6 In a piece called 'What is Feminism?'

7 Betty Miller's novel *On the Side of the Angels* was first published in 1945 and was reissued in 1985 by Virago with an interesting introduction by her daughter, Sarah Miller.

8 Milan Kundera: *The Unbearable Lightness of Being,* transl. Michael Henry Heim (Faber & Faber, 1984), p. 200.

9 There is no single source for this brief summary of Gramsci's ideas about hegemony. I have drawn on *Selections from the Prison Notebooks of Antonio Gramsci,* ed. and transl. Quintin Hoare and Geoffrey Nowell-Smith (Lawrence & Wishart, 1986) and on essays from Anne Showstack Sassoon's *Approaches to Gramsci* (Writers & Readers, 1982). I have also been helped by Raymond Williams's chapter 'Hegemony' in his *Marxism and Literature* (Oxford University Press, 1977).

10 Toril Moi: *Sexual/Textual Politics. Feminist Literary Theory* (Methuen, 1985), p. 169.

11 From an essay by Julia Kristeva included in Elaine Marks and Isabelle de Courtivron (eds): *New French Feminisms. An Anthology* (Harvester, 1981), p. 137.

12 ibid. Corresponding doubts are sometimes voiced as to whether Kristeva is a feminist.

13 I am thinking of Michel Foucault: *The History of Sexuality. Volume One. An Introduction,* transl. Robert Hurley (Penguin, 1981).

14 Pierre Choderlos de Laclos: *Les Liaisons Dangereuses* (1782).

15 Verse 194 from Canto I of Byron's *Don Juan.*

16 All references to Samuel Richardson's *Clarissa* are to the 1985 Penguin edition, here p. 883.

17 ibid. p. 1468.

18 J.S. Mill: *The Subjection of Women* (Virago, 1983), p. 76.

19 Richardson: *Clarissa,* p. 883.

20 ibid., p. 1349.

21 ibid., p. 417.

22 ibid., p. 441. Richardson is rewording Pope's 'But every woman is at heart a Rake' from 'Of the Characters of Women: An Epistle to a Lady' (1735). In an essay called 'Wild Nights: Pleasure/Sexuality/Feminism', in *Sea Changes. Essays on Culture and Feminism* (Verso, 1986), Cora Kaplan asks why Mary Wollstonecraft's *A Vindication of the Rights of Woman* (1792), is 'so suffused with the sexual, and so severe about it?' Kaplan's essay begins with a quotation from Wollstonecraft which echoes Pope and Richardson: 'till women are led to exercise their understandings, they should not be satirized for their attachment to rakes; or even for being rakes at heart, when it appears to be the inevitable consequence of their education. They who live to please – must find their enjoyments, their happiness in pleasure!' I have found this essay about sexuality, feminism and class very useful.

23 Richardson: *Clarissa,* p. 720.

24 ibid., p. 77.

25 ibid., p. 557.

26 ibid., p. 1388.

27 ibid., p. 1367. Catherine Clément's wonderful *Opera or the Undoing of Women* (Virago, 1989) is illuminating and funny about the sublime lamentations with which women celebrate their own deaths in operas.

28 Richardson: *Clarissa*, p.609. Lovelace quotes lines from Dryden's play *Aureng-Zebe*, which begin: 'It is resistance that inflames desire'. This is conventional wisdom, of course, but worth dwelling on here for the way in which the novel implicates the woman in the seductiveness of these resistances.
29 Richardson: *Clarissa*, p. 658.
30 Jane Austen: *Sense and Sensibility* (1811), ch. 15.
31 ibid., ch. 31.
32 ibid., ch. 47.
33 ibid., ch. 33.
34 ibid., ch. 44.
35 ibid., ch. 45.

2 The One Great Silent Area

1   Raymond Williams: *Resources of Hope*, ed. Robin Gable, with an Introduction by Robin Blackburn (Verso, 1989). The last chapter of *Towards 2000* is called 'Resources of a Journey of Hope'.
2   'You're a Marxist, Aren't You?' was first published in Bhiku Parekh (ed.): *The Concept of Socialism* (Croom Helm, 1975).
3   Williams: *Resources of Hope*, p. 74.
4   ibid., p. 75.
5   Raymond Williams: *Marxism and Literature* (Oxford University Press, 1977). Williams was working on this between 1972 and 1976.
6   Terry Eagleton: 'Resources for a Journey of Hope: The Significance of Raymond Williams', *New Left Review*, no. 168, March/April 1988, p.8.
7   'Culture is Ordinary', in Williams: *Resources of Hope*. This was first published in 1958 in Norman MacKenzie (ed.): *Convictions* (MacGibbon & Kee), p. 5.
8   Raymond Williams: *The Country and the City* (Paladin, 1975; first published 1973). Williams appears to have started working on this in 1965.
9   Williams: *Marxism and Literature*, p. 46.
10 ibid.
11 Raymond Williams: *Politics and Letters. Interviews with New Left Review* (Verso, 1981), p. 144.
12 Williams: *The Country and the City*, p. 368.
13 Francis Mulhern: '"Towards 2000": News from You-Know-Where', *New Left Review*, no. 148, November/December 1984, p. 27.
14 Williams: *Marxism and Literature*, p. 21.
15 Williams: *Politics and Letters*, p. 148.
16 Raymond Williams: *The Long Revolution* (Penguin, 1975; first published 1961), p. 135.
17 Raymond Williams: *Culture and Society 1780–1950* (Penguin, 1963; first published 1958).
18 ibid., p. 314.
19 ibid., p. 318.

20   ibid., p. 314.
21   ibid., p. 318.
22   Williams: *Politics and Letters*, p. 148.
23   Juliet Mitchell: 'Women: The Longest Revolution' was republished in a book with the same title, subtitled *Essays in Feminism, Literature and Psychoanalysis* (Virago, 1984). The original essay was first published in 1966 in *New Left Review*.
24   Juliet Mitchell: *Woman's Estate* (Penguin, 1971), p. 99.
25   Williams: *Politics and Letters*, p. 149.
26   ibid., p. 23.
27   Christine Delphy: *Close to Home* (Hutchinson, 1984), p. 132.
28   Williams: *The Country and the City*, p. 11.
29   ibid., p. 62.
30   ibid. p. 70.
31   ibid.
32   *The Country and the City*, p. 67.
33   ibid., p. 44.
34   ibid., p. 79.
35   ibid., p. 81.
36   ibid., p. 83.
37   ibid.
38   This view of the urban poor is one I discuss at greater length in Chapter 3 in relation to Clara Collet's work and the Charity Organisation Society, to which she belonged.
39   Williams: *The Country and the City*, p. 127.
40   ibid., p. 255.
41   ibid.
42   Williams: *Politics and Letters*, p. 150.
43   Delphy, p. 72.
44   Cynthia Cockburn: 'Macho Men of the Left', *Marxism Today*, April 1988.
45   The Australian writer Sylvia Lawson puts this powerfully in a review of Germaine Greer's *Daddy, we hardly knew you:*
     The first chapter is called 'The Quest', and that announces both the intensity of the writer's commitment and her sense of the perils ahead. What's exhilarating there and throughout is the nerve it takes to appropriate the mythic dimension, to understand unwaveringly that your own story is worth it, and claim for the female warrior in these contemporary battlefields the full scope of the aspiration accorded time out of mind to the male. *(London Review of Books*, vol. 11, no. 8, 20 April 1989)
46   Williams: *The Country and the City*, p. 75.
47   ibid., p. 318.
48   Raymond Williams: *Border Country* (The Hogarth Press, 1988; first published 1960, after many rewritings).
49   Raymond Williams: *Second Generation* (The Hogarth Press, 1988; first published 1964).
50   Raymond Williams: *The Fight for Manod* (The Hogarth Press, 1988; first published 1979).

51 Williams: *Politics and Letters*, p. 273.
52 ibid., p. 272.
53 ibid.
54 *Politics and Letters*, p. 293.
55 Seamus Heaney: 'Digging', in *Death of a Naturalist* (Faber & Faber, 1966), p. 13.
56 Williams: *Border Country*, p. 9.
57 ibid., p. 10.
58 ibid.
59 *Border Country*, p. 20.
60 ibid., p. 15.
61 ibid., p. 234.
62 ibid., p. 54.
63 Williams: *Politics and Letters*, p. 288.
64 Eagleton, p. 8.
65 Williams: *Politics and Letters*, p. 287.
66 Williams: *Second Generation*, p. 133.
67 Williams: *Politics and Letters*, p. 272.
68 ibid., p. 289.
69 Raymond Williams: *The Volunteers* (The Hogarth Press, 1985; first published 1978).
70 Williams: *The Fight for Manod*, p. 206.
71 ibid., p. 68.
72 Williams: *Politics and Letters*, p. 106.
73 Williams: *The Fight for Manod*, p. 156.
74 Williams: *Politics and Letters*, p. 27.
75 ibid., p. 28.
76 ibid., p. 78.
77 ibid., p. 147.
78 Mark Lawson: 'Storey Lines', *The Independent Magazine*, 8 April 1989.
79 Carolyn Steedman: *Landscape for a Good Woman. A Story of Two Lives* (Virago, 1986).
80 ibid., p. 33.
81 Ruqaiya Hasan: 'The Ontogenesis of Ideology: An Interpretation of Mother–Child Talk', in Terry Threadgold, E.A. Grosz, Gunther Kress and M.A.K. Halliday (eds): *Semiotics, Ideology, Language*, Sidney Studies in Society and Culture, no. 3 (1986).
82 Cathy Urwin: 'Constructing motherhood: the persuasion of normal development', in Carolyn Steedman, Cathy Urwin and Valerie Walkerdine (eds): *Language, Gender and Childhood* (Routledge & Kegan Paul, 1985). This illuminating chapter demonstrates just how the 'normalising apparatuses' of developmental psychology and of childcare manuals promote principles of 'child-centredness' and cumulatively work to undermine women's sense of their own needs and their own capacity to make judgements about the bringing up of their own children.
83 Williams: *Politics and Letters*, p. 164.

84 Williams: *Second Generation,* p. 338.
85 Steedman: *Landscape for a Good Woman,* p. 5.
86 ibid., p. 14.
87 ibid., p. 6.
88 Raymond Williams: 'Desire', a review of *Landscape for a Good Woman, London Review of Books,* vol. 8, no. 7, 17 April 1986.
89 ibid., p. 8.
90 ibid.
91 Michèle Barrett: *Women's Oppression Today. Problems in Marxist Feminist Analysis* (Verso, 1980), p. 256.
92 Steedman, Urwin and Walkerdine (eds): *Language, Gender and Childhood,* p. 7.
93 Raymond Williams: *Towards 2000* (Chatto & Windus, 1983), p. 249.
94 ibid.
95 Just as I finished writing this chapter I read Carol Watts's 'Reclaiming the Border Country: Feminism and the Work of Raymond Williams' in an issue of *Oxford English Limited* devoted to Raymond Williams. (*News from Nowhere, Raymond Williams: Third Generation, Oxford English Limited* no. 6, February 1989.) Watts's most accomplished piece ends with a call for feminists to return to the strengths of Williams's work and to constructive debate with it:

> . . . what can be found, in a body of work so committed to an understanding of the present formation, is, on the one hand, a practical belief in the forging, through action and argument, interaction and communication, of a hard-won solidarity. And, on the other hand, a sustained materialist analysis which vitally connects certain necessary theoretical abstractions to the complex social relations from which they have been derived, the determinations of culture to the agency of women and men – without reduction, and beyond what Williams would regard as the *impasse* of modernist formalism. If this is a time for the women's movements to take stock, to get back 'to the apparently duller procedures of what, where and how', it may be that there is a debate to be had with the work of Raymond Williams. (p. 107)

3 An Odd Woman

1 Some of these letters are still unpublished and in the possession of the author's family. Two letters from Karl Marx to Collet Dobson Collet, dated 10 November and 9 December 1876, concerning Gladstone's relations with the Russian government, have been published, with editorial notes and an introduction, by Royden Harrison, in 'Marx, Gladstone and Olga Novikov', *Bulletin of the Society for the Study of Labour History,* no. 33 (Autumn 1976), pp. 27–34.
2 Collet Dobson Collet was the author of *History of the Taxes on Knowledge. Their Origin and Repeal* (2 vols), Introduction by George Jacob Holyoake (T. Fisher Unwin, 1899). The book was started by its author when he was eighty-one and completed when he was eighty-five.

3 An injunction I have carried with me uneasily all my life. Clara wrote, edited and published privately a quantity of family records and letters.

4 For a detailed discussion of just how hobbled this could be, see Hilda Martindale: *Women Servants of the State 1870–1938. A History of Women in the Civil Service* (George Allen & Unwin, 1938) and Martha Vicinus: *Independent Women, Work and Community for Single Women 1850–1920* (Virago, 1985). See also Julia Parker: *Women and Welfare. Ten Victorian Women in Public Social Service* (Macmillan, 1988).

5 Beatrice Potter, who married Sidney Webb, was Clara's almost exact contemporary. She was born in 1858 into a Unitarian family and was to claim, many years after her father's death: 'He was the only man I ever knew who genuinely believed that women were superior to men, and acted as if he did.' The differences between Clara and Beatrice were differences of class and money and, perhaps by extension, of education. Both women would have conceded, I think, that Clara's remaining unmarried while Beatrice married constituted another important difference. When referring to Beatrice Webb I have made extensive use of her four-volume *Diary*, edited by Norman and Jeanne MacKenzie (Virago and the London School of Economics, 1982–5).

6 This is a constant theme in her work and leads her to views which are uncomfortable to contemplate today: for instance, that middle-class married women should not work because they were taking work from unmarried women, who needed it more.

7 Martindale, pp. 46–51. For a detailed account of women's position in the Civil Service in this century, see Meta Zimmeck: 'Strategies and Stratagems for the Employment of Women in the British Civil Service, 1919–1939', *The Historical Journal*, vol. 27, no. 4 (1984), pp. 901–24.

8 Martindale; Zimmeck.

9 This is taken from Clara's unpublished diary, which is in my possession. The Modern Records Centre, University of Warwick Library, contains copies of most of the material to which I refer here. This entry was made on 4 October 1898.

10 COS are the initials which were commonly used to stand for the Charity Organisation Society, of which Clara was at one time a member and to whose journals, the *Reporter* and the *Review*, she regularly contributed. This society is central to an understanding of the debate about poverty (most particularly London's poverty) which raged during the last twenty-five years of the nineteenth century. For a most illuminating and critical account of the society's role in this debate, see Gareth Stedman Jones's *Outcast London. A Study in the Relationship between Classes in Victorian Society* (Penguin, 1984). For a more partisan account of the COS see Charles L. Mowat: *The Charity Organisation Society 1869–1913* (Methuen, 1961). See also Vicinus, ch. 6.

11 I own the copy Clara must have given to her sister Carrie of *Labour and Life of the People*, vol. 1, *East London*, edited by Charles Booth and published by Williams & Norgate in 1889. This also contains sections by

Beatrice Potter on 'The Docks', 'Tailoring' and 'The Jewish Community'.

12 Sophia Dobson Collet (1822–94). Apart from writing a number of articles on atheism and on the relation of Hinduism to Christianity, she was the compiler and editor of *The Life and Letters of Raja Rammohun Roy*, privately published by her nephew, Harold Collet, after her death, in 1900. The Brahmo Somaj (of which Roy was founder) was a branch of Hinduism regarded at the time as opportunistic apostasy by many contemporary Indians, but welcomed by many Liberal British imperialists for its responsiveness to certain aspects of Christianity and for its abandonment of some traditional Hindu beliefs and practices. Sophia was also a member of the circle which gathered round Emerson in London in the earlier part of the century.

13 Wyggeston Girls' School, which opened in the year Clara went there (1878), continued into the 1980s and is now a sixth-form college. Miss Leicester, its first headmistress, who did not retire until 1902, is remembered for her words: 'I want all you girls to be clever, but above all I want you to be good women.'

14 Beatrice Potter met Eleanor Marx in the British Museum refreshment room in 1883 and argued with her about Christianity. She gives an interesting account of Clara's old friend:

> In person she is comely, dressed in a slovenly picturesque way with curly black hair flying about in all directions. Fine eyes full of life and sympathy, otherwise ugly features and expression, and complexion showing the signs of an unhealthy excited life, kept up with stimulants and tempered by narcotics. Lives alone, is much connected with Bradlaugh set, evidently peculiar views on love, etc., and I should think has somewhat 'natural' relations with men! Should fear that the chances were against her remaining long within the pale of 'respectable' society. (*The Diary of Beatrice Webb*, vol. 1. pp. 87–8).

Yvonne Kapp, in her *Eleanor Marx,*, vol 1 (Virago, 1972) responds robustly to Webb's comments:

> That Eleanor Marx should fall below the standards of the railway magnate's daughter is not altogether a surprise – it is conceivable that their papas would not always have seen eye to eye – but the opinion that Eleanor was something of a slut and a drug addict into the bargain does seem a shade bizarre considering her attitude to narcotics – 'not much better than dram-drinking and ... almost ... as injurious' – and the innumerable testimonies to her neat if not modish attire. (p. 284)

15 Clara transcribed, edited and privately published selections of family letters entitled *William Whiston's Disciples. In correspondence with each other 1723–1768* and *Letters of Dr. John Collet of Newbury to his Brother Joseph.* In the first of these there is a letter written by Sam Collet (referred to by Clara as the Patriarch) to his children in 1723, which engages in discussion with them about the significance of the Holy Ghost in the Bible. This suggests (and there is evidence and family belief to

support it) that Sam Collet, who was born in 1682, turned towards Unitarian beliefs at an early age. Clara, as editor, appends a characteristic footnote to this letter: '[In future these lectures on the Bible will be omitted from these extracts.]' The letter and its footnote provide a kind of implicit commentary on a very fundamental transformation of Unitarianism: from the passionate rereading of the Bible of its earliest days to the rationalism and humanism of the forms of Unitarianism with which Clara was familiar.

16 Clara transcribed and edited (and published privately) *The Letters of John to Eliza*, which she subtitled 'A Four Years' Correspondence Course in the Education of Women, 1806–1810' – the letters written by her grandfather, John Collet, to his future wife, Elizabeth, on this very question.

17 The South Place Ethical Society is described on a plaque in its present location in Conway Hall as: 'founded in 1793, the society is a progressive movement, whose aim is the study and dissemination of ethical principles based on humanism and the cultivation of a rational way of life'.

18 This piece, the second half of a chapter on secondary education in London, was published in *Labour and Life of the People*, vol. 2, *London continued* (Williams & Norgate, 1891).

19 Clara has sometimes been regarded as the first woman to get an MA in Political Economy. John Halperin, in his *Gissing, A Life in Books* (Oxford University Press, 1982), takes this view. He also describes her as 'involved in some of the most advanced political and social organizations of the time' (p. 189), a view she would vehemently have pooh-poohed.

20 Stedman Jones, pp. 305–6.

21 ibid. In Stedman Jones's argument, the COS comes to stand for the most damaging attitudes to London's poverty in the 1860s and 1870s: 'The COS repeatedly stressed that its function was not primarily to give relief but to organize charitable activity. Ideally, all local relief was to be channelled through the charity office and the local committee would decide whether the applicant was deserving before passing him on to the relevant specialized charitable agency or to the Poor Law', p. 256, and 'by systematically investigating each individual applicant, the COS was a pioneer of "casework" and thus laid the foundations of modern social administration.' See also Mowat; and Helen Bosanquet: *Social Work in London 1869 to 1912. A History of the Charity Organisation Society* (John Murray, 1914).

22 Clara remarks a little sadly in her diary that Clementina Black, the editor of *Married Women's Work* (Virago, 1983, first published 1915), 'thoroughly believes in the utility of her work'.

23 'Maria Edgeworth and Charity' was published in *The Charity Organisation Review*, vol. 5, 1889, pp. 418–24.
Amongst Clara's papers is the manuscript of 'A Statistical Survey of Pre-Victorian Novels'. Its rather formal abstract lays out two principal objectives:

(1) an occupation census of the inhabitants of any novel throwing light on the morals, manners and social conditions of the period described; and (2) a brief estimate of the value of the novel under consideration as first-hand evidence, presented by an author, contemporaneous with its inhabitants during the period of time selected and personally acquainted with the country and social groups to which they belong.

Not a currently fashionable way of reading novels, it might be said, though it has something in common with recent feminist trawling of novels for a variety of understandings.

24 Martindale, p. 46.
25 George Gissing: *London and the Life of Literature in Late Victorian England. The Diary of George Gissing Novelist,* ed. Pierre Coustillas (Harvester Press, 1978), 19 March 1892, p. 273.
26 Halperin, p. 175.
27 George Gissing's *Diary,* 18 July 1893, p. 310.
28 Clara Collet's Diary MSS. 14 May 1905.
29 Halperin, chs. 4 and 5. Some of these events were used by Gissing in his novels *Born in Exile* and *The Nether World*.
30 George Gissing: *The Odd Women* (Virago, 1980; first published 1893), p. 101.
31 Unpublished letter from George Gissing to Clara Collet, 17 June 1894.
32 This is the view taken by Halperin, but also by Gillian Tindall in *The Born Exile: George Gissing* (Chatto & Windus, 1974).
33 MSS. 29/3/13/4 (Modern Records Centre, University of Warwick Library): 'Clover King': 'Undercurrents'.
34 Gloom has always been the quality people have associated with Gissing's novels. Patrick Parrinder recalls Raymond Williams advising him not to read George Gissing's novels in the winter (Patrick Parrinder: 'Uncle Raymond', *The Cambridge Review,* vol. 109, no. 2301, June 1988).
35 Pierre Coustillas (ed.): *The Letters of George Gissing to Gabrielle Fleury* (New York Public Library, 1964), 16 February 1899.
36 A large collection of letters written by Gabrielle Fleury to Clara Collet between 1904 and 1928 is in the author's possession.
37 Clara never revealed to Gabrielle that she had known from the beginning that Morley Roberts meant to produce a novel about Gissing rather than a biography.
38 Clara Collet's Diary MSS., 12 February 1909.
39 From 'Women's Work' in Charles Booth (ed.): *Labour and Life of the People,* vol. 1, *East London* (1889), pp. 406–77 (p. 461).
40 Stedman Jones, pp. 334–5.
41 In *The Diary of Beatrice Webb,* vol. 3. Between pages 11 – the day, 23 November 1905, when she was appointed to the Commission – and 106, 'the day after the reception of the reports of the Poor Law Commission'. Webb was always more at ease with politicians and with political negotiation than Clara was.
42 Clara Collet's Diary MSS., 19 August 1910.

43 Martindale.
44 Clara E. Collet: *Educated Working Women. Essays on the Position of Women Workers in the Middle Classes* (P.S. King & Son, 1902).
45 ibid. ('Prospects of Marriage for Women', p. 64).
46 ibid. (Preface).
47 ibid. ('The Economic Position of Educated Working Women', p. 3).
48 ibid., p. 6.
49 ibid. p. 102. I am indebted to Carolyn Steedman for pointing out that this book is in fact called *The Governess, or The Little Female Academy,* and was written by Sarah Fielding and published in 1749. She also points out that Clara was unfair to the book.
50 Clara E. Collet: ibid. ('The Age Limit for Women', p. 95).
51 ibid. ('The Economic Position of Educated Working Women', p. 24).
52 ibid. ('The Age Limit for Women', p. 91).
53 ibid. ('Mrs Stetson's Economic Ideal', p. 122).
54 This essay was originally published in *The Charity Organisation Review,* vol. 7, 1890, pp. 134–43.
55 Clara E. Collet: *Educated Working Women* ('The Economic Position of Working Women', pp. 15–16).
56 Stedman Jones, p. 336.
57 Unpublished notes for the consideration of the Chairman: *Employment of Women Committee.* Memorandum on the Employment of Married Women. Undated, but probably 1917 or 1918.
58 Clara E. Collet: *Educated Working Women* ('Through Fifty Years. The Economic Progress of Women', p. 140).

4 Imperial Seductions

1 Charlotte Brontë: *Villette,* (Everyman edn, p. 180, first published 1853). Jean Rhys, who 'rewrote' Bronte's Creole madwoman in *Jane Eyre* in her own novel, *Wide Sargasso Sea,* pointed out in a letter to Diana Athill that

> Charlotte had a 'thing' about the West Indies being rather sinister places – because in another of her books, 'Villette', she drowns the hero, Professor Somebody, on the voyage to Guadeloupe, another very alien place – according to her. (From Francis Wyndham and Diana Melly (eds): *Jean Rhys Letters 1931–1966.* (Penguin, 1985), p. 297.

2 In Shakespeare's *Antony and Cleopatra.*
3 Naila Kabeer: 'Subordination and Struggle: Women in Bangladesh', *New Left Review,* no. 168, March/April 1988, pp. 95–121.
4 Studs Terkel, in an interview broadcast on BBC Radio, 7 November 1988.
5 Anna Davin: 'Imperialism and Motherhood', *History Workshop Journal,* vol. 5, Spring 1978, pp. 9–65.
6 Frantz Fanon: *Toward the African Revolution* (Writers & Readers, 1980; first published 1964), p. 39.
7 Antonio Gramsci: *Selections from The Prison Notebooks,* ed. and

transl. Quintin Hoare and Geoffrey Nowell-Smith (Lawrence & Wishart, 1986), p. 447.

8 Edward W. Said: *Orientalism* (Penguin, 1985), p. 28.
9 ibid., p. 203.
10 ibid., p. 6.
11 Ahdaf Soueif: Review of *An Egyptian Journal* by William Golding, *London Review of Books*, vol. 7, no. 17, 3 October 1985.
12 I am thinking particularly here of Said's books *The Question of Palestine* and *Covering Islam*.
13 Said: *Orientalism*, p. 325.
14 ibid.
15 Edward W. Said: *The World, the Text, and the Critic* (Faber & Faber, 1984, p. 14. It is clear from this and other parts of Said's work that he has been strongly influenced by both Gramsci and Williams.
16 Said: *Orientalism*, p. 6.
17 ibid., p. 187.
18 Rana Kabbani: *Europe's Myths of Orient* (Pandora, 1986), pp. 47–8.
19 ibid.
20 Said: *Orientalism*, p. 311.
21 ibid.
22 *Orientalism*, p. 328.
23 See, for instance, Huda Sharawi's *Harem Years. The Memoirs of an Egyptian Feminist* (Virago, 1986).
24 Kabeer, p. 101. A vegetarian version of Richardson's carniverous view of marriage. See p. 32.
25 Joanna Trollope: *Britannia's Daughters. Women of the British Empire* (Cresset Women's Voices, 1983), p. 121.
26 Brontë: p. 447.
27 Gayatri Chakravorty Spivak: *In Other Worlds. Essays in Cultural Politics* (Methuen, 1987), in 'The Politics of Interpretation' p. 129; the reference is to Wayne Booth's 'Freedom of Interpretation: Bakhtin and the Challenge of Feminist Criticism', *Critical Inquiry* 9, September 1982, in which Booth delivers himself of a somewhat perfunctory *mea culpa* by implicating Bakhtin, as I shall too in the next chapter, for evading the question of women and their relation to texts.
28 Simone de Beauvoir: *The Second Sex* (Four Square, 1966; first published 1949), p. 30.
29 ibid. p. 56.
30 Frantz Fanon: *Black Skin White Masks* (Paladin, 1970; first published 1952), p. 108.
31 ibid., p. 94.
32 ibid., p. 93.
33 ibid., p. 127.
34 ibid., pp. 35–6.
35 Jacques Lacan: 'The Mirror Stage as Formative of the Function of the I', in *Ecrits: A Selection*, transl. Alan Sheridan (Tavistock, 1977).
36 Fanon, p. 114.
37 Vygotsky's theory of human development as always social and cultural

is argued and demonstrated in two books: *Thought and Language,* newly revised and edited by Alex Kozulin, MIT Press, 1986; and *Mind in Society* (Harvard University Press, 1979).

38 V.N. Vološinov: *Marxism and the Philosophy of Language* (Harvard University).

39 M.M. Bakhtin: *Speech Genres and Other Late Essays* (University of Texas Press, 1986).

40 This is not to say, of course, that we can look to less economically and culturally elaborate societies for recognition of women's centrality. A fine study of this theme in relation to contemporary rural and agricultural France is to be found in Christine Delphy's *Close to Home* to which I referred in Chapter 2, (Hutchinson, 1984).

41 Outstanding examples of this are to be found in Nawal El Saadawi's *The Hidden Face of Eve. Women in the Arab World* (Zed Books, 1980); Mai Ghoussoub's 'Feminism – or the Eternal Masculine – in the Arab World', *New Left Review*, no. 161, January/February 1987. See also the critique of this by Reza Hammami and Martina Rieker: 'Feminist Orientalism and Orientalist Marxism', *New Left Review*, no. 170, July/August 1988, and Ghoussoub's reply in the same issue.

For a most useful feminist theoretical discussion of colonialism, see Chandra Mohanty: 'Under Western Eyes: Feminist Scholarship and Colonial Discourses', *Feminist Review*, no. 30, Autumn 1988. See also Pratibha Parmar: 'Gender, race and class: Asian women in resistance', in Centre for Contemporary Cultural Studies: *The Empire Strikes Back* (Hutchinson, 1982).

42 Jane Austen: *Selected Letters 1796–1817*. Selected and Edited by R.W. Chapman (Oxford University Press, 1981), pp. 188–9.

43 Sahar Khalifeh: *Wild Thorns* (Al Saqi Books, 1985).

44 Toni Morrison, in an interview broadcast on BBC television in October 1987.

45 Toni Morrison: *Beloved* (Chatto & Windus, 1987), p. 73.

46 ibid., p. 180.

47 ibid., p. 155.

48 Morrison, in interview, as above.

49 Morrison: *Beloved*, p. 88.

50 ibid., p. 149.

51 ibid., p. 97.

52 ibid., p. 272.

53 ibid., p. 251.

54 ibid., p. 273.

55 ibid., p. 268.

56 In Jane Miller: *Women Writing about Men* (Virago, 1986) and *Many Voices. Bilingualism, Culture and Education*, Routledge & Kegan Paul, 1983).

57 Cora Kaplan: 'Keeping the Color in *The Color Purple*', in *Sea Changes. Culture and Feminism* (Verso, 1986), p. 182.

5 Feasters and Spoilsports

1   See, for instance, the chapter by Thom Gunn in Ronald Hayman (ed.): *My Cambridge* (Robson Books, 1977).

2   Carlo Ginzburg: *The Cheese and the Worms. The Cosmos of a Sixteenth-Century Miller* (Routledge & Kegan Paul, 1980) p. xxii.

3   M.M. Bakhtin: *Rabelais and His World* (Indiana University Press, 1984), p. 240.

4   See, for instance, Julia Kristeva's 'Word, Dialogue and Novel', in *The Kristeva Reader*, ed. Toril Moi (Basil Blackwell, 1986). It is significant as well that it was Kristeva who introduced Bakhtin to the West, though it is often to Raymond Williams's rather later work on Bakhtin and Vološinov (in *Marxism and Literature*, 1977) that British interest in their work is attributed.

5   Bakhtin, p. 72.

6   Kristeva, p. 49.

7   Bakhtin: *Rabelais and His World*, p. 97.

8   ibid., p.10.

9   ibid., p. 212.

10 ibid., p. 118.

11 This phrase is used by D.B. Wyndham Lewis in his introduction to François Rabelais: *The Heroic Deeds of Gargantua and Pantagruel*, transl. Sir Thomas Urquhart and Peter Le Motteux (J.M. Dent, 1933; first published 1653), p. viii.

12 For this and other quotations from Rabelais I have used Urquhart's extraordinary translation. This passage is discussed by Bakhtin in *Rabelais and His World*, p. 206.

13 Bakhtin: *Rabelais and His World*, p. 205.

14 ibid., p. 190.

15 See Wayne C. Booth: 'Freedom of Interpretation: Bakhtin and the Challenge of Feminist Criticism', *Critical Inquiry*, 9, September 1982.

16 Bakhtin: *Rabelais and His World*, p. 229.

17 ibid., p. 239.

18 ibid.

19 *Rabelais and His World*, p. 240.

20 ibid., p. 105.

21 ibid.

22 *Rabelais and His World*, p. 106.

23 ibid., p. 223.

24 M.M. Bakhtin: 'The Problem of Speech Genres', in *Speech Genres and Other Late Essays* (University of Texas Press, 1986).

25 ibid., p. 60.

26 ibid., p. 71.

27 ibid., p. 69.

28 Ken Hirschkop: 'Bakhtin, Discourse and Democracy', *New Left Review*, no. 160, November/December 1986, p. 103.

29 V.N. Vološinov: *Marxism and the Philosophy of Language* (Harvard University Press, 1973), p. 23.

30   M.M. Bakhtin: *Problems of Dostoevsky's Poetics* (University of Minnesota Press, 1984), p. 30.
31   Hirschkop, p. 106.
32   ibid., p. 110.
33   ibid., p. 105.
34   This is in Michael Holquist's Introduction to Bakhtin's *Speech Genres and Other Late Essays,* p. xiii.
35   Vološinov, p. 102.
36   B. Megson and J. Lindsay: *Girton College 1869–1959. An Informal History* (W. Heffer & Sons Ltd, 1961), p. 66.
37   See, for instance, Michel Foucault: *Discipline and Punish* (Penguin, 1982), pp. 26, 27 and *passim:* and Pierre Bourdieu: 'Systems of Education and Systems of Thought', in Michael F.D. Young (ed.): *Knowledge and Control. New Directions for the Sociology of Education* (Collier-Macmillan, 1971). See Shirley Brice Heath: *Ways with Words* (Cambridge University Press, 1983) for a comparative ethnographical account of the literacy practices of three communities in America: a mixed urban group of teachers and two small rural communities, one black and one white. Brice Heath offers invaluable insights into the gaps between home and school literacy practices and how these come to be disabling. Brian Street's *Literacy in Theory and Practice* (Cambridge University Press, 1986) compares literacies developed for local and commercial purposes and those learned in the context of Koranic studies in contemporary Iran. See also Hilary Minns: *Read it to me now! Learning at Home and at School* (Virago 1990).
38   L. Vygotsky: *Mind in Society. The Development of Higher Psychological Processes* (Harvard University Press, 1978), p. 86.
39   I am enormously grateful to my colleague John Hardcastle for letting me use this material from his own classroom.
40   Derek Walcott: 'Mass Man', in *The Gulf* (Jonathan Cape, 1969).
41   For an account of one school's struggle to introduce work by black writers into an A level syllabus, see Peter Traves: 'A Better A Level', in Jane Miller (ed.): *Eccentric Propositions. Essays on Literature and the Curriculum* (Routledge & Kegan Paul, 1984). See also Suzanne Scafe: *Teaching Black Literature* (Virago, 1989).
42   Ginzburg, p. xxii.
43   ibid., pp. 33, 51.
44   ibid., p. 53.
45   ibid., p. 5. This advice was given to Menocchio by his childhood friend, the vicar of Polcenigo, Giovanni Daniele Melchiori.
46   Paul Willis: *Learning to Labour: How Working Class Kids Get Working Class Jobs* (Saxon House, 1977).
47   Vološinov, p. 23.
48   Margaret Atwood: *Cat's Eye* (Bloomsbury, 1989), p. 410.
49   ibid., p. 98.
50   ibid., p. 249.
51   ibid., p. 126.

52   ibid.
53   *Cat's Eye*, p. 138.
54   ibid., p. 267.
55   ibid., p. 420.
56   Marina Warner: *Alone of All Her Sex. The Myth and the Cult of the Virgin Mary* (Picador, 1985), p. 58.
57   ibid.

Bibliography

Adams, Ruth M., 'George Gissing and Clara Collet', *Nineteenth Century Fiction* XI (June 1956), pp. 72–7

Adams, Ruth, L. M., 'Reviews', *Victorian Studies* V (March 1962), pp. 271–2

Anderson, Benedict, *Imagined Communities*, Verso, 1983

Attar, Dena, *Wasting Girls' Time. The History and Politics of Home Economics*, Virago, 1990

Atwood, Margaret, *Cat's Eye*, Bloomsbury, 1989

Auerback, Erich, *Mimesis, The Representation of Reality in Western Literature*, transl. Willard R. Trask, Princeton University Press, 1974

Austen, Jane, *Sense and Sensibility* (1811)

Austen, Jane, *Selected Letters 1796–1817*, Selected and ed. R.W. Chapman, Oxford University Press, 1981

Bakhtin, M.M., *The Dialogic Imagination. Four Essays*, ed. Michael Holquist, transl. Caryl Emerson and Michael Holquist, University of Texas Press, 1981

Bakhtin, M.M., *Problems of Dostoevsky's Poetics*, ed. and transl. Caryl Emerson, Introduction by Wayne C. Booth, University of Minnesota Press, 1984

Bakhtin, M.M., *Rabelais and His World*, transl. Hélène Iswolsky, Indiana University Press, 1984

Bakhtin, M.M., *Speech Genres and Other Late Essays*, transl. Vern W. McGee, ed. Caryl Emerson and Michael Holquist, University of Texas Press, 1986

Barrett, Michèle, *Women's Oppression Today. Problems in Marxist Feminist Analysis*, Verso, 1980

Barrett, Michèle, '*Max Raphael and the Question of Aesthetics*', *New Left Review*, no. 161, January/February 1987

Barrett, Michèle and McIntosh, Mary, 'Ethnocentrism and Socialist-Feminist Theory', *Feminist Review*, no. 20, Summer 1985

de Beauvoir, Simone, *The Second Sex*, Four Square, 1966 (1949)

Benhabib, Seyla and Cornell, Drucilla, (eds), *Feminism as Critique*, Polity Press, 1987

Benjamin, Jessica, *The Bonds of Love, Psychoanalysis, Feminism and the Problem of Domination*, Virago, 1990

Bennett, Tony, *Formalism and Marxism*, Methuen, 1979

Bernheimer, Charles and Kahane, Claire (eds), *In Dora's Case: Freud. Hysteria. Feminism*, Virago, 1985

Black, Clementina (ed.), *Married Women's Work*, Virago, 1983. (1915)

Blackburn, Robin, 'Raymond Williams and the Politics of A New Left', *New Left Review*, no. 168, March/April 1988

Booth, Charles (ed.), *Labour and Life of the People*, vol. 1, *East London*, Williams & Norgate 1889

Booth, Charles (ed.), *Labour and Life of the People*, vol. 2, *London*, Williams & Norgate, 1891.

Booth, Charles (ed.), *Life and Labour of the People in London*, Series 1, 2 and 3, Macmillan, 1902

Booth, Wayne C., 'Freedom of Interpretation: Bakhtin and the Challenge of Feminist Criticism', *Critical Inquiry*, 9, September 1982

Bosanquet, Helen, *Social Work in London 1869 to 1912. A History of the Charity Organization Society*, John Murray, 1914

Boumelha, Penny, *Thomas Hardy and Women. Sexual Ideology and Narrative Form*, Harvester Press, 1982

Bourdieu, Pierre, 'Systems of Education and Systems of Thought', in Michael F.D. Young (ed.), *Knowledge and Control. New Directions for the Sociology of Education*, Collier-Macmillan, 1971

Brice Heath, Shirley, *Ways with Words*, Cambridge University Press, 1983

Brontë, Charlotte, *Villette*, Everyman edn 1966, (1853)

Byron, Lord, George, Gordon, *Don Juan* (1819)

Cameron, Deborah, 'Sexism and Semantics', *Radical Philosophy*, Spring, 1984

Cameron, Deborah, *Feminism and Linguistic Theory*, Macmillan, 1985

Carby, Hazel, 'White woman listen! Black feminism and the boundaries of sisterhood', Centre for Contemporary Cultural Studies, *The Empire Strikes Back: Race and Racism in 70s Britain*, Hutchinson, 1982

Césaire, Aimé, *The Collected Poetry*, transl. Clayton Eshleman and Annette Smith, University of California Press, 1983

The Charity Organisation Reporter, vols. 1–13, 1872–84

The Charity Organisation Review, vols. 1–12, 1885–96; vols. 1–22, 1897–1906 Longmans, Green, and Co.

Clark, Katerina and Holquist, Michael, *Mikhail Bakhtin*, Harvard University Press, 1984

Clément, Catherine, *Opera or the Undoing of Women*, transl. Betsy Wing, Virago, 1989

Cockburn, Cynthia, 'Macho Men of the Left', *Marxism Today*, April 1988

Collet, Clara E., 'Maria Edgeworth and Charity', *The Charity Organisation Review*, vol. 5, 1889

Collet, Clara E., 'The Economic Position of Educated Working Women', South Place Ethical Society, 1890

Collet, Clara E., 'Foreign Competition', *The Charity Organisation Review*, vol. 6, 1890

Collet, Clara E., Review of Mrs Stetson's *Women and Economics*, *The Charity Organisation Review*, vol. 7. 1890

Collet, Clara E., 'Charity Organisation' in *Charity Organisation Review,* vol. 7, 1891

Collet, Clara E., *Educated Working Women. Essays on the Economic Position of Women Workers in the Middle Classes,* P.S. King & Son, 1902

Collet, Clara E., 'Women in Industry', London Women's Printing Society, 1911

Collet, Clara E., *The Private Letter Books of Joseph Collet, sometime Governor of St. George, Madras, (1717–1720),* Calcutta Superintendent Government Printing, India, 1924

Collet, Clara E. (ed.), *Letters of Dr. John Collet of Newbury to his Brother Joseph,* privately published, 1933

Collet, Clara E. (transcribed and edited), *William Whiston's Disciples. In correspondence with each other 1723–1768,* privately published

Collet, Clara E. (transcribed and edited), *The Letters of John to Eliza. A Four Years' Correspondence Course in the Education of Women, 1806–1810,* privately published, 1949

Collet, Clara E., see also under Charles Booth for her investigative pieces on subjects like girls' schools, home work, women in particular trades, etc

Collet, Collet Dobson, *History of the Taxes on Knowledge. Their Origin and Repeal,* 2 vols. Introduced by George Jacob Holyoake, T. Fisher Unwin, 1899

Collet, Sophia Dobson, *The Life and Letters of Raja Rammohun Roy,* privately published, 1900

Collie, Michael, *George Gissing. A Bibliography,* Dawson, 1975

Coustillas, Pierre (ed.), *The Letters of George Gissing to Gabrielle Fleury,* New York Public Library, 1964

Coustillas, Pierre (ed.), *Collected Articles on George Gissing,* Frank Cass and Co. Ltd, 1968

Coustillas, Pierre, (ed.), *Henry Hick's Recollections of George Gissing Together with Gissing's Letters to Henry Hick,* Enitharmon Press, 1973

Coustillas, Pierre (eds.), *London and the Life of Literature in Late Victorian England. The Diary of George Gissing Novelist,* Harvester Press, 1978

Davidoff, Leonore, 'Class and Gender in Victorian England', in Judith L. Newton, Mary P. Ryan and Judith R. Walkowitz (eds), *Sex and Class in Women's History,* History Workshop Series, Routledge & Kegan Paul, 1983

Davidoff, Leonore, l'Esperance, Jean and Newby, Howard, 'Landscape with Figures: Home and Community in English Society', in Juliet Mitchell and Ann Oakley (eds), *The Rights and Wrongs of Women,* Penguin, 1976

Davies, Emily, *The Higher Education of Women (1866).* Introduced by Janet Howarth, The Hambledon Press, 1988

Davies, Llewelyn, Margaret (ed.), *Maternity. Letters from Working Women,* Virago, 1978

Davin, Anna, 'Imperialism and Motherhood', *History Workshop Journal*, vol. 5, Spring 1978. pp. 9–65

Delphy, Christine, *Close to Home, A materialist analysis of women's oppression*, transl. and ed. Diana Leonard, Hutchinson in association with The Explorations of Feminism Collective, 1984

Dyhouse, Carol, *Girls growing up in late Victorian and Edwardian England*, Routledge & Kegan Paul, 1981

Eagleton, Terry, 'Resources for a Journey of Hope: The Significance of Raymond Williams', *New Left Review*, no. 168, March/April 1988

Eisenstein, Zillah R. (ed.), *Capitalist Patriarchy and the Case for Socialist Feminism*, Monthly Review Press, 1979

Ellmann, Mary, *Thinking About Women*, Virago, 1979

Fanon, Frantz, *Black Skin White Masks*, Paladin, 1970 (1952)

Fanon, Frantz, *Toward the African Revolution*, Writers & Readers, 1980 (1964)

Fanon, Frantz, *The Wretched of the Earth*, Penguin, 1983 (1961)

Foucault, Michel, *The Archaeology of Knowledge*, transl. A.M. Sheridan Smith, Tavistock Publications, 1982 (1969)

Foucault, Michel, *Discipline and Punish. The Birth of the Prison*, transl. Alan Sheridan, Penguin, 1982 (1975)

Foucault, Michel, *The History of Sexuality. Volume One. An Introduction.* transl. Robert Hurley, Penguin, 1981

Gallop, Jane, *Feminism and Psychoanalysis. The Daughter's Seduction*, Macmillan, 1982

Gavron, Hannah, *The Captive Wife*, Routledge & Kegan Paul, 1966

Ghoussoub, Mai, 'Feminism – or the Eternal Masculine – in the Arab World', *New Left Review*, no. 161, January/February 1987

Ginzburg, Carlo, *The Cheese and the Worms. The Cosmos of a Sixteenth-Century Miller*, transl. John and Anne Tedeschi, Routledge & Kegan Paul, 1980

Gissing, George, *Born in Exile* (1892)

Gissing, George, *The Odd Women* (Virago, 1980), (1893)

Gissing, George, see also under Pierre Coustillas and under Manuscript Sources at the end of Bibliography

Gramsci, Antonio, *Selections from Cultural Writings*, ed. David Forgacs and Geoffrey Nowell-Smith; transl. William Boelhower, Lawrence & Wishart, 1985

Gramsci, Antonio, *Selections from the Prison Notebooks of Antonio Gramsci*, ed. and transl. Quintin Hoare and Geoffrey Nowell-Smith, Lawrence & Wishart, 1986

Greenberg, Caren, 'Reading Reading: Echo's Abduction of Language', in Sally McConnell-Ginet, Ruth Borker and Nelly Furman (eds), *Women and Language in Literature and Society*, Praeger, 1980

Greer, Germaine, *Sex and Destiny. The Politics of Human Fertility*, Picador, 1984

Halperin, John, *Gissing, A Life in Books*, Oxford University Press, 1982

Hammami, Reza and Rieker, Martina, 'Feminist Orientalism and Orientalist Marxism', *New Left Revie,* no. 170, July/August 1988

Hardwick, Elizabeth, *Seduction and Betrayal. Women and Literature,* Random House, 1974

Hare, David, 'Cycles of Hope and Despair', an article on Raymond Williams and Cambridge in the Sixties, *Weekend Guardian,* 3–4 June 1989

Harrison, Royden (ed. and intro), 'Marx, Gladstone and Olga Novikov', *Bulletin of the Society for the Study of Labour History,* no. 33 (Autumn 1976)

Hart, Nicky, 'Gender and the Rise and Fall of Class Politics', *New Left Review,* no. 175, May/June 1989

Hasan, Ruqaiya, 'The Ontogenesis of Ideology: An Interpretation of Mother–Child Talk', in Terry Threadgold, E.A. Grosz, Gunther Kress and M.A.K. Halliday (eds), *Semiotics, Ideology, Language,* Sidney Studies in Culture, no. 3, 1986

Haug, Frigga, 'How gender can guide socialism', a review of Claudia Koonz's *Mothers in the Fatherland: Women, the Family and Nazi Politics.* Jonathan Cape, 1987, *New Left Review,* no. 172, November/December 1988

Hayman, Ronald (ed.), *My Cambridge,* Robson Books, 1986

Heaney, Seamus, *Death of a Naturalist,* Faber & Faber, 1966

Hirschkop, Ken, 'Bakhtin, Discourse and Democracy', *New Left Review,* no. 160, November/December 1986

Hornsby, Jennifer, 'Philosophers and Feminists on Language Use', *Cogito,* vol. 2, no. 3, Autumn 1988

Jardine, Alice and Smith, Paul (eds), *Men in Feminism,* Methuen, 1987

Jones, Gareth Stedman, *Outcast London. A Study in the Relationship between Classes in Victorian Society,* Penguin, 1984 (1971)

Kabbani, Rana, *Europe's Myths of Orient,* Pandora, 1988

Kabbani, Rana, *Letter to Christendom,* Virago, 1989

Kabeer, Naila, 'Subordination and Struggle: Women in Bangladesh', *New Left Review,* no. 168, March/April 1988

Kaplan, Cora, 'Radical Feminism and Literature', in Mary Evans (ed.), *The Woman Question. Readings on the Subordination of Women,* Fontana, 1982

Kaplan, Cora, *Sea Changes, Essays on Culture and Feminism,* Verso, 1986

Kapp, Yvonne, *Eleanor Marx,* vol. 1, *Family Life 1855–1883;* vol. 2, *The Crowded Years 1884–1898,* Virago, 1972, 1976

Khalifeh, Sahar, *Wild Thorns,* Al Saqi Books, 1985

Kristeva, Julia, *Desire in Language. A Semiotic Approach to Literature and Art,* ed. Leon S. Roudiez, transl. Thomas Gora, Alice Jardine and Leon S. Roudiez, Basil Blackwell, 1980

Kristeva, Julia, see Toril Moi (ed.) *The Kristeva Reader*

Kundera, Milan, *The Unbearable Lightness of Being,* transl. Michael Henry Heim, Faber & Faber, 1984

Lacan, Jacques, *Ecrits: A Selection*, transl. Alan Sheridan, Tavistock Press, 1977

Laclos, Pierre Choderlos de, *Les Liaisons Dangereuses* (1782)

Ladurie, Emmanuel Le Roy, *Carnival in Romans. A People's Uprising at Romans*, Penguin, 1980

Lawson, Mark, 'Storey Lines' *The Independent Magazine*, 8 April 1989

Lawson, Sylvia, 'Greeromania', a review of Germaine Greer's *Daddy, we hardly knew you*, in *London Review of Books*, vol. 11, no. 8, 20 April 1989

Lovibond, Sabina, 'Feminism and Postmodernism', *New Left Review*, no. 178 November/December 1989

MacKenzie, Norman (ed.), *Connections*, MacGibbon & Kee, 1958

Marks, Elaine and de Courtivron, Isabelle (eds), *New French Feminisms. An Anthology*, Harvester, 1981

Martindale, Hilda, *Women Servants of the State 1870–1938. A History of Women in the Civil Service*, George Allen & Unwin, 1938

Megson, B. and Lindsay, J., *Girton College 1869–1959. An Informal History*, W. Heffer & Sons Ltd, 1961

Meulenbelt, Anja, Outshoorn, Joyce, Sevenhuijsen, Selma and de Vries, Petra, *A Creative Tension. Explorations in Socialist Feminism*, Pluto, 1984

Mill, John Stuart and Mill, Harriet Taylor, *The Subjection of Women* and *Enfranchisement of Women*, Virago, 1983 (1869, 1851)

Miller, Betty, *On the Side of the Angels*, Virago, 1985 (1945)

Miller, Betty, 'Amazons and Afterwards', *The Twentieth Century*, Special number on women, vol. 164, no. 978, August 1958

Miller, Jane, *Many Voices. Bilingualism, Culture and Education*, Routledge & Kegan Paul, 1983

Miller, Jane (ed.), *Eccentric Propositions. Essays on Literature and the Curriculum*, Routledge & Kegan Paul, 1984

Miller, Jane, *Women Writing about Men*, Virago, 1986

Miller, Karl, 'Are you distraining me?', in *Doubles*, Oxford University Press, 1985

Miller, Karl, *Authors*, Oxford University Press, 1989

Minns, Hilary, *Read it to me now! Learning at home and at school*, Virago, 1990

Mitchell, Juliet, *Woman's Estate*, Penguin, 1971

Mitchell, Juliet, *Psychoanalysis and Feminism*, Penguin, 1974

Mitchell, Juliet, *Women: The Longest Revolution. Essays in Feminism, Literature and Psychoanalysis*, Virago, 1984

Mitchell, Juliet, An interview with Angela McRobbie, *New Left Review*, no. 170, July/August 1988

Mitchell, Juliet and Oakley, Ann (eds), *The Rights and Wrongs of Women*, Penguin, 1976

Mitchell, Juliet and Oakley, Ann (eds), *What is Feminism?*, Basil Blackwell, 1986

Mitchell, Juliet and Rose, Jacqueline (eds), *Feminine Sexuality. Jacques*

Lacan and the Ecole Freudienne, transl. Jacqueline Rose, Macmillan, 1982

Mohanty, Chandra, 'Under Western Eyes: Feminist Scholarship and Colonial Discourses', *Feminist Review*, no. 30, Autumn 1988

Moi, Toril, *Sexual/Textual Politics. Feminist Literary Theory*, Methuen, 1985

Moi, Toril (ed.), *The Kristeva Reader*, Basil Blackwell, 1986

Morrison, Toni, *Beloved*, Chatto & Windus, 1987

Morson, Gary Saul, (ed.), *Bakhtin. Essays and Dialogues on His Work*, University of Chicago Press, 1986

Moss, Gemma, *Un/Popular Fictions*, Virago, 1989

Mowat, Charles L., *The Charity Organisation Society, 1869–1913*, Methuen, 1961

Mulhern, Francis, '"Towards 2000": News from You-Know-Where', *New Left Review*, no. 148, November/December 1984

Mulvey, Laura, *Visual and Other Pleasures*, Macmillan, 1989

Naipaul, V.S., *An Area of Darkness*, Penguin, 1984 (1964)

Parekh, Bhiku (ed.) *The Concept of Socialism*, Croom Helm, 1975

Parker, Julia, *Women and Welfare, Ten Victorian Women in Public Social Service*, Macmillan, 1989

Parmar, Pratibha, 'Gender, race and class: Asian women in resistance', in Centre for Contemporary Cultural Studies, *The Empire Strikes Back. Race and Racism in 70s Britain*, Hutchinson, 1982

Parrinder, Patrick, 'Uncle Raymond', *The Cambridge Review*, vol. 109, no. 2301, June 1988

Patel, Vibhuti, 'Women's Liberation in India,' *New Left Review*, no. 153, September/October 1985

Phillips, Anne, *Divided Loyalties, Dilemmas of Sex and Class*, Virago, 1987

Pinchbeck, Ivy, *Women Workers and the Industrial Revolution 1750–1850*, Virago, 1981 (1930)

Poovey, Mary, *Uneven Developments. The Ideological Work of Gender in Mid-Victorian England*, Virago, 1989

Rabelais, François, *The Heroic Deeds of Gargantua and Pantagruel*, transl. Sir Thomas Urquhart and Peter Le Motteux, J.M. Dent, 1933 (1653)

Richardson, Samuel, *Clarissa*, Penguin, 1985 (1747,8)

Ridley, Annie E., *Frances Mary Buss And Her Work for Education*, Longmans, Green and Co., 1895

Rorty, Richard, *Contingency, Irony, and Solidarity*, Cambridge University Press, 1989

Rose, Jacqueline, *The Case of Peter Pan or The Impossibility of Children's Fiction*, Macmillan, 1984

Rowbotham, Sheila, 'What Do Women Want? Woman-Centred Values and the World As It Is', *Feminist Review*, no. 12, Summer 1985

El Saadawi, Nawal, *The Hidden Face of Eve. Women in the Arab World*, Zed Books, 1980

Said, Edward W., *The Question of Palestine*, Vintage, 1979

Said, Edward W., *The World, the Text, and the Critic*, Faber & Faber, 1984

Said, Edward W., *Covering Islam*, Routledge & Kegan Paul, 1985

Said, Edward W., *Orientalism*, Penguin, 1985

Said, Edward W., *After the Last Sky*, with photographs by Jean Mohr, Faber & Faber, 1986

Said, Edward W., 'Jane Austen and Empire', in Terry Eagleton (ed.), *Raymond Williams. Critical Perspectives*, Polity Press in association with Basil Blackwell, 1989

Scafe, Suzanne, *Teaching Black Literature*, Virago, 1989

Segal, Lynne, *Is the Future Female? Troubled Thoughts on Contemporary Feminism*, Virago, 1987

Sharawi, Huda, *Harem Years. The Memoirs of an Egyptian Feminist*, Virago, 1986

Shiva, Vandana, *Staying Alive. Women, Ecology and Development*, Zed Books, 1988

Sassoon, Anne Showstack (ed.), *Approaches to Gramsci*, Writers & Readers, 1982

Soper, Kate, Review of *Feminism as Critique* (eds Seyla Benhabib and Drucilla Cornell, Polity Press, 1987), *New Left Review*, no. 176, July/August 1989

Soueif, Ahdaf, Review of *An Egyptian Journal* by William Golding, *London Review of Books*, vol. 7, no. 17, 3 October 1985

Spivak, Gayatri Chakravorty, *In Other Worlds. Essays in Cultural Politics*, Methuen, 1987

Stanley, Liz and Wise, Sue, *Breaking Out: Feminist Consciousness and Feminist Research*, Routledge & Kegan Paul, 1983

Steedman, Carolyn, *Landscape for a Good Woman. A Story of Two Lives*, Virago, 1986

Steedman, Carolyn, *Childhood, Culture and Class in Britain, Margaret McMillan, 1860–1931*, Virago, 1990

Steedman, Carolyn, Urwin, Cathy and Walkerdine, Valerie (eds), *Language, Gender and Childhood*, History Workshop Series, Routledge & Kegan Paul, 1985

Street, Brian, *Literacy in Theory and Practice*, Cambridge University Press, 1986

Sturrock, John (ed.), *Structuralism and Since. From Lévi-Strauss to Derrida*, Oxford University Press, 1979

Suleiman, S.R. (ed.), *The Reader in the Text*, Princeton University Press, 1980

Terkel, Studs, Interview on BBC Radio, 7 November 1988

Thompson, Ann and Wilcox, Helen (eds), *Teaching Women, Feminism and English Studies*, Manchester University Press, 1989

Tindall, Gillian, *The Born Exile: George Gissing*, Chatto & Windus, 1974

Todoro, Tzvetan, *Mikhail Bakhtin: The Dialogical Principle*, transl. Wlad Godzich, University of Minnesota Press, 1984

Tomalin, Claire, 'The Sage of Polygon Road', a review of *The Works of*

Mary Wollstonecraft, vols. 1–VII, ed. Janet Todd and Marilyn Butler, Pickering and Chatto, 1989, *London Review of Books*, vol. 11, no. 18, September 1989

Tracy, Lorna, *Amateur Passions. Love Stories?* Virago, 1981

Traves, Peter, 'A Better A Level', in Jane Miller (ed.), *Eccentric Propositions*, (see above)

Trollope, Joanna, *Britannia's Daughters. Women of the British Empire*, Cresset Women's Voices, 1983

Urwin, Cathy, see Steedman, Carolyn, Urwin, Cathy and Walkerdine, Valerie (eds), *Language, Gender and Childhood*, Routledge & Kegan Paul, 1985

Vicinus, Martha (ed.), *A Widening Sphere. Changing Roles of Victorian Women*, Methuen, 1980

Vicinus, Martha, *Independent Women. Work and Community for Single Women, 1850–1920*, Virago, 1985

Vološinov, V.N., *Marxism and the Philosophy of Language*, transl. Ladislav Matejka and I.R. Titunik, Harvard University Press, 1973

Vološinov, V.N., *Freudianism. A Critical Sketch*, transl. I.R. Titunik and ed. in collaboration with Neal H. Bruss, Indiana University Press (1976–87)

Vygotsky, Lev, *Thought and Language*, transl. newly revised and ed. Alex Kozulin, MIT Press, 1986

Vygotsky, Lev, *Mind in Society. The Development of Higher Psychological Processes*, ed. Michael Cole, Vera John-Steiner, Sylvia Scribner and Ellen Souberman, Harvard University Press, 1978

Walzer, Michael, *The Company of Critics. Social Criticism and Political Commitment in the Twentieth Century*, Peter Halban, 1989

Walcott, Derek, *The Gulf*, Jonathan Cape, 1969

Warner, Marina, *Alone of All Her Sex. The Myth and the Cult of the Virgin Mary*, Picador, 1985

Watts, Carol, 'Reclaiming the Border Country: Feminism and the Work of Raymond Williams', in *News from Nowhere. Raymond Williams: Third Generation, Oxford English Limited*, no. 6, February 1989

Webb, Beatrice, *The Diary of Beatrice Webb*, 4 vols. ed. Norman and Jeanne MacKenzie, Virago and the London School of Economics, 1982–5

Whitbread, Hilary and Zanker, Kathryn, (eds), *Wyggeston Girls' Centenary 1878–1978*

Weir, Angela and Wilson, Elizabeth, 'The British Women's Movement', *New Left Review*, no. 148, November/December 1984

Wells, H.G., *Ann Veronica* (1909)

Williams, Raymond, *Culture and Society 1780–1950*, Penguin, 1963 (1958)

Williams, Raymond, *The Long Revolution*, Penguin, 1975 (1961)

Williams, Raymond, *The Country and the City*, Paladin, 1975 (1973)

Williams, Raymond, *Keywords*, Flamingo, 1984 (1976)

Williams, Raymond, *Marxism and Literature,* Oxford University Press, 1977

Williams, Raymond, *Politics and Letters. Interviews with New Left Review,* Verso, 1979

Williams, Raymond, *Towards 2000,* Chatto & Windus, 1983

Williams, Raymond, *The Volunteers,* The Hogarth Press, 1985 (1978)

Williams, Raymond, 'Desire', a review of Carolyn Steedman, *Landscape for a Good Woman* (see above), *London Review of Books,* vol. 8, no. 7, 17 April 1986

Williams, Raymond, *Border Country,* The Hogarth Press, 1988 (1960)

Williams, Raymond, *Second Generation,* The Hogarth Press, 1988 (1964)

Williams, Raymond, *The Fight for Manod,* The Hogarth Press, 1988 (1979)

Williams, Raymond, *Loyalties,* The Hogarth Press, 1989 (1985)

Williams, Raymond, *Resources of Hope,* ed. Robin Gable, Verso, 1989

Willis, Paul, *Learning to Labour: How Working Class Kids Get Working Class Jobs,* Saxon House, 1977

Wolff, Joseph J. (compiler and editor), *George Gissing. An Annotated Bibliography of Writings About Him,* Northern Illinois University Press, 1974

Wollstonecraft, Mary, *A Vindication of the Rights of Woman,* Penguin, 1985 (1792)

Wyndham, Francis and Melly, Diana (eds), *Jean Rhys: Letters 1931–1966,* Penguin, 1985

Yates, May, *George Gissing. An Appreciation,* Manchester University Press, 1922

Zimmeck, Meta, 'Strategies and Stratagems for the Employment of Women in the British Civil Service, 1919–1939', *The Historical Journal,* vol. 27, no. 4 (1984), pp. 901–24

Manuscript Sources

Modern Records Centre, University of Warwick Library MSS. 29 Clara Collet Papers. This small collection was made from the originals belonging to Clara's nephew (my father), Robert Collet, in 1974. The originals are now in my possession (JM)

Also in my possession are originals and copies of letters written by Karl Marx to Clara's father, Collet Dobson Collet, and letters from George Gissing and Gabrielle Fleury to Clara Collet

Index

Other Virago Books of Interest

WOMEN WRITING ABOUT MEN
Jane Miller

'*Women Writing About Men* is one of the most intelligent works of feminist literary criticisms that I have read' – *Literary Review*

'An absorbing and extremely intelligent addition, from an original angle, to the canon of feminist critiques of women's writing ... shows women "transforming themselves from men's heroines to the tellers of their own stories"' – *Hermione Lee*

This fascinating book is about novels by women and about the men in them. It is also about women reading, and the sense we make of other women's accounts of the world. Its focus is the novel as a form which women writers, from the early nineteenth century to the present day, have used to question and challenge men's appropriation of women's experience, and to explore their own perspectives on men as husbands, fathers, brothers, sons and lovers. Drawing on the works of writers from Jane Austen, the Brontës and George Eliot, to Dorothy Richardson, Rebecca West, Virginia Woolf, Doris Lessing, Christina Stead, Angela Carter, Alice Walker and many more, Jane Miller's exciting and original study offers important new perspectives on women and men and on writing.

VIRTUE OF NECESSITY: English Women's Writing 1649-88
Elaine Hobby

'This courageous book is full of information and new ideas ... It opens up whole new areas ... splendid' – *Christopher Hill*

In this fascinating survey of some two hundred women's writings between 1649-88, Elaine Hobby draws on the extraordinary range of genres in which women expressed themselves in petitions, prophecies and religious writings, autobiography and biography, fiction, plays, poetry, and books on housewifery, medicine, midwifery and education. Living under the 'necessity' of their subjection, their writings show us how they were able to make a virtue of this – to turn constraints into permissions, into little pockets of liberty or autonomy, thus constantly defining and redefining existing concepts of femininity. In the upheavals of civil war and regicide, many women travelled the country and even the world, campaigning for social change and explaining their beliefs. In 1649, for example, Joanna Cartwright appealed for Jews to be re-admitted to England and many petitions sought parliamentary reforms for women.

After the restoration of the monarchy in 1660, women such as these were driven back into quiescence. Others turned to love poetry and plays, often ridiculing male conventions of panting lovers and coy mistresses: Aphra Behn, reviled for her success as a woman playwright, nevertheless wove together with wit and humour, music and spectacle, the dilemmas that she and her sisters faced in the debauchery of the Restoration. *Virtue of Necessity* makes a major contribution to our understanding of women's literary activity and lives in the seventeenth century.

THE SIGN OF ANGELLICA: Women, Writing and Fiction 1660-1800
Janet Todd

'A model of clarity and careful construction ... hugely informative ... an indispensible book' – *Helen Wilcox, Times Higher Education Supplement*

In this scholarly and entertaining work, Janet Todd takes as her subject the entry of women into literature as a profession in the Restoration and eighteenth century. She richly explores the various signs that women deployed during this crucial period for the construction of the modern ideology of femininity. Angellica in Aphra Behn's *The Rover* deliberately hangs out a seductive sign of womanhood the better to sell herself. Over a hundred years later Mary Wollstonecraft also asserted that femininity was a cultural construction and that writing was an act of self-assertion for women. But between Behn and Wollstonecraft lies a century of changing strategies of authorship employed by women: the erotic and witty invitations to men in the Restoration; the sentimental appeal to modesty, passivity, chastity in the mid-century in which the authors kept their signs indoors, writing simply as 'a lady' or 'one of the fair sex'; the assumption of moral authority at the century's close.

Janet Todd studies private letters as well as public dramas, but it is fiction in particular that is seen as self-expression; as an investigation of women's social and psychological predicament, and as a communal female dream. Extended essays on authors such as the Duchess of Newcastle, Eliza Haywood, Charlotte Lennox, Sarah Fielding, Ann Radcliffe, and Fanny Burney elaborate her engaging and persuasive thesis.

UNEVEN DEVELOPMENTS: The Ideological
Work of Gender in Mid-Victorian England
Mary Poovey

'Great skill and clarity ... a unique contribution to Victorian
Studies' – *Catherine Gallagher, University of California*

In *Uneven Developments*, Mary Poovey undertakes a brilliant
analysis of how notions of gender shape ideology. Asserting
that the organisation of sexual difference is a social, not
natural, phenomenon, and that beneath the smooth veneer
of Victorian society lay disturbing contradictions and inconsistencies, she focuses on the ways in which representations
of gender were simultaneously, but unevenly, constructed,
deployed and contested in five major institutions: in medicine,
where controversy raged over the use of anaesthesia in childbirth; in law and the wrangle over the first divorce legislation;
in literature and the struggle by literary men to enhance the
prestige of writers; in education and work, which the figure
of the governess brought together, and in nursing.

Ranging across sources from *David Copperfield* to Parliamentary debates, Florence Nightingale to Mrs Beeton, this
closely argued and immensely readable book provides fascinating insight into mid-Victorian culture and ideology by challenging both the isolation of literary texts from other kinds
of writing and the isolation of women's issues from economic
and political histories.